IMAGES OF THE "INDIAN"
IN FOUR NEW-WORLD LITERATURES

Cover:

The cover photo is of Kiontwogky or "Cornplanter" and is taken from the painting made in 1788 and taken to England. A copy was brought back to the United States and engravings made from it which have been used in several works and are found in the United States Archives in Washington, DC. The main nineteenth-century reference work to use these paintings, James Hall's and Thomas McKinney's *Bibliographical Sketches and Anecdotes of Ninety-Five of 120 Principal Chiefs from the Indian Tribes of North America*, (first publication of volume one in Philadelphia by Edward C. Biddle in 1836), describes Cornplanter as a Seneca chief who had a white (likely Irish) father. Cornplanter grew up speaking English in a white community. He is best known for a letter he wrote to the governor of Pennsylvania decrying the situation of the Seneca. In it he used imagery and poetic language. In himself, Cornplanter is emblematic of some of the authors discussed in this work. His image on the cover of the book, however, reflects its entirety.

IMAGES OF THE "INDIAN"
IN FOUR NEW-WORLD LITERATURES

Mikle Dave Ledgerwood

Native American Studies
Volume 4

The Edwin Mellen Press
Lewiston•Queenston•Lampeter

Library of Congress Cataloging-in-Publication Data

Ledgerwood, Mikle D., 1954-
   Images of the Indian in four new-world literatures / Mikle Dave
Ledgerwood.
      p. cm - (Native American studies ; 4)
   Includes bibliographical references.
   ISBN 0-7734-8462-0 (hardcover)
   1. Indians in literature. 2. Literature, Modern--History and
criticism. 3. Semiotics and literature.   I. Title. II. Series.
PN56.3.I6L43   1998
809'.933520397--dc21   97-38499
                                                                                CIP

This is volume 4 in the continuing series
Native American Studies
Volume 4 ISBN 0-7734-8462-0
NAS Series ISBN 0-88946-482-0

A CIP catalog record for this book is available from the British Library.

The Edwin Mellen Press   The Edwin Mellen Press
          Box 450   Box 67
    Lewiston, New York   Queenston, Ontario
    USA 14092-0450   CANADA L0S 1L0

The Edwin Mellen Press, Ltd.
Lampeter, Ceredigion, Wales
UNITED KINGDOM SA48 8LT

Printed in the United States of America

TABLE OF CONTENTS

ACKNOWLEDGEMENTS

I would like to thank many people here for their contributions to this endeavor. First, I would like to thank the department of Romance Languages at the University of North Carolina at Chapel Hill and Ms. Joanne Kucharski of UNC. I would also like to thank Dr. Paul Barrette of the University of Tennessee, Knoxville, Dr. Jack Warwick of York University, Dr. John Barrett and the faculty at the University of South Carolina at Sumter, a few individuals at Rhodes College, Memphis—especially Ms. Margie Stoner of the Language Center there as well as those individuals who chose me for two Faculty Development Grants and one Faculty Rotation Grant, and several people at the State University of New York at Stony Brook, especially Kris Vandenberg who helped with making the manuscript camera ready.

For help with the theoretical parts of this book, especially those presented in the concluding chapter, I would like to thank several individuals of the Semiotics Society of America and all of the members of the Southern Semiotics Circle, especially Katherine Stephenson, Terry Prewitt, Michele Magill, and Charles Pearson. They all argued with me and made important suggestions. They should NOT, however, be held responsible for my theoretical conclusions which are all my own.

Most importantly of all, however, I would like to thank my family, my children Rhiannon, Ian, and Will and my wife, Fayanne Thorngate, without whose help at important junctions in my career this book would never even have been begun, much less finished.

INTRODUCTION TO THE PROBLEM OF "INDIANS" IN COMPARATIVE NEW-WORLD LITERATURE

"Why Indians, why the Americas?"

"Because they're there?"

"No, because they're us."

Indians from the moment of their first "discovery" have always been popular subjects in Europe and the European-derived cultures of the Americas. The number of Indian movies — the popularity of "Dances With Wolves", "The Black Robe", and "The Deerslayer" — remind us of the fascination of this subject. Yet "Indians" have always served European and European-inspired art, whether it be film, literature, music, or concrete art as objects, as "others", for those who use them. For those artists who are from the Americas these "Indians" are an "other" which is solely their own, not Europe's, Asia's, or Africa's, but still an *object* of interest not identical with the author using them.

This fascination is not unique. Indeed the whole written history of man, especially history dealing with military and cultural affairs, is filled with episodes of the meetings of two groups of humans, unknown to each other. Very rarely do these two groups manage to come to a complete understanding of each other's strengths and weaknesses; instead they find it necessary to fight in order to discover who is physically stronger. Only later, and sometimes much later, is any effort made to determine which group is stronger culturally or intellectually. From the viewpoint of the defeated people, this examination usually takes the form of self-accusation, attempting to discover what inherent faults led to their defeat. The stories of the victors are often more interesting. After producing their hymns of self-congratulation, they might begin to examine the positive aspects of the defeated people. This may be done in order to make their victory over the foes more glorious than before, or in order to concentrate on certain unsavory aspects of their own culture. The long history of literature provides examples of all of these types of examinations, but only with the discovery of the New World does this comparison of groups acquire a major role in literature.

Before 1492, the world was considered to be fairly well mapped. China had been known since the 1200's; Africa was being discovered by the Portuguese. All that remained to do was to close the gap between Europe and Asia. Although more intellectual thinkers might have wondered about the distance between the two continents and might have remembered the legends of spirit-inhabited islands, bold adventurers denied the ancient estimates of the world's circumference and decided to close the gap between the continents once and for all. In fact, the Europeans were so sure that the newly discovered land was simply a hinderance, they spent another two centuries looking for a Northwest Passage around it. Only slowly did they realize that they had found something "new".

Until the ways of thinking rediscovered during the Renaissance penetrated intellectual thought, all knowledge was considered to be circumscribed by Greek and Roman writings and only repeated by medieval writers.[1] The idea that the Ancients had no knowledge of the lands in the West separating Western Europe and Eastern Asia was disturbing. The fact that they were populated by hitherto unknown beings was even more disturbing. Where did these beings belong in the history of the Bible? Were they different from men of the Old World, and if so, how? How could they add to man's knowledge of the world? These questions would perplex writers for many centuries to come.

In considering any early answer to these questions, it is important to remember that the early European settlers considered these new people, who would

---

[1] Clive Staple Lewis, The Discarded Image, an Introduction to Medieval and Renaissance Literature (Cambridge: Cambridge University Press, 1964).

later be called "American Indian"[2] natives, either East Indians or some kind of primitive men. Indeed they were often viewed just as an impediment in European attempts to travel to Asia. As a result, at first the Europeans did not view the cultures of these newly discovered peoples as physically or intellectually superior. The early conquered "Indians" were part of a defeated culture, doomed to servitude. Only later when the European had completed his conquest of these previously unknown inhabitants could he even consider these peoples to have a culture. Indeed, it was only when the Indian was no longer a real threat to the European that the European and his/her descendants could re-evaluate ideas about Indians and the latter's civilization.

Quite clearly, any new opinions then would have to be based upon a change in the European's own viewpoint and their own particular interests, not those of the Indian. This explains one of the problems of critical distance in any discussion of the New World[3] . Since history (and literature) is usually written by the victors, then the stories of New World civilization and culture have been written by the descendants of the Europeans. Thus all New World literatures are essentially Eurocentric ones writtten in European languages and it is their view of the Indian, that is a European-influenced view, which becomes the basis of New-World or Inter-American literature[4]. This is not to say that the New World literatures

---

[2] I use the term Indian in this work as a type of shorthand. It is a well-known fact that the term "Indian" is indeed a misnomer. However, the term "red" (as opposed to "black" or "white") is not acceptable due to its other connotations. The other terms such as "native American" or "native New-World inhabitant" are too long for continuous use. Finally, the majority of "native American" groups actually seem to have few problems, themselves, with the term, Indian, recognizing that it addresses a unity visible only to non-"Indian" eyes. Therefore I will use the term Indian as an abbreviation, keeping in mind its etymology.

[3] Claude Lévi-Strauss, Tristes Tropiques (Paris: Union générale des éditions, 1955) is an excellent example of this phenomenon.

[4] I use the words "American", "New World", and "Inter-American" to mean those countries or cultures of the Western Hemisphere which had no historical European contact prior to Columbus' voyages. This includes both the Indian and the new white cultures.

slavishly imitate European models and show no originality of their own. As most critics will attest this is not true, especially in the twentieth century. Still, it is easy to trace the path literary trends took as they developed in Europe and then circumnavigated the globe through the subject cultures of colonial powers. The European enlightenment engendered a pan-American enlightenment; European romanticism led to American romanticism; European symbolism, naturalism, and surrealism were emulated by American writers. It is true that New World *literati* can equal those of Europe even when using European literary models. Writers such as James Fenimore Cooper, Edgar Allen Poe, Gonçalves Días, Machado de Assis, or Clorinda Matto de Turner are indeed geniuses in their own right. It also must be said that some of them influenced European writers. Nevertheless, until the middle of the twentieth century, the European hand continued to weigh heavily over the New World in cultural matters. It must be said that cultural independence lagged behind political independence. The problem of European influence was exacerbated by the failure of New-World countries to communicate with each other in an organized fashion. Due to jealousy, residual resentment, or feelings of inferiority, a climate was not created that was conducive to the sharing of each other's culture until relatively recently.

Europe, with its philosophers, linguists and the power of the Catholic Church, broke down cultural barriers fairly early, even if political and military ones still remained. Even after the fall of Latin as Europe's intellectual language, a great deal of literature and philosophy was translated from one language to another. Intellectuals from all over the European world met in the cultural capital of their particular period whether it was a city in Italy, France, Britain, or Germany. There is nothing equivalent to this in the New World, although such a center may now be developing in New York City, California, or Miami[5].

---

[5] Some critics argue that only with the growth of New York, Los Angeles, San Francisco, and Miami since 1950 as cultural centers for "Pan-American" culture has this fact changed. Personally, I find New York to be the most convincing center for discussions of Inter-American literature. I am also interested to note that no non-U.S. American cities have been promoted as centers for Pan-American cultural discussions. However, I do not wish to derive any conclusions from this.

Petty resentments and failure to appreciate the relative value of the literatures and cultures of other Western-Hemisphere countries has left each nation in the New World unaware of the richness of the others' cultures until recently. An exception to this statement might be made for cultures sharing the same language. But even then, when one compares the influence of other New-World versus European works, s/he finds the advantage weighing heavily in favor of the Europeans. This is all the more surprising when one considers how similar the histories of New World countries have been, when viewed from a cultural perspective such as all of them suffering from feelings of inadequacy in expressing their non-European existence. Yet even today the idea of comparative Inter-American literature is still buried in the mire of misunderstanding. The field of comparative literature until very recently has been normally restricted to purely European literatures or to an analysis of one non-European and several European literatures. The concept of inter-American comparative literature is a logical one, yet few examples of it exist. This type of comparison, however, is what I propose to do here.

Our already-described task of considering the ways "Indians" are used in New World literatures is an obvious point of departure for our example of Inter-American comparative literature. As we will discover, the human beings found in these new lands helped to create new "national" literatures since this human being, the Indian, is something each culture has in common in the New World. S/he is a "native American" and most definitely not European by heritage. In classical literary terms s/he is a symbol of what is new and different in the New World, as well as a common component of all of these cultures. Thus comparing her/his function in New-World literatures would seem to be able to serve as an ideal area of comparison among New-World or American literatures. His/her civilization had been defeated by the Europeans, with all of its attendant ramifications, but its memory had not been eradicated from the minds of his/her conquerors and their American descendents. As such, it serves as an antithesis to what would later be known as a "progressive world-view" or the Whig philosophy of history. Most important of all to us here, however, is the fact that the Indian becomes unimportant to European literature at the same time s/he becomes important to New World literatures. The New World adopts the Indian as its anti-European symbol first and then keeps the Indian on as a figure throughout its literary and cultural history. It appears that any consideration of the Indian as literary myth and image, then, has to take account of her/him in New World literature as well as in European literature of the sixteenth, seventeenth, eighteenth and early nineteenth centuries.

Unfortunately the hope of exhaustively examining the history of Indians in all New-World literatures from their beginnings until the present cannot be realized in a single book-length study. Certain compromises will have to be made. My first compromise is to spend less space discussing earlier European literatures than some critics may wish. My reasons are quite simple, however. There has already been a lot of critical attention paid to the problem of Indians in these literatures and in these periods and I have no reason to "re-invent already excellent wheels". As a result, my discussion of this period will be more a consideration of certain key figures and conclusions that will be essential to my own study of later periods than any attempt to plow new ground in these earlier periods. Secondly, there have been very few studies of the ways Indians are used as literary myths and images in the nineteenth and twentieth centuries. To exacerbate this paucity of analysis, most of these studies have treated only one national literature. There has been little attempt to discover whether certain uses of Indians are repeated in other literatures. Therefore, since the last two centuries of literary use of the Indian need to be studied more intensely and since it is New World countries who are the primary creators of the Indian literature of these centuries, I have decided to concentrate on nineteenth- and twentieth-century New-World literature for my analyis.

A second series of compromises revolve around the number of literatures treated and the third around the number of literary genres to be treated. All twenty or more New World literatures and all literary genres cannot be treated exhaustively in a book-length text. Yet this is not to say that a good *overview* of the problem cannot be accomplished in a work of this length. However a good overview depends upon a careful selection of material that can suggest, through its content, what it does not treat in an extremely detailed fashion. For a more manageable study, let one genre be chosen for detailed analysis: the novel, and four different literatures: Brazilian, Peruvian, French Canadian and English Canadian.

The novel is the logical genre to choose. Theater dealing with the Indian did not appear until fairly recently in some of these cultures. In fact, theater was the last literary genre to establish itself in the New World. The short story, although more common, is on the whole a late nineteenth- and a twentieth-century phenomenon and is less important in Amercan literatures than European literatures until very recently. Poetry, on the other hand, is very important in the Americas from an early period. In addition there are some key poems that contain Indian characters. Certain poems will have to be discussed here to add to our understanding of a specific culture's or literature's viewpoint on Indians. A few other works from other genres may also be mentioned, but, generally speaking, it is the novel in which the Indian makes his most important appearance. In the greater length of a novel, the author can develop secondary characters, and Indians are very often secondary rather than primary characters. In the novel with its possiblilities for sub-plots and long descriptions, Indian characters can be used more effectively. Therefore the novel is the logical genre to choose.

Choosing only a few literatures from the more than twenty New-World literatures was very difficult. I chose the four cited above for several reasons. In the interest of completeness and in the interest of suggesting that which was not to be treated directly at length, I wanted a literature from each of the four major languages spoken in the New World. I also wished to include literatures from both North and South America; and both Catholic and Protestant influences needed to be represented. With these considerations in mind, two choices were obvious. Brazil is the only major New-World country in which Portuguese is spoken. It has, as well, a very rich Indian-inspired literature with some of the hemisphere's best examples of the "Indianist" novel[6]. Its Portuguese-influenced culture is distinct from that of other Latin American countries. French Canadian or Québécois

---

[6] See chapters three and four for a discussion of "Indianist" and "Indigenist" novels.

10

literature was the only other obvious choice. With the exception of Haiti, and perhaps Louisiana, Quebec has the only francophone literature in the New World. It is also interesting in that it forms a part of North America, and although Catholic, it has had to deal with influences from neighboring Protestant countries.

The other two choices were not so simple to resolve. Although there are only two major English-language literatures in the New World, they are quite separate. The literature of the United States[7] deals with the Indian from many interesting and diverse points of view, and some works, especially the James Fenimore Cooper novels, influenced European and other New-World books dealing with the Indians. However, U.S. American literature is a vast subject studied intensely in this country. It is not comparable to Brazilian or Québécois literature in terms of the amount of works it has produced or in terms of the amount of critical attention paid to it. Most importantly, however, U.S. American literature does not appear to be unique in the New World in any of its uses of the Indian in its literature.

In contrast to U.S. American literature, English Canadian is more manageable, and resembles the other literatures picked for study in the extent to which it has been explored critically in the United States or even in Canada. As late as 1950 Canadian critics were arguing as to whether a separate Canadian literature even existed[8]. The establishment of the Journal of Canadian Literature and university degree programs in Canadian literature have finally rendered the question moot. Nevertheless, this is still a relatively new and fruitful area of study. Secondly, the relationship between French and English Canadian literature is an interesting one, and will be discussed somewhat here. Indeed the relatively new study of "Comparative Canadian Literature" reflects on a smaller scale what I am

---

[7] Once again there is a problem of nomenclature. The name "United States of America" is often confusing since there is a "United States of Brazil" and a "United States of Mexico" and both of these countries are located in America. However I will use "United States of America" and its abbreviations to refer to the country whose capital is in Washington, D.C.

[8] See the Journal of Canadian Literature, 1 (1956).

proposing to do with my interest in comparative New-World literature. Another reason for choosing Canadian literature is that English Canada is still primarily a Protestant country, although it is not as heavily influenced by Puritanism as is the United States. A last reason for choosing Canadian literature is that its culture has been profoundly influenced by the U.S. American culture. Certain attitudes found in English Canadian society and literature are reflections of those seen in the United States or those heard in English speakers in other developed countries. In as much as this is true, it allows us to see Canadian literature as a microcosm of the larger Anglo-Saxon world attitude (or to use the more precise German term, the Englischeweltanschauung), and helps to validate the selection of Canadian instead of U.S. American literature.

The last choice to be made for detailed treatment was the most difficult. Argentina, Mexico, Guatemala, and Ecuador in addition to Peru could all make claims to being selected as the Hispanic Latin American literature. There are some important reasons for giving preference to Peru, however. Guatemala was not selected because of the relative political and economic unimportance of the country. Argentina was not chosen because, although its literature was crucial in early Latin American writing on the Indian and it inaugurated the gaucho narrative, its consequent literary treatment of the Indian was not nearly as well-developed as that of Peru. Ecuadorian literature could have been chosen, but its treatment of the Indian varies little from that of Peruvian literature. Even Bolivian and Chilean literature generally reflect the same Andean interests as that of Peru. Mexican literature, however, is as rich as Peruvian in its use of the Indian, and it has its own interesting characteristics. Peruvian literature, nevertheless, offers some important advantages. First, it is a South American literature and its treatment of the Indian is not overly influenced by English North America unless all Hispanic literatures are. Second, as stated before, it is representative of all Andean literature, and third, Peruvian literature initiated what we will later call the indigenista novel with Clorinda Matto de Turner's Aves sin nido. For these reasons Peruvian literature will be the primary Hispanic literature treated, with mention being made of important works from other Hispanic literatures.

The four ethnic or national groups responsible for these literatures vary enormously in their relations with the Indian. In Brazil there was a large Indian population which was, until recently, being systematically eliminated by government policies. Even today there are still primitive Indian tribes living in the Amazon basin who have little knowledge of white civilization. Peru is a country currently trying to rectify past wrongs done to its Indians. It has had a long history of Indian enslavement, both political and economic. Even the recent Maoist and fascist initiatives in Peru have failed to ease the lot of this large minority, perhaps because of a failure to understand the different culture of its Indians. English Canada still has a number of Indians who are concentrated in the Western provinces. In the past, most Canadian literature was written from an Ontarian perspective where the actual presence of the Indians became relatively unimportant early in its history. However, there has been a recent growth of interest in the Indian fueled by new works from the Western provinces. In Quebec the Indian presence is the slightest of all; however, its large number of Eskimos in the far north of Ungava and its Indians living on reservations in the south have recently erupted, seeking political, economic, and constitutional rights—reminding the Québécois as well as other Canadians that minority rights are important to them as well as to Canada's Francophones. The number of Indians, therefore, differs greatly in the four countries or provinces. One would imagine that this fact would influence their literatures. This assumption will be tested.

Yet even this lesser, compromised, undertaking, trying to follow even one characters composite image—the Indian—through the history of four literatures, is a difficult process. To make it a bit clearer, yet, let us outline what each chapter of the book contains and what types of questions it raises. The first chapter is a continuation of the introduction. It includes a general consideration of the history of European writing about non-Europeans showing the parameters of how Europeans have traditionally written about "others". This is followed by a more detailed discussion of the important early European writers on Indians, including Spanish, French, English, and Portuguese writers' notions about the native Americans written during the sixteenth, seventeenth, and eighteenth centuries. Neither analysis is a detailed one, but rather a type of summary intended to show the background canvas upon which later literature would paint.

In the second chapter there is a more obviously theoretical consideration of literary myth and literary images as they apply to literature in general—with specific emphasis on how they apply to the problem of the images of the Indian. This will involve a more theoretical, and less anecdotal, discussion of how Europeans have looked at different *non-European*, cultures. The second chapter also presents two sample summarized mythic images, taken from eighteenth-century French literature. Finally semiotic theory is used here to show how a specific text may be related to the notions of "general myth" and "mythology" as proposed in this chapter.

The third and fourth chapters take up where the first chapter stopped, giving the general history of the image of the Indian in the nineteenth and twentieth centuries, with specific mention made of the uses of the types of images and texts appropriate to the four literatures, the eight novels chosen for primary analysis, and the two centuries.

In the conclusion, the results of this comparative study, will be focussed in a different way. I will take specific descriptions from the eight nineteenth- and twentieth-century novels and compare them using semantic tables created from a content analysis of these passages. Semiotic theory will aid in determining what types of sign-functions and what sign-qualities are presented by the descriptions of the Indians and the eight novels as a whole. If the sign-attributes of the descriptions and the novels show certain basic similarities, then this would invalidate the assumption that differences in socio-political organization will be necessarily reflected in a country's culture as expressed in its literature. Indeed, if similarities are found among literatures, considering how different the actual conditions of these country's Indian populations and socio-economic conditions are, then this would be a powerful argument for the validity of this study's contention that it is time to take the notion of Inter-American literature seriously.

CHAPTER 1:

EARLY NON-EUROPEANS IN EUROPEAN LITERATURE

In Renaissance England, at the time it set out to colonize America, at least two opposing ideas of history—the progressive and the retrograde—identical to those that were dominant in ancient thought shaped the historian's imaginations in the classic image[1].

Europeans have long had ambivalent feelings about peoples from other cultures and lands. Their view of the people who would later be known as American Indians proves to be no exception to this general observation and the quotation given above reflects this ambivalence. The opposing ideas had their origins in schools of thought which antedate the European discovery of the New World by over a thousand years. In any consideration of images of American Indians, it is necessary to begin with an overview of pre-Columbian European considerations of peoples considered not to be "civilized". This discussion will then set the stage for a presentation of the types of descriptions Europeans used for the inhabitants of the New World discovered in the early modern period and will provide necessary background for understanding the discussions of the literary myth of the New-World native presented in the later chapters of this book.

In the introduction the parameters of the creation of these two schools of thought have been presented. The school which believes that all societies which differ from one's own are inferior is the school which predominates in the vast majority of human writing about other cultures. Yet in European writing there is

---

[1] Elemire Zolla, The Writer and the Shaman: A Morphology of the American Indian, (New York: Harcourt, Brace, and Jovanovich, 1973) 5.

an important minority of writers who allot certain superior virtues to groups that might be considered inferior. Since this will become an important element in European and Inter-American Indian images, let us now discuss some of the key contributors to this idea. One of the most important and powerful schools of European writing on "uncivilized societies" was inaugurated by Plato in his dialogues. In his Laws and his Timeaus he speaks of societies which have been corrupted by the "advances" of civilization and need to return to the purity of the state espoused in the Republic[2]. Plato's vision of a golden age uncorrupted by secularism or luxuries has much in common with the Greek myths of the golden age of Saturn. It was a pure society, simple and innocent, in complete harmony with the gods. As a result, although Plato did not perhaps intend this, what is simple and untainted by luxury became associated with purity and superior virtues. Much later then the idea of simplicity and even savagery could logically be considered superior as well.

In Hellenic thought the sudden rise to power of Alexander could only be explained in terms of his philosophical education and his important tutors, but the fact remained that he came from a barbarian and primitive people, i.e. not one of the civilized city states, and yet he managed to create one of the greatest empires the world has ever known. The Platonically-inspired vision of splendid innocence certainly helped to explain Alexander's rise out of innocence, as well as his fall, when he discarded his primitive virtues for the luxuries of the defeated Persian Empire.

The idea of the superior barbarian later was seen in a literary context in Tacitus' histories. His writings appeared at a time when some of the first intimations of mortality presented themselves to the Roman empire. His characterization of the Germans was not that of an unambiguously morally-superior civilization, yet it was sympathetic and pointed out quite clearly the deficiencies of Roman society as they existed during its decline. Once again

---

[2] Plato, The Dialogues of Plato, trans. B. Jewett, (New York: Scribner, Armstrong and Co., 1873).

one sees simplicity expressed as a virtue while the luxuries of a rich society become vices: as Civilis, the German chief, speaks to his prisoner after a victory saying, "Roman subjects, resume again the customs and manner of your own country and throw off those luxurious habits which enslave Roman subjects more effectively than Roman arms."[3]   It could be that Tacitus was merely echoing Stoic philosophers and writers such as Marcus Aurelius but the fact remains that barbarians were assigned certain moral advantages.

Elemire Zolla has pointed out that some later medieval thinkers, such as Gower, Chaucer, and Bocaccio also shared a vision of ancient purity[4] as illustrated by their reflections on the mythical Roman age of Saturn. They equated innocence and purity or other higher virtues with an "uncivilized state of being" as characteristics of this "Golden Age" and seem to advise using this age as a guide for the creation of a higher society, perhaps cynically, but nonetheless persuasively. Other late medieval thinkers emphasized that the Golden Age of Saturn was mythical and not historical and thus not to be used as a guide. Still, although one should not underestimate the import of reflections on the specifically Roman mythic (and originally Greek-described) past seen often mentioned in the late medieval age, it is important to realize that this vision of golden age innocence and simplicity is present in the mythologies of many different religions and cultures and is not unique to ancient Rome. Greek, Celtic, and non-European cultures, even that of the Native American, all contain references to an Edenic golden age of a distant past.

In fact, twentieth-century thinkers such as R.D. Laing argue that all mythology is iconic to the embryology of the human race.[5] Thus the golden age is a period of perfect peace equivalent to the security of the fetus in the womb, which

---

[3]   Tacitus, <u>The Histories,</u> trans. W. Hamilton Fyfe, 2 vols., (Oxford: The Clarendon Press, 1912) 2:75.

[4] Zolla 6.

[5] R. D. Laing, <u>The Facts of Life,</u> (New York: Ballantine Books, 1972) 38.

18

all cultures have subsequently stored in the collective unconscience and put into their mythology as a moment of perfection which was once enjoyed, but never will be again in this life. The Biblical story of the Garden of Eden, or the mythical world before the misadventure of Pandora, are examples of that perfection which cannot exist again. This is an age of humanity which is only disturbed by humankind's accession to knowledge, memory, or civilization. As a result, one's whole life on Earth is spent trying to recreate that primitive goodness or trying to propitiate the gods in order to live that life again after death. Any earthly resemblance to this lost innocence thus becomes almost irresistible. Since most Europeans became conditioned to acceptance of a Greco-Judaic order, especially as interpreted by Hellenized Christian Romans, the Garden of Eden and the Greek Golden Age became intertwined in the minds of philosophers and people. Simplicity, or the lack of worldliness and cynicism, as a positive trait was ascribed to these eras.

As a result the culture in which the philosophers lived could not hope, in its current state, to regain this innocence. It could only be achieved by corporate purification of the soul and body in order to wash away the defects of character acquired through too much involvment with the civilized world. In seeking this redemption, examples of the successes and failures of other cultures would be helpful as guides. Tacitus' histories are only one example of such a search for the perfect in other cultures. In later times, and indeed in our own culture, the mythology of the Norse, the Celts and the New-World Indians, among others, would be studied in order to discover the secrets of primitive moral superiority.

A tradition which accompanies that of the ancient utopia is the literature of the fantastic, especially when it makes reference to a golden age culture and a golden age man. In Titus-Livy, Pliny, Ptolemy, Strabo, and Herodotus, we may, at times, see the germ of a superior man existing in a vastly different culture.[6] At least, certain positive features are given to other civilizations, even those civilizations which seem most fantastic. Plato and his view of Atlantis come to

[6] For one example of a discussion of this, see James Romer "Rabelais and the Voyages to the New World," dissertation, University of North Carolina, Chapel Hill, 1977.

mind again here, and the later utopias and negative utopias of Sir Thomas More, Rabelais, and Voltaire are also relevant. Medieval literature continues this tradition of description of fantastic customs and places. It also begins to associate it with the old ideals of primitive golden age virtue. The early popularity of the Byzantine novels continues the Western tradition that wisdom and wealth are often found in faraway and exotic locales—a belief that the late medieval writings of Marco Polo propagated.

A tradition influential in the growth of fantastic literature, and one associated with the mysterious West, is that of the Celts who believed in a western paradise beyond the sea: the legendary land or island of Avalon, so imprecisely described. In some traditional narratives it appears as a place of rest for warriors, in others it is a paradise where life never ends and pain is unknown. Marie de France in her Lais refers to this place, especially in her "Lanval".[7] In Celtic mythology it is also associated with the twilight of the elder gods. Some later narratives treat it quite differently, however. The legend of St. Brendan tells of rather concrete western lands which are not described in a wholly utopic light. There are frightening visions of sea serpents and other horrors, as well as some more pleasant places.[8] The link between these tales and the European fear of the great Western sea should be obvious. One especially interesting horror story of the Western lands is one told by Adam of Bremen in which he claims to quote Norse accounts. Although the Norse did indeed reach the New World, it is difficult to say how many intermediaries there were between the original version of this story and that told by Adam of Bremen. The passage quoted here is especially interesting, as it purports to give the first description of the New World inhabitant:

---

[7] Marie de France, Les lais, ed. Jean Rychner (Paris: Librairie Honoré Champion, 1977).

[8] St. Brendan, The Anglo-Norman Voyage of St. Brendan by Benedeit, A Poem of the Early Twelfth Century, ed. Edwin George Ross Walters (1928; Geneva: Slatkine Reprints, 1974).

Et iam periculum caliginis et provintiam frigoris evadentes, inseparate appulerunt ad quandam insulam altissimis in circuitu scopulis ritu oppidi munitam. Huc visendorum gratia locurum egressi, reppererunt homines in antris subterraneis meridiano temore latitantes; pro quorum foribus infinita iacebat copia vasorum aureorum et eiusmodi metallorum, quae rara mortalibus et preciosa putantur. Itaque sumpta parte gazarum quam sublevare poterant, laeti remiges festine remeant ad naves, cum subito retro se venientes contemplati sunt homines mirae altitudinis, quos nostri appellant Cyclops; eos antecedebant canes magnitudinem solitam escedentes eorum quadrupedum.[9]

This cyclopean New Worlder, even if totally fantastic and wealthy, presents us for the first time with its discussion of precious metals with a linking of the West, a Golden Age, and a "Fairyland". It also presents another view of history promulgated in the ancient world and described by Zolla as the "Virgilian progressivist" philosophy, presented in stark contrast to the Platonistic one.[10] In this view, man has always been progressing, step by step, from primitive ignorance and darkness into greater and greater light. Lucretius' Epicureanism taught the same idea. Francis Bacon, as Zolla indicates, is, perhaps, a logical follower in this line of thought with his famous aphorism "Veritas, filia temporis". Although this thought could be considered to advocate a type of relativism, Bacon's own followers would later take such ideas farther and create the Whig progressivist ideas of history which would help justify the destruction of native New World civilizations. In the medieval period however, this Lucretian/Baconian notion was buried for a while, or at least did not have the same importance that it would later.

Nevertheless, some medieval chroniclers believed that the idea of progress was indeed important. These include the writers of the Scriptorium at the court of Alfonso Sábio in Spain and Philippe de Commyne's chronicles of Burgundy's

---

[9] K. P. Harrington, ed., <u>Mediaeval Latin</u> (Chicago: University of Chicago Press, 1962), 253–54.

[10] Zolla 5.

Charles the Bold. A more literary support for this view, and one related to the traditional Christian view comes from Dante's <u>Divina Commedia</u>. In his portrayal of the Elysian Fields, the great thinkers of the ancients could live a life in a type of earthly paradise, yet could not go to heaven, since they had no knowledge of God and Jesus Christ. Thus even though the ancients were revered in Dantes's time for their wisdom and knowledge, they still had to be thought of as deficient and imperfect because they were not Christian.

In the 1400's, however, the Academmia of Florence began to question such a view of the ancients, and indeed the traditional Judeo-Christian view of original sin. The writers associated with the Academmia were certainly not the first men to address these questions; but due to their exchanges of ideas with thinkers in Spain, Portugal, and France, they influenced a large number of Europeans including the Genoan who would provide Europe with a new focus for its thoughts on the nature of man—the American Indian.

Thus in this extremely brief sketch of the development of the European vision of the non-European world we come up with two contrasting views. They are not contradictory philosophies so much as they are two sets of opposing connotations given to a single set of denotations (in Umberto Eco's sense of these two concepts).[11] The basic historical facts used by these two philosophies concerning non-Europeans were stories common to both sets of thinkers, but the interpretations given to them varied radically. This sort of acquisition of a story and putting it to work for the benefit of one's personal viewpoint will be seen time and time again in the literature on the New World about the Indian and discussed in more detail later. Before going on to consider the myths associated with these two philosophies and the methodology associated with an analysis of specific literary mythic instances, let us develop these two connotational sets in more detail and expand them to fit the earliest European writers writing specifically about the New World Indians in the sixteenth, seventeenth, and eighteenth century respectively.

---

[11] Zolla 6, and Umberto Eco, <u>A Theory of Semiotics</u>, (Bloomington, IN: Indiana University Press, 1979).

The Sixteenth Century

Before Columbus sailed to the New World, while thinking he was sailing to the Indias, the intellectual ferment of the Renaissance in Europe had already begun. The church had suffered greatly as many of its fifteenth-century leaders became more and more complacent and corrupt. The stage was set for the development of the ideas that led to both Protestant and Catholic reform and the quickening of interest in new opinions about man and his institutions. Therefore Columbus' venture, although treated at first as a failure, was soon to reveal information about a new man, unknown to the ancient world.

Unlike the account of Adam of Bremen, the first men Columbus met were gentle beings who appeared genuinely happy to see him and helped him in his quest for knowledge and treasure. At the same time the newly discovered men, themselves, told stories of men in other islands who were fierce and warlike cannibals, these men being more similiar to the Cyclopeans of the Norse tale. Although Columbus did not meet these cannibals, he assumed that their existence was indeed real even though he did not have actual proof. Such stories were probably at least partially at the root of Montaigne's famous chapter on "Des cannibales" written fifty years later.[12] Nevertheless, even if Columbus did not have proof of cannibal Indians, he still managed to satisfy both groups of thinkers who pondered the nature of the new human beings discovered; he found both "virtuous innocents" and "heathen devils".

Columbus had set the scene for the philosophic discussions of the sixteenth century about the newly discovered beings. Two early explorers in New Spain expanded the scope of the discussion. In the early sixteenth-century, Francisco Pizarro discovered the Incas, and Hernán Cortés discovered the Aztecs. Cortés, with his earlier discovery and dramatic narrative style in his <u>Cartas de relación</u>, was

---

[12] Michel de Montaigne, <u>Essais</u>, ed. Maurice Rat, 2 vols., (Paris: Editions Garnier Freres, 1962).

much more influential than Pizarro.[13] In contrast to the sweet, simple natives that Columbus found in the Carribean, Cortés discovered a rich, corrupt, bloodthirsty civilization that practiced human sacrifice. Nevertheless Cortés did see good in this heathen culture. In his letters detailing it, he adapted literary conventions and created a type of epic tragedy which chronicled the fate of a doomed society. In fact, Cortés' leading dramatic figure was Moctezuma who was depicted as a tragic Nero, if indeed such a figure of contrasting characteristics can be imagined. Perhaps Cortés' portrayal is a function of the literary conventions of his age, which were based upon Roman models depicting conquering adversaries as worthy opponents to be remembered and celebrated. Nevertheless, in some respects this portrayal was the most multi-faceted to appear for many years, even if many readers did not read past the tales of the horrors of Aztec human sacrifice, the terror of the "Noche triste", and the seeming barbarity of this non-Christian civilization. As a result the Aztec became an early representative of a powerful opposing force which had to be conquered. In the space of twenty years, two different views of primitive men, Columbus' of the pure virtuous innocent, and Cortés' of the wild bloodthirsty barbarian, had been exemplified by Spanish writers in the New World.

The pace of New World discoveries was such that the Spanish explorers were not the only ones to travel to, or to write about the New World. Magellan's voyage, the logical outcome of earlier Portuguese ventures in Africa and Asia gave differing impressions of non-Europeans. In Pigafetta's account of the voyage one sees beautiful naked natives who, friendly as they might first appear, later become violent and kill Magellan himself. In this variation on Columbus' savage, one encounters a native who is sly enough or simply savage enough to appear friendly until it is within his power to demonstrate his mastery over the European. This image also parallels the view of Moctezuma presented by Cortés although without presenting a parallel to Moctezuma's tragic side.

Verrazano, Jacques Cartier, and Vespucci however, also generally give a favorable impression of the first natives, whereas Peter the Martyr in De Novus

---

[13] Hernán de Cortés, Cartas de relación de la conquista de México, 5th ed., (Madrid: Espasa-Calpa, 1970).

Orbus tends to take Pigafetta's accounts and expand upon them.[14] Cartier's views would become much more important in French Canada, as he was one of the first Europeans and the first Frenchman to view the natives in this habitat. Cartier's natives are presented in contrast to Pigafetta, Cortés, or Pizarro. They are generally simple unassuming people similiar to Columbus' natives. As Gilbert Chinard describes them in Cartier's work, the natives take on the image of poor devils with no hope of salvation whose life is one of slow and deadening tedium and savagery, although they are capable of enjoying their primitive dancing and feasts.

Thus, in contrast to Spain, from the very first, the image of the native reported back to France from the French explorers was positive. It was tempered, however, by Cartier's implicit criticism that the natives' nature had developed out of ignorance of other ways of life—not from a well-thought out attempt to develop a superior civilization. In other words, their goodness was a goodness brought about by ignorance not the superior goodness of civilized Christian humans.[15] Despite this amendment Cartier's conclusion was a positive one and appears to have influenced Rabelais and later Rousseau, as a result of this implied criticism, more than he did Montaigne's "Des cannibales".[16]

At the same time that Cartier was traveling in the New World, the first descriptions of the natives of this region were being collected and published in volumes, such as those of Peter Martyr and later, Benzoni. Many of these accounts were descriptions of voyages, in which the discussions of the native inhabitants function only as minor motifs. However, they were enormously popular, were translated into all of the major European languages, and succeeded in making the scholars of Europe aware of the newly discovered human beings and societies of the Western Hemisphere.

---

[14] Zolla pp 5–20.

[15] Gilbert Chinard, <u>L'éxotisme américain dans la littérature française au XVIe siècle d'après Rabelais, Montaigne, etc.</u>, (Paris: Hachette et Cie., 1911) 44–45.

[16] Chinard 44–50.

In addition to these voyage accounts there were also an important group of accounts written by writers who had actually lived in the New World for a period of years. The most relevant writer in developing later Francophone opinion was a Swiss Protestant pastor, Jean de Léry.

Just a few years later than Cartier de Léry published his tales of life among the Indians in Brazil, at that time a region partially under French control. The aspect of his writing which was perhaps the most influential upon later French thinkers, including Montaigne, was his use of Indians as a means to criticize European customs. De Léry's account of his sojourn during the 1560's gave a glowing picture of the Indian population which he encountered. As an example of his opinion of them, the following citation may be studied:

> Les sauvages de l'Amerique habitant en la
> terre du Brésil, nommés Toupinambaoults, avec
> lesquels j'ai demeuré et fréquenté familièrement
> environ un an, n'étant point plus grands, plus gros ou
> plus petits de stature que nous sommes en Europe,
> n'ont le corps ni monstrueux ni prodigieux à notre
> égard, bien qu'ils soient plus forts, plus robustes et
> replets, plus dispos, moins sujet à maladie et même
> il n'y a presque point de boiteux, de borgnes,
> contrefaits, ni maladies entre eux.[17]

Thus his savages were at least physically well-made, even if their cultural simplicity did not lead him to describe them as superior in intellectual capacity.

Four other early writers who observed the New World Indian in his/her native habitat and influenced early Spanish writers on the Indian were Fray Bartolomé de Las Casas, Fray Antonio de Montesinos, Francisco Oviedo, and Garcilaso de la Vega el Inca, the latter of whom was himself one of the first products of the racial mixing of the Old and the New World. Las Casas' Brevísima relación de la destrucción de las Indias (1552) and his Historia de las Indias (1561) give descriptions of the Indians such as this one quoted by Concha Melendez:

---

[17] Jean de Léry, Indiens de la Renaissance, Anne-Marie Cheuser ed. (Paris: Episa éditeurs, 1972) 88.

> [son] gentes mansuetísimas, humilísimas,
> inermes y sin armas, simplisísimas, y sobre todos
> que de hombres nacieron sufridas y pacientes.[18]

As Melendez so aptly indicates, Las Casas was indeed a predecessor of Rousseau, giving the natives the qualities of intelligence, virtue, and "prontísima diligencia para recibir la santa fé". He even goes so far as to praise the Indians beyond the limits of prose; his description becomes rather poetic. Las Casas was joined in his crusade by Fray Antonio de Montesinos. Montesinos went farther than Las Casas in some respects, especially in his preaching on the need for protecting the Indians.

> Decíd, ¿con qué derecho y con que justícia
> tenéis en tan cruel y horrible servidumbre e estos
> índios? ¿Con qué autoridad habéis hecho tan
> detestables guerras a estas gentes que estaban en sus
> tierras mansas y pacíficas, donde tan infinitas delas,
> con suertes y estragos nunca oídos habéis
> consumido?[19]

The preaching of Montesinos and the writings of Las Casas quickly became known throughout Europe. Las Casas' work went through several editions in Spain and was soon translated into other languages, increasing its dissemination. His influence on sixteenth-century writers such as Montaigne is uncertain, but his influence is apparent in seventeenth-century Europe when Spain, Spanish customs and Spanish literature were in fashion in the rest of Europe. During the same period, Spanish influence was paramount in Portugal. Indeed Spain's political control over the country enabled Spanish authors to use the presses of Lisbon—this close relationship ending only with the overthrow of the Spanish in 1640. Even in England Spanish literature was well-known; many early Spanish works were

---

[18] Concha Melendez, La novela indianista en Hispanoamerica 1832–1889, (Madrid: Imprensa de la Libreria y Casa Editorial Hernando, 1934) 18–19.

[19] Aída Cometta Manzoni, El Indio en la novela de America, (Buenos Aires: Editorial futuro, 1960) 9.

translated into English. In fact, one of the most important early English works dealing with the New World was Hakluyt's <u>Voyages</u> which made extensive use of the Spanish writers already cited. As a result, Las Casas, Montesinos, and other Spanish writers had a more extensive audience than the Spanish court. A large part of intellectual Europe was aware of their opinions about New World inhabitants.[20]

It must not be said, however, that these pro-Indian opinions had no opposition from other Spanish thinkers. Francisco Oviedo was a member of Cortés' expedition and did not share Cortés' opinions. In his own account of Cortés' handling of the situation that led to the "Noche triste" his view of the Indians, and that of de Sepúlveda, was not nearly as favorable as those previously cited. Oviedo considered the Indians weak and ignobly savage. Since he was an actual observer of the natives in their own habitat his conclusions had some force. Sepúlveda brought the issue to the moral level and added a new dimension to Oviedo's description. He was unsure whether the non-Christian natives could be thought of as simple creatures of pure virtue. The notion that men could exist, isolated in some equivalent of the Garden of Eden, without Christian instruction was heretical and therefore indefensible. The propogation of opinions reflecting his ideas is an important development in the process of European thinking on the native New Worlder. It would become a clear counterweight to the view already set out by Las Casas and de Léry. This "Christian" viewpoint would influence the opinions of the English settlers in the New World and their apologists, but it would also affect images of the Indian in later literature, even that of the twentieth century.

Negative opinions were not limited to Spaniards either. A French contemporary of Jean de Léry, André Thévet, agreed with Oviedo and presented a French opinion on this side. He was horrified and repulsed by what he believed were pure unadulterated savages. However, in an example of the saying "a picture is worth a thousand words", and in clear testimony of the problems his view would encounter, the plates in Thévet's work were done by an Italian artist who drew the

---

[20] Zolla 139.

Indians as classical gods. In fact it seems these drawings had more influence upon French intellectuals than the text itself.[21]

Thus the early explorers' accounts, far from altering a debate based upon connotational divergences from the unchanging base denotation of non-European humans, merely added fuel to the fire as each explorer perceived his experiences in the light of existing thought about non-European human beings. As modern social scientists have discovered, humans are able to be at least somewhat "objective" or dispassionate in regard to inanimate objects, but when they view another representative of their species become subjective since the object of discussion is essentially a reflection of the human who is its discussant.

So for these Europeans all of their historic "cultural baggage" came together when they finally realized that the land Columbus had discovered was indeed a land not previously known. It was then, perhaps, inevitable that old ideas about barbarians who were to be treated as "others", about Avalon and other lands beyond the setting sun, and about all that was so primitive as to be unsettling or even frightening would be associated with the New World discovered. It was even more inevitable that the humans of this world would be discussed in great detail.

Thus far we have indescriminately lumped together all types of writers writing about the native inhabitants of the New World. Until the final complete separation of literature from natural philosophy in the nineteenth century it is defensible to consider "philosophical" treatises such as those of the eighteenth century philosophes as being not far distant from the novels of the same writers in terms of the disparate work's aims and goals. Only in the nineteenth century do writers of literature and writers of "factual accounts"—the predecessors of social scientists—develop different interests.

In many ways, indeed, the presentation of an ideological truth, not a "philosophical" truth is the reason for much early philosophical writing on Indians. As even the early explorers' narratives disagreed about fundamental aspects of the

---

[21] David Driver, The Indian in Brazilian Literature, (New York: The Hispanic Institute, 1942) 17.

New World native, philosophical or literary narratives could hardly be expected to present a united front in their opinions of these newly-discovered beings. Surprisingly, however, there is a great amount of similarity in the literary presentations of the native, inasmuch as one can separate philosophical discussions and works from literary ones. Indeed, one of the problems with discussing the early images of the native New Worlders results from this difficulty, that is the fact that the earliest presentations of the new human were written, discussed and read by all types of readers, both the more and less "philosophically-inclined" readers.

However, let us now attempt to concentrate as much as possible on literary works dealing with American Indians. We will need to discuss a few non-literary works but, for the most part, from the sixteenth century on, the literary works seem to influence the philosophical works and not the obverse.

The first literary work of any merit and influence in creating images of the New World Indian was written in 1569 in Madrid. Alfonso de Ercilla y Zuñiga's La Araucana is the first widely-popular literary work to dramatize the Indian and present him/her as a heroic figure.[22] At the time of its appearance, Spanish control over its New World provinces appeared secure and the process of revisionist historical writing, referred to earlier, had begun. Las Casas' view of the nature of humankind had become widely accepted among the Spanish literati during the reign of the Hapsburg emperor Charles V (1519–1557). Although Phillip II worked to establish Spain as a pure, religiously orthodox state (a Catholic city on the hill) and severed ties with humanism at the time Ercilla was writing the Araucana, a "progressive" mentality was still accepted in Spain; its practioners represented an important, if secondary, force at the court.

With Las Casas' descriptions and Columbus' and Cortés' letters from the New World, there was a clear precedent for a literary work on the Indian which could ascribe noble characteristics to him, as well as violent ones. The great European interest in the New World also worked in Ercilla's favor. Tales

---

[22] Alfonso de Ercilla y Zuniga, La Araucana, (Santiago de Chile: Escritores coloniales de Chile, Editorial universitaria, 1969).

emphasizing the exotic nature of the country and its people could be counted on to give an author a large readership and renown. The only issue remaining to an author then was what kinds of elements would an Indian story have and what form it would take. The answer to that question resides in another important work: Jorge de Montemayor's La Diana.[23]

La Diana established the Italian sub-genre of the Arcadian narrative of Jacopo Sannazaro on a solid Iberian basis. Since Montemayor was Portuguese but wrote in a modified Castillian, his influence was felt equally in both of the countries of the peninsula with his tales of shepherds and shepherdesses whose endless lover's quarrels and emotional misunderstandings could only be sorted out through a visit to the enchantress Felicia (felicitas) and her magic fountain. The importance of the Diana to Ercilla and his imitators lay in its emphasis on love and beautiful exotic settings with nature playing an important part in the setting of the narrative, as described in a relatively pure poetic manner. Certain specific Arcadian traits which are found time and time again in later poetry with Indian characters are the timeliness of the world created, its few links with any sort of concrete reality, its emphasis on nature, and the highly intellectual nature of the speech of its supposedly rustic inhabitants.

Of course the use of the Arcadian narrative poem as a popular sub-genre was not unique to the Italian originators such as Boccaccio or Sannzaro or even Montemayor and Ercilla. Almost all of Spain's important writers attempted some kind of Arcadian narrative. In fact, part of the humor of the second volume of Miguel de Cervantes' Don Quixote comes from his showing how absurd any attempt at living life in an Arcadian manner would be; although Cervantes, too, wrote an Arcadian novel. In France the enormous work of Urfé entitled L'Astrée, along with that of his numerous imitators, definitely springs from La Diana as well as the Italians' works. In England nymphs and shepherds appear frequently in

---

[23] Jorge de Montemayor, Los siete libros de la Diana ed. Enrique Moreno Baez, (Madrid: Editora Nacional, 1976).

works by many authors, including both Spenser and Shakespeare.[24] The Spanish role in its creation of the first literary image of the Indian is not limited to deriving it from the Italian Arcadian poem. There is also the Spanish chivalric romance to consider, including the epic poem of El Cid and the more recent courtly work, Amadís de Gaula from which the Spanish developed their tradition of noble honor so often ridiculed by the English.[25] The remembrance of the struggle against the Moors (who were finally completely defeated in 1492) and Spain's lead in the exploration of the New World brought about a feeling of pride that was accompanied by this growth in the Spanish concept of honor. Thus at the time Ercilla was writing, the Spanish were interested in medieval romances as well as the Arcadian poem. The Quixote itself presents a good example of this by establishing a strong link between the two genres with its hero wavering between the two literary ideals in his bouts of madness. Nevertheless, there are some qualities in common in these sub-genres of Arcadian poem and the chivalric romance. Both are concerned with utopic and bucolic states, in direct opposition to the reality of the time in which they were written: that of socio-economic and religious strife. Probably nostalgia as well as exoticism played an important role in the growth of popularity of each sub-genre.

Ercilla managed to combine the qualities of both the chevalric hero and the Arcadian hero in his Indians of the Araucana. He described a land far away that had almost no relationship to the New World as described by the explorers. His Indian heroes, in keeping with their chevalric and Arcadian heritage, also had little kinship with the Indians described by Columbus or Cortés. These were not simple ignorant people who were totally unacquainted with European mores. They were, instead, warriors cast almost completely in medieval terms. As Julio Caillet-Bois says in his Análisis de la Araucana,

---

[24] Louise K. Horowitz, Honoré d'Urfé, Boston: Twayne Publishers, 1984), Miguel de Cervantes, Don Quijote de la Mancha, 2 vols, Juan Bautista Avalle-Arce ed. (Madrid: Editorial Alhambra, 1976).

[25] Amadís de Gaula, Edwin B. Place ed., (Madrid: Consejo Superior de Investigaciones Cientificas, Instituto Miguel de Cervantes, 1971).

> Como en el Orlando Furioso se borran los limites
> entre la guerra y el torneo, los araucanas en ésta,
> como los saracenas y paranos en aquél son
> caballeros practicantes de las normes de Bretaña.26

As proof of this assertion this series of citations from the Araucana, points out the Arcadian irreality of setting and the chevalric nature of the Ercillan Indian hero:

> En fin, el hado y clima desta tierra,
> si su estrella y pronósticos se miran,
> es contenida, furor, discordia, guerra,
> y a solo ésto los ánimos aspiran;
> todo su bien y mal aquise encierra:
> son hombres que de súbito se airan,
> de condición feroces, impacientes,
> amigos de domán extrañas gentes.
> (...) Son de gestos robustos, desbardados,
> bien formados los cuerpos y crecidos,
> espaldas grandes, pechos levantados,
> recios miembros de niervos bien fornidos,
> legiles, desenvueltos, y alientados,
> animosos, valientes, atrevidos,
> duros en el trabajo y sufridores
> de fríos mortales hambres y calores.27

Therefore it seems clear now that Ercilla has created a protagonist who has combined in him both Arcadian and chivalric features. Indeed he was the true "savage" in its derivation from the Latin selvaticus—that pertaining to a forest. In this sense he and his tribe could become "valientes caballeros a quien solo el valor natural de la persona os trujo a descubrir el austral polo".28 They were true children of the woods.

In French literature the Ercillan archetype of the pastoral Indian did not immediately become popular. In fact, with one notable exception, the Indian was

---

26 Julio Caillet-Bois, Análisis de la Araucana, (Buenos Aires: Centro Editor de America latina, 1967) 29.

27 Ercilla 28–29.

28 Melendez 23–27.

not a popular character in sixteenth century. There were a few allusions to the New World in the poetry of the Pléiade and some of Rabelais' fantastic adventures of Pantagruel and Gargantua, including some episodes that could be considered to be influenced by New World voyages. However, the tenor of most of these chapters is more similiar to those of St. Brendan than Cartier. Nevertheless, although Rabelais does seem to have been interested in the voyages of discovery in the New World, he may have written his works too early to have been intrigued by the possibilities of the New World savage inhabitant. His particular interests in writing were more aligned with his need to popularize his version of humanism as a learned philosophy, rather than with showing how the natural state of primitive man is a humanistic one.[29] It can be also argued that the nature of primitive man did not become a popular topic in France until the work of Las Casas and de Léry became widely known during the later part of the century; since it is known that they influenced the other great writer of the French sixteenth century, Michel de Montaigne.[30]

It has always proven difficult to define the generic category under which Montaigne's work belongs. Indeed, in English, the word "essai" has simply become "essay" and Montaigne's literary work serves as the first model of the genre of the essay. Although my purpose is not to do a thorough analysis of non-fictional writing, the influence of his essay, "Des cannibales" is extremely important. This essay is not necessarily a re-telling of a true story, nor is it exactly a purely literary work such as La Araucana or other Arcadian narratives. Neither is it a purely philosophical proposition devoid of emotional impact, dealing only with the abstract or metaphysical nature of primitive man. Montaigne creates the image of the noble "cannibal", who in spite of this particular repugnant anti-Christian characteristic, exemplifies in many other ways the tenets of Christian doctrine. The narrative is accomplished through the device of a conversation between the author and a cannibal from the New World. In the dialogue the native is allowed to

---

[29] See Romer.

[30] See De Léry.

describe his <u>Weltanschauung</u> in an eloquent and sympathetic manner. Montaigne then inserts his own opinion and moral force on behalf of the native to complete the chapter.[31]

Although his chapter might have been based upon a real meeting between Montaigne and an Indian (or a native of any non-European part of the world), the author's exposition created a literary text independent of any necessary link with real events. His cannibal, and his race of noble cannibals in their literary exemplification, present Montaigne's thesis more eloquently and persuasively than any simple statement of perceived fact or philosophical premise. Montaigne, before Rousseau, described the "noble savage" in the original antithetical meaning of a savage who is nevertheless noble. At the same time, he makes the savage, the savage's characteristics, and nature the important elements in a moral and philosophical debate that continues to the present day. Perhaps even more importantly Montaigne begins a French philosophical tradition of considering the American native as the ideal test case in any discussion of the nature of primitive man, although this tradition would be complemented later by that of Spanish, Portuguese, English and other European writers of the seventeenth and eighteenth centuries.

In England, the sixteenth century is the period of the break with the Roman church, the Spanish armada, and "bloody" Mary. Writing on the Indians in the New World was not the exciting issue that it was in other countries due to the domestic excitement which occupied the citizen's attention. However, some important works on the New World were written. The first work written in English which contains an important Indian character describes him as a creature having no king, no master, or God, who has everything owned in common, going about covered in feathers like beasts, without any reason. The author even goes so far as to insist that their diet was primarily composed of family members. "The man eateth his wife, his chylderne as we have also seen and they hange also the

---

[31] Montaigne 230–245.

bodyes of persons fleeshe in the smoke as men do with swynes fleshe."[32] William Cunningham goes equally far in 1559 in saying, "There is no law or order observed of wedlock; for it is lawful to have so many women as they affect, and to put them away without any daunger. They be filthy at meate, and in all secrete acts of nature, comparable to beasts."[33]

But the early English writers did not uniformly hold a negative image of the New World inhabitants. Richard Hakluyt, the most famous chronicler of English exploration in the sixteenth century, described the New World in terms more familiar to other writers in Europe. He thought of the discovered lands as a perfect Eden for commerce and industry. Hakluyt quoted Sir Walter Raleigh as saying that the natives were physically superior to Europeans.[34] Hakluyt's follower, Purchas, continued the descriptions of the newly discovered lands, and went farther than Raleigh. He compared the newly discovered people with both the Britons of King Arthur and the character of Ariel in Shakespeare's The Tempest. Arthur Barlowe described the Indians in terms fitting of Las Casas. To him, in 1584, they were a people "most gentle, loving, and faithfull, voide of all guile and treason and such as live after the manner of *the Golden Age*" [author's emphasis].[35] Still, only with the seventeenth-century story of John Smith does English literature really begin to deal with the Indians as literary characters. In some respects this story should be considered an archetypal account, that is one which influenced later writers in the English-speaking New World, and perhaps served as a way of discussing the sexual relationships between European men and Indian women. The obvious fact that the first English settlers in Virginia were almost all men and that Indian women followed a different system of moral teachings is enough to explain the cross-cultural relationships; yet John Smith's apologia was not the only

[32] Zolla 13.

[33] Zolla 13.

[34] Zolla 14.

[35] Zolla 15.

story of its kind. What is perhaps more important than its relation to any real situation is the fact that these stories ascribed "noble" characteristics to a given group of native Americans (i.e. women) while describing the Indian men as savages, thus launching what would become a tradition of writing about both the ignoble and the noble aspects of Indians in the same work. It also inaugurated an English tradition of noble savage women and ignoble savage men.

The Seventeenth Century

In Spain early during this century, writing on New World inhabitants took on new importance when Bernardo de Balbuena published his Grandeza Mexicana and Garcilaso (Inca) de la Vega published his Comentarios, both in 1604.[36] These writers chronicled fallen civilizations which they knew would never rise again. It is interesting to note the nostalgic value they assigned to their respective societies. In Garcilaso's case this is even more poignant due to his mixed parentage. Garcilaso admired Spanish culture and indeed wrote his work in Spanish, but he also admired what he saw as the many positive aspects of Inca rule. The fact that the Incas themselves were a type of colonial power was not important to his view of the past. Instead, he emphasized their noble rulers and the tragedy of the ultimate Incan defeat upon the arrival of the Spanish. In this sense Garcilaso supplied the historical background for later novelists and playwrights, giving them an adequate topic to use in their consideration of more global questions. He also added further fuel to any philosophical consideration of the Indian as a new form of human being.

Also in Spain, a work by a Spaniard who had resided in Chile caught the public's imagination. This was Francisco Nuñez de Pineda's Feliz cautiverio en Chile (1630).[37] In this work Nuñez de Pineda describes how his dreaded captivity

---

[36] See Melendez 23, 28–30.

[37] Francisco Nuñez de Pineda, Feliz cautiverio en Chile, quoted in Melendez, 30–32.

among the Indians had become a rather pleasant stay as he became more accepting of the Indian tribe. This allowed him to propagate his Christian beliefs among the younger members of the tribe, who enthusiastically embraced the ideals proclaimed. Although the emphasis upon conversion is rather strong in this narrative, Nuñez de Pineda also gives praise to the Indian, describing how honorably the non-Christian chief treated him and how he had to resist the temptation of the Indian women—especially one "que sobresalía por blanca, por discreta, y por hermosa".[38] In short, although he believed that the Indians needed to be converted to Christianity, there can be no doubt about the positive nature of his description of the Indians he encountered. As such it is written in stark contrast to some other captivity narratives that will be discussed later. His Indians, indeed, seem to fall in the tradition established by Ercilla.

In Portugal, which regained its independence from Spain in 1640, and in Brazil, the early Jesuit priests were the first writers of any importance to deal with the Indians. Fathers Anchieta, Nobrega, and later Father Viera all wrote about the simple, savage, and at times touching nature of the Indian. However as they, and the French D'Evreux and Abbéville also writing about the Brazilian Indians discovered, the Indian they saw was far from perfect.[39] He was indeed a savage, even if he often was appealing. He seemed to be lazy, quarrelsome, and, most importantly, his religion was totally philosophically inadequate. He was a child to these writers, a most pleasing child perhaps, but a child who did not act according to the dictates of the Christian religion. As a result, the Portuguese and the French priests in Brazil could be considered the least affected of any early writers by the humanism of Las Casas or the mercantilism of the colonial governments, yet this is not the case. Their descriptions show they believed that many of the positive traits first described by Columbus and Las Casas existed, but that these traits were insufficient to characterize the Indians without a clear indication of the Indian's acceptance of Christian doctrine, and consequently of European civilization. Thus,

---

[38] Melendez 32.

[39] See Driver.

38

force should be used to convert them just as it had been used for the Jews who had stayed in Spain.

A more appealing tactic than force was Father Anchieta's attempt at persuasion with his morality plays written in Guarani (an Indian language), intended to teach the Indians the advantages of Christianity. Still even though the priests recognized deficiencies in the Indian's religion and society, they also found themselves obliged to defend his basic good nature. Father Viera, writing almost a hundred years later than Fathers Anchieta and Nobrega, had his life threatened on several occasions for daring to defend enslaved Indians against the injustices of their masters. As David Driver ably points out in his The Indian in Brazilian Literature, Viera was no Father Montesinos nor Las Casas. He described the natives using the image of a rough block of stone whose beauty lay in what the accomplished sculptor could chisel out of it, but whose beauty was no less real for its being potential and not actual.[40]

It is also important here to note that these three Portuguese priests and the two Frenchmen were the only important writers discussing what were to become Brazil's Indians before Basílio de Gama wrote his Uruguai at the end of the eighteenth century. This could be due to a variety of factors, the most important being Portugal's continued use of the Index de librorum prohibitorum and the Spanish-influenced Inquisition. As the commercial element in both countries was satisfied to let the church and government continue in repressing the Indians, the number of published works opposed to these tenets naturally declined. Just as Spain began to close itself off to the rest of Europe in 1585, so did Spanish-controlled Portugal. Although Portugal did not follow Spain's lead in prohibiting any students to study outside of Spain or Bologna, Italy, its cultural importance began to fade as quickly as its economic strength. In a parallel effect Portugal became more and more isolated and insulated from new ideas as its government drew a tighter control over its people and policies.

---

[40] Driver 66–67.

Spain's decline in literature can only be traced after the death of the last generation of its writers influenced by the Renaissance. For the same reasons mentioned above for Portugal, Spanish interest in any new literary ideas flagged and only nostalgic rewriting of previous literary motifs sparked any interest among literate Spaniards. This is not to say that the late seventeenth century and the eighteenth century were literary deserts, as many critics seem to believe. There were some interesting baroque and neo-classical poems written, as well as a few novels patterned after the work of Cervantes. However, any type of unveiled criticism of the official governmental policies reminiscent of Las Casas or even Cervantes was not acceptable. Purveyors of such ideas were liable to persecution by the Inquisition. As a result liberal ideas were hidden in tortured baroque prose, or later, were contained only in classically-inspired allusions. Finally, the growth of an urban bourgeoisie, which influenced the type of literature produced in Northern Europe, did not occur in Spain or Portugal to the same extent. The rigid Iberian class structure helped kill innovation. Thus, it was left to England, and especially to France, to continue the renaissance ideals propagated by Iberian writers.

In England in the seventeenth century, the Pocahontas story started a short-lived trend of New World romances. Quickly, the literate English settlers living in the New World responded with another view of the Indian. This view was expressed especially strongly in North America's only independent philosophical center, as well as the only one with a printing press—Puritan New England. Early Puritan sermons tended to label the Indians as examples of God's creatures who had fallen from grace, who were not regenerate, and who could not be expected to be counted among the elect. From there it was but a short step to identify them as being followers of Satan, as their barbaric rituals proved. It was not until 1679, however, that a literary expression was given to this sentiment. In that year Mary Rowlandson published her <u>Captivity Among the Indians</u>.[41] In harrowing detail she described Indian excesses, barbarism, and cruelty. She did

[41] Zolla 56–57.

40

give some examples of savage kindness, but these were explained as proof that the loving-kindness of God can penetrate even the blackest of evil hearts. In short, what she produced was the first in a long series of English-language captivity narratives whose popularity as a type remains undiminished even in the twentieth century.[42] Here, at last, is the first clear example of what will be defined in the next chapter as the progressivist mentality which writers such as Buffon will adapt for their own needs in the eighteenth century.

It is now appropriate to reconsider Elmire Zolla's description of the conflict between ideologies presented in the beginning of this chapter. Zolla gives examples of Englishmen supporting both ideologies. He shows how some Englishmen did not support the Puritan, Mary Rowlandson's, view of the Indians and instead presented another view which he calls the Libertine-Enlightenment attitude, only seen in the seventeenth century in such writers as John Archdale and perhaps William Penn and Lord Shaftesbury. In this view of the Indian, which would become much stronger in the eighteenth century, the early traditions of Montaigne, Las Casas, and Barlowe become fused together into a new exoticism that often explicity adds eroticism. Writers such as Shaftesbury discuss the New World savage as a creature who lets his impulses and instincts become predominant and as a result is at home in nature.[43] William Penn's well-known fair dealings with the Indians exemplify a current of Quaker writers who discussed the Indian in the same way as Shaftesbury. They used the words "simple", "simplicity", and "innocence" to describe the New Worlder they found which in their pietistic interpretation of Christian teaching were positive expressions. Let us return to eighteenth-century English ideas after examining seventeenth-century French

---

[42] See Perry Miller, The New England Mind: The Seventeenth Century, (Cambridge, MA: Harvard University Press, 1954). See also some recent Hollywood offerings, including "A Man Called Horse" and "The Return of a Man Called Horse" or the "bad" Indians in "Dances With Wolves", "The Black Robe" or "The Deerslayer".

[43] Zolla 56–70.

literature dealing with the Indian and what Zolla calls their "bible", Baron de Lahontan's work.

France, from the seventeenth century through the nineteenth century is the most important European center for the discussion of notions of the nature of the Indian, viewed as the exemplary primitive man. As such, it is the focal point of the Indian question. In a sense this importance reflects France's predominant position in Europe, politically and economically. But it also reflects the importance of both Montaigne and Descartes. Montaigne is important for his introduction of the moral problem of the noble savage, as viewed in a philosophical manner. Descartes is important to the French consideration of the Indian question in that he encouraged a rational system of thinking which relied upon experimentation and hypothesis. His methods were based upon the notion that man, as a whole, was a rational being who could understand his surroundings through his observations and rational deductions. Thus while the English in England and the Puritans in the New World both attempted to see the Indians as a very concrete problem who was either maltreated or maltreating, and the Spanish wrote about him as a fierce honorable warrior who lived in an Arcadian world, the French in the late seventeenth century, and more so in the eighteenth century, saw the Indian as the turning point in the various philosophical arguments about the nature of man. In some sense this was due to Montaigne himself and his treatment of the New World man in "Des cannibales"; however, it is no less due to Cartesian influence. As conclusions must be drawn upon observations and experimentation, the only possible way to learn about the nature of man was to abstract it from the most isolated and primitive beings possible—the American native. Since few French philosophical or literary writers showed much interest in leaving their hearths for a first-hand experience in the wilderness, they had to rely upon the published letters and reports of those who had this experience. As a result the previously mentioned reports of Las Casas, de Léry, D'Evreux and Abbéville interested the French literati, as well as other first-hand narratives to be discussed later.

Gilbert Chinard discusses many of these sources for the eighteenth-century writers and at the same time shows how even these writers were influenced by earlier literary figures. Most interesting is his account attempting to prove that Jacques Cartier was influenced by the Arcadian writers. As an example, he gives Cartier's account of certain native customs, including that of the native women stripping and meeting visitors in the nude. While Chinard presents an interesting argument, later travelers to Canada were definitely more Arcadian-influenced than Cartier. Included among these were Fathers Lescarbot and Sagard who wanted to attract more settlers to Canada and would not shy away from using sexually-inspired narratives to do so. Chinard even describes Lescarbot's narrative as quite, "Rabelaisian in tone",[44] especially his tales of the wild voyages he made in the interior and the amount of liquor he consumed. In fact one of Lescarbot's greatest reproaches to the Indians is their ignorance of wine, "Je ne sçay si je ne doy mettre entre les plus grands aveuglements des Indiens Occidentaux d'avoir le fruit le plus excellent que Dieu nous ait donné et de n'en savoir l'usage".[45] At the same time he defends them against charges of brutality, stupidity, and slow-wittedness that evidentally were commonplace during this period. He even went so far as to say that they had "autant d'humanité et plus d'hospitalité que nous", comparing the Indians and their customs to the ancient Lacedoemians.[46]

Father Gabriel Sagard and later Father Hennépin would continue the refrain of Indian nobleness. As Sagard has been accepted by the Québéçois as one of the first French Canadian writers, it is instructive to realize to what extent he enobles the Indian. Although at one point in his description he calls them rather sarcastically, just as Champlain did, "les pauvres dégenerés", he later discusses them as being more virtuous than the majority of the French inhabitants of the early colonial period. Then, while still insisting upon their paganism, he described them

---

[44] Gilbert Chinard, L'Am rique et le r ve exotique dans la litt rature française au XVIIeme sicle, (Paris: E. Droz, 1934).

[45] Chinard 103.

[46] Chinard 107.

in tones worthy of Las Casas.[47] In a sense, since Sagard is now quoted in the standard Quebec literary anthologies as an individual, he is more important to twentieth-century Quebec literary mythology than to the eighteenth. As part of a group of priests, especially the early Jesuit priests, Fathers Hennépin and Sagard wrote descriptions paralleling those of Charlevoix and Lescarbot.

Although Sagard and Hennépin have little individual importance in the eighteenth century, they have a great collective impact when their writings are put together with other Jesuit priests. It was as if there were some kind of unified accord on the worth of the early Huron Indians to which all of the priests writing back to Europe had to subscribe. This unified opinion only came to the attention of French writers and philosophers later in the seventeenth century and in the eighteenth century.

Before going on to the important eighteenth-century accounts it is necessary to consider the more literary narratives of the seventeenth century in France. Chinard cites several writers of the Arcadian school as being important to later writing on the New World. Du Perier's Pistion is a work in keeping with this tradition, in which the forests of the newly discovered lands become mysterious woods (or the haunts of Venus and her court) and in which the natives participate in a medieval tournament. Gomberville's La Corithée and Polexandre owe as much to L'Astrée, and ultimately to La Araucana, as they do to any intended realism. All of its fantastic notions about the New World are presented as facts and the volumes' plots become rather byzantine in their complexity. At the same time the theme of the lover searching for his beloved remains the paramount interest of their intrigues.[48]

Other early novelists using the New World as the setting for their love stories are no more interested in departing from the popular Arcadian conventions. The New World might as well be an island located in the Bay of Biscay settled by Ercilla and his family as the real terra habitata of the Indians.

---

[47] Chinard 110.

[48] Chinard 135–140.

More important in its influence upon the eighteenth century was the work of Baron de Lahontan. His <u>Dialogues du Baron de Lahontan avec le sauvage du bon sens</u> (1703)[49] became well-known in both France and England from the time inhabitants that could have served as the focal point of later philosophical discussion, although it was the work of a man who may never have made any of the voyages to the interior, or the <u>pays d'en haut</u>,[50] that he claimed to have made. His opinion of Canadian Indians differed somewhat from those of his priest predecessors. He had good reason for being opposed to the Church, as it had taken over his barony, so he was not concerned whether or not Indians were Christian.

After his work was first published, another writer, Guedéville, rewrote the dialogues and changed some of their meaning. Although proclaiming himself as an editor, he introduced the idea of the evil of private property into the third dialogue. It could be argued, however, that he was merely extending the ideas written in Lahontan's original volume in which doctors, wives, and the power of wealth were all attacked. What is most interesting is the narrator's conclusion about the Indians; he says that "ils sont libres et nous sommes esclaves."[51] Lahontan's savage, Adario, is even given what would become "<u>philosophe</u>" thought to express. In one passage Adario says, "La loi est cette impulsion naturelle gravée dans nos âmes qui nous préscrit ou qui nous défend une chose, suivant que cette chose est conforme ou opposée à la justice et à la droite raison."[52]

It is most likely the words of the savage, Adario, would have had little or no meaning to a non-European educated New World native. In fact in the eighteenth century these words only acquired their full meaning when read by a small group of European <u>literati</u> who were acquainted with the ideas contained in them.

---

[49] See Chinard and Zolla 65–66 and 77.

[50] This term comes from Jack Warwick, <u>The Long Journey, Literary Themes of French Canada</u>, (Toronto: University of Toronto Press, 1966).

[51] Chinard 177.

[52] Chinard 181.

In contrast to Lahontan's historical fiction, Huet's <u>Le faux Inca</u> reflected the importance of Garcilaso de la Vega and other Spanish and French chroniclers, including P. Bergeron's <u>Traité de la navigation et des Voyages de Descouvertes et Conquestes modernes et principalement des François</u>, the anonymous <u>Mercure américain</u>, Gabriel Foigny's <u>La terre australe connue</u>..., and Cyrano de Bergerac's works.[53] All of these works share the theme of a fantastic voyage, with little or no relation to reality. In a sense these voyages are all like those of Rabelais or the medieval narrators already described. They deal with unlikely and marvelous occurences and share some subject matter with medieval tall tales. The best of the later works, such as those of De Bergerac, remind one of Thomas Mores's <u>Utopia</u>. At times there is a serious attempt to portray an entire utopic society in which foreign ways are shown as being better. Unlike the case of Rabelais, where the best societies are those of the reformed Europeans (the Gargantuan and Pantagruelian philosopher-king societies), here there are positive non-European civilizations. Even if these societies are merely European projections onto existing cultures, they are still significant as sources of the superior savage stories that become important during the last three centuries of this milennium.

So it is the superior savage, that of the forward-looking Lahontan and the utopic writers, instead of that of the backward-looking Huet who sets the stage for the twist the image of the Indian receives in the eighteenth century in France. And, it is France who will develop this image and make it a focal point of philopsophical debate.

The Eighteenth Century

If the sixteenth century viewed the New World inhabitant as a child, sometimes sweet-natured but an oddity of no real importance, and the seventeenth

---

[53] Chinard and Cyrano de Bergerac, <u>Voyage dans la lune</u>, Maurice Lauguaa, ed., (Paris: Garnier-Flammarion, 1970).

century viewed him as an ignorant child, either basically good who could be taught the teachings of the church or basically evil who could never learn about God and had to be pushed aside; then, in the eighteenth century he seems to become the child of nature living in a simple but highly refined society whose ignorance of the institutions of private property, organized religion, and urban life are viewed as characteristics of a superior society.[54]

However, the older images of the Indian do not die out in the eighteenth century. While the philosophical problem of the New World native begins to dominate French writing, the Ercillan-, Arcadian, love-story never disappears—especially in Spanish and Portuguese America where it continues to dominate writing on Indians. In France this love-story becomes a sub-current which re-emerges at the end of the century in Bernardin de St. Pierre's discussion of Caribbean blacks, and of course in the nineteenth-century work of Chateaubriand.

One of the first French literary works to express the new image of the Indian was not a novel or a poem, but a play. This is Louis François de la Drevetière Deslisles' L'Arlequin sauvage,[55] presented for the first time in 1721. In this play a Canadian Huron is brought back to France for the amusement of a sea captain's mistress. Here for the first time in France a whole work is devoted to the reactions of a native New Worlder to the vagaries of European culture. Among the different institutions that puzzled the Indian, Arlequin, (whose commedia dell'arte name was given to him due to the fact that L'Arlequin sauvage was first presented at the Théâtre Italien), are European laws and codes created to enforce decent behavior. He was amazed when told that if it were not for these laws, France and other European countries would soon be in the hands of looters and other criminals. To him this abridgement of freedom and this lack of self-control were unthinkable. The coquettery of French women of the court also astounded him.

---

[54] For the classic treatment of these ideas, see especially Gilbert Chinard, L'éxotisme américain dans l'oeuvre de Chateaubriand, (Paris: Hachette et Cie., 1910).

[55] Chinard 226–227.

As he explained, in Canada a woman either accepted an amorous offer or she refused it. She would be shown a match that a brave held in his hand. If she blew out the match, she accepted the offer; if she let the match burn the brave's fingers then the offer was rejected. Continuing with ideas expressed in the dialogues of Lahontan and Guedéville, the ownership and distribution of private property, was the most difficult thing for Arlequin to comprehend. Arlequin finally cries out in desperation at his European mentors:

> Vous êtes des fous, car vous cherchez avec une
> infinité de soin des choses inutiles; vous êtes
> pauvres, parce que vous bornez vos biens dans
> l'argent, ou d'autres diableries, au lieu de jouir
> simplement de la nature comme nous, qui ne
> voulons rien avoir afin de jouir plus librement de
> tout. Vous êtes des esclaves de toutes vos
> possessions que vous préférez à la liberté...Enfin,
> vous êtes ignorans, parce que vous faites consister
> votre sagesse à savoir les lois, tandis que vous ne
> connaissez pas la raison.[56]

Jean-Jacques Rousseau enjoyed the play and knew it well. In a sense it is a continuation of Molière's and Lope de Vega's comedies which tried to teach moral lessons as well as entertain. The value of common sense is again put forward by someone not of the noblesse or the bourgeoisie. But now, the speaker of good sense was even more of an outsider, since he is not European or even Christian, and his critique goes deeper. Although this play did not present ideas not already being discussed or debated in the salons, it did present them in a convincing, straightforward manner in the realm of a popular theatrical performance. It also put these ideas in the mouth of a bon sauvage fashioned upon Lahontan's Adario. Finally it anticipated the point of view of Montesquieu's Lettres persanes by some twenty years.

The fashion of the bon sauvage, especially le bon Huron of la Lahontan, spred to every major French writer in the eighteenth century. For a while, the

---

[56] Chinard 229–230.

48

philosophical ideas of Adario and Arlequin were replaced by purely love stories as the most popular theme in literature containing Indians, with the savage serving only to give the writer a convenient exotic focal point. Yet, as already evidenced by Arlequin, the savage could be involved in a love story while spouting philosophical doctrines in an exotic setting. Thus philosophy, exoticism, and love, the beloved themes of eighteenth-century literature, could all be presented using a single subject in a single work and all three would be important in French works using Indians.

The sub-genre of works treating the Indians or other non-European peoples in exotic settings, sporting much of the same philosophy as that of Adario and Arlequin, became important throughout eighteenth-century Europe. An obvious example of this trend is Montesquieu's Lettres persanes, in which a Persian noble and his entourage came to Paris and commented on French life much in the same way as did Arlequin.[57] In a sense it is unjust to compare Deslisle's somewhat inelegant and theatrical Arlequin with Montesquieu's biting, witty, and masterful use of the epistolary form. It is perhaps equally unjust to compare Montesquieu's skilled use of humor and style written in such clear prose with the simplicity of ideas inherent in most of the theatrical productions of the eighteenth century. Nevertheless, both works do share many of the same notions: the injustice of private property, the absurdity of courtly sexual behavior, and the problems of an disobedient people. The contrast between Persian opulance and Indian simplicity might appear to render comparisons between the two groups difficult, but the device of using non-Europeans to critique Europeans still meant their similarities would be more numerous than their differences since the Indians and the Persians who were both created by Parisian intellectuals would be likely to find the same failings in Europeans.

---

[57] Charles de Secondat, Baron de Montesquieu, Lettres persanes, (Paris: Garnier, 1975).

Another member of the sub-genre of the exotic non-European story is Diderot's Supplement au voyage de Monsieur de Bougainville.[58] Here Diderot's Tahitian could be Adario in a tropical setting with other parallel views on religion, property, and sex. If anything, Diderot goes farther than Lahontan with his insistence on absolute freedom of the individual. For Didetot's Tahitian the only law is the law of nature. As a result this new character can be considered as much of a bon sauvage as Adario. It could be that Didero's change of locale and not of native attributes was due either to wanting a new non-Canadian superior being to describe the glowing reports of Tahiti with its warm climate, or to the Buffon-Rousseau controversy about the native (to be discussed in the chapter two).

Voltaire also used New World characters. Along with his many philosophical essays, some of which touched on the Indians, he was also a playwright. One of his plays, Alzire, specifically treated the New World natives. Alzire differs significantly from the Deslisle play, Arlequin sauvage, or the earlier views of the Indians given by Lahontan and his followers. Voltaire seems to return to the opinions of the seventeenth century. Perhaps the reason for this surprising retour en arrière is the fact that Voltaire uses Peruvian Incas and not Canadian Hurons as his protagonists and is thus relying upon Spanish and not French sources for his play. Still, Voltaire seems to be attempting to prove that even the highest non-European civilization in the New World should be considered inferior to European society, both militarily and morally. As a result, what should have been a purely tragic play with a well-defined situation, in which two groups are in inalterable opposition, is suddenly changed by the Spanish captain's acceptance of his own death as a sacrifice given in order to insure peace. He forgives his Indian slayer, and as a result paves the way for the Indian chief's conversion to Christianity. The tragedy à la Corneille is transformed into a melodrama worthy of twentieth-century television, which perhaps explains why the play was only performed seven times before a critical Parisian audience. Whether this was a

---

58 Denis de Diderot, Oeuvres philosophiques, Paul Vernière, ed., (Paris: Garnier, 1964).

result of its poetic verse, its somewhat old-fashioned themes, or its imperfect plot is hard to say. Some critics go so far as to insist that, although the purported point of the play was its pro-Christian views, the dramatic interest is so connected with the principal figure of the play, the Indian maiden, Alzire, that her point of view and especially her denounciation of private property are the high points of the play.[59] She becomes a type of Racinian Andromaque caught in the web of a melodrama.

Therefore, although Voltaire did use an Indian heroine to express his views, he did not use her in the same way as writers discussed earlier did. Rather, he used a character from another world, not a New World noble savage, to expound his philosophical ideas in his Micromegas, one of his most didactic works. Although his use of another planet has some fantastic elements in common with some works dealing with the New World and Cyrano de Bergerac it cannot be claimed to be a work dealing with Indians. In Voltaire's Candidé as well, the savages that the European heroes met in South America were for the most part, real savages quite unenobled. Although Voltaire did have a positive primitive character in Le Huron ou l'Ingénu, the possible superiority of primitive man over civilized man was normally a horrifying thought to him.[60]

L'Abbé Prévost is also somewhat of a throwback to earlier times. His Clèveland and his Manon Lascaut[61] include travels to the New World and descriptions of different places there. But the Indians do not figure as central characters in his works. Exoticism, however, is an important element in Manon Lescaut, and his descriptions of Louisiana were well-known, albeit a Louisiana without Indians. Only in his Clèveland did he describe the savages in detail. He decided that they could be accepted in their inferior state, but also believed that they should be taught certain lessons, such as respect for their elders and a "purer" religion. In Clèveland Prévost seems to share Voltaire's repugnance for true

---

[59] Chinard 232–239.

[60] Chinard 237.

[61] Chinard 291–293.

savages. Prévost only enobles them in terms of their potential to be civilized after being educated in the European manner. A play that goes farther than Prevost's in describing the Indians as ignoble savages is Piron's <u>Fernand Cortez</u> (1744). It shows Cortes as a true Christian hero who has to eradicate the excesses of savage barbarism to make way for an improved society. For him the Aztecs were "Anthropopages impies et sanguinaires qui déshonoraient le genre humain".[62]   Although Prévost does not go this far, Voltaire at times seems to. His savage "Oreillons" in Candide look and act like monkeys. They bear no resemblance to his hero in <u>Le Huron ou l'Ingénu</u>. We can say that for Voltaire only French and not Spanish Indians are fit to be enobled.

As demonstrated in the second chapter Piron, Prevost, and normally Voltaire represent one common French attitude towards the Indian discussed and expanded upon in Buffon's <u>L'Histoire de la nature</u>.[63]   At the same time they remind us of well-known early American attitudes such as those of the early Puritan preachers and Mary Rowlandson in her captivity narrative. Therefore, even during the period of the greatest acceptance of the image of the noble savage, in the country best known for this image, the counter-image of the ignoble savage also had some powerful supporters. Thus both dichotomous images discussed at the beginning of this chapter are seen in eighteenth-century France, reflecting their development over two hundred and fifty years.

Nevertheless the image, soon to be the myth, of the noble savage dominated French thought about primitive man in the period before the revolution of 1789. As the greater part of the French aristocracy became more firmly entrenched in their attitudes and resistant to the changes recommended by the <u>philosophes</u>, the philosophers struggled harder to induce the aristocrats to accept some change. As a result, the noble savage became more of a political sign; s/he represented a unified

---

[62] Chinard 243.

[63] Georges Louis LeClerc Buffon, <u>A Natural History, General and Particular</u>, William Smellie trans., (London: Henry Augustus Chambers, 1917).

52

corpus of reformist thought as expressed through the works of <u>philosophes</u> and other writers detailing social abuses. A good example of this use of the noble savage is Jean-Jacques Rousseau's discourse on the nature of inequality from which his view of primitive humankind will be abstracted and discussed in the next chapter.[64]

In addition to the previously mentioned well-known examples, there were other French writers who dealt with the Indians as positive reformist signs. Examples are the Canadian missionaries, Lafitau and Charlebois, who continued the trend begun in the last century. They described the Indian as exceedingly adaptable to the Catholic faith, having only to be instructed in it to appreciate its inherent worth.[65] In this sense Indians were born to be noble Catholics due to the lack of the corrupting influences of civilization.

Writers other than the missionaries continued to provide ammunition for philosophical writing. There was a continuation in popular writing of the type of work created by Deslisle with his <u>Arlequin sauvage</u>. Numerous plays used the idea of the innocent and naively-wise Arlequin in establishing a sub-genre of noble savage plays, a fad which continued until the outbreak of revolution in 1789.

The last important eighteenth-century French work presenting the noble savage and a work that definitely influenced nineteenth-century New World literature is Marmontel's novel, <u>Les Incas</u>. Later Latin-American writers found appealing its strong denunciation of Spanish religious fanaticism and the fact that a French <u>philosophe</u> used New World history to explicate his ideas. They also admired its complicated plot full of love interests and non-romantic true-to-life descriptions. It is often cited in nineteenth-century Latin American writings, even though its worth as a literary work of art is debatable.[66]

---

[64] Jean-Jacques Rousseau, <u>Oeuvres completes</u>, 2 vols. (Paris: Garnier frères, 1965).

[65] For a discussion of these missionaries' reports and other early Jesuit ideas on French Canada, see Warwick 10–33.

[66] Melendez 44–45.

Before discussing further the influence of French sources on nineteenth-century literature, it is necessary to leave France to show how the images of noble and ignoble savages were reflected in other eighteenth-century European literatures.

In Spain and Portugal, the old ideas of Las Casas and Garcilaso were not forgotten, even if the freedom to write libertine works resembling those of Diderot and Rousseau did not yet exist. The eighteenth century is generally considered one of the least interesting periods of Iberian and Latin American literature due to the paucity of new themes and new ideas. In terms of its treatment of the Indian question the accuracy of this opinion is proven true. There were only a few works written this period that are interesting enough to cite here and one of them is from the end of the century—the period of the French revolution. This is the <u>Siripo</u> of José Manuel de Lebardón. It must be cited here even though only the second act has been preserved. With its celebration of its New World setting and characters, Concha Melendez, whose work on Indians in nineteenth-century Latin American literature remains authoritative, calls it "cronologicamente, el primero (drama) en la expresión literaria de la argentinidad."[67] with Lebardón's <u>Oda al majestuoso río Paraná</u> (1801) being perhaps the first poetic expression of "Argentineity", that is a work exalting a non-Spain controlled world.

A more interesting work is the drama <u>El Ollantay</u> written in Quechua and performed in Peru in the eighteenth century.[68] Although it is not my purpose here to deal with works written in an indigeneous language by either whites or by the Indians themselves, the scarcity of Indianist writing and the Spanish authorities' reaction to it makes it worthwhile to note. According to researchers delving into accounts of colonial history, it was presented to the Inca José Gabriel Condorcanqui, and it was written by a Father Valdés. It is known that later Condorcanqui revolted against the Spanish authorities, taking the name of

---

[67] Melendez 36–37.

[68] Melendez 34.

Tupac-Amaru II, and that after his defeat the Spanish forbade all drama written in Quechua. <u>El Ollantay</u> therefore was not performed again for many years. When it was translated into Spanish a hundred years later, however, it was very popular and went through six editions. In translation it was known for the beauty of its verse, even if its unbelievably happy ending was not very popular with the nineteenth-century devotees of melodrama. Finally, as Concha Melendez stresses, this repression of pro-native literature could explain, at least in the case of colonial Peru, why Peruvian literature dealing with the Indian only appears after the success of the revolt against Spain.[69] In Portugal the literary situation resembled that of Spain. There were some writers of note, both in Portugal and in Brazil, who wrote interesting neo-classical and neo-baroque poetry.[70] In terms of writings dealing with the Indian, only two works are of any importance. However one of them is perhaps the most striking example of an Indian-influenced poem written in an Iberian language before 1840. This is <u>O Uruguai</u> published in 1769 by José Basílio da Gama.

Before <u>O Uruguai</u> Diego Garção Tinoco wrote a poem in 1689 about the Bandeirantes—the first explorers of the São Paulo region. Although much of it was lost, the part that was preserved was a section in the prologue to Claudio da Costa's poem <u>Villa Rica</u> published in 1773. Included in it is a description of the main Indian character:

> Era o silvestre moço valeroso.
> Sobre nervudo, de perfídio alheio.
> O gesto respirava um ar brioso,
> Que nunca conhecerá o vá receio.

---

[69] Melendez 34–35.

[70] See Driver for a thorough discussion of the early Brazilian Indianist literature 21–40.

Pintado de urucu vinha pomposo,
E o labio baixo roto pelo meio
Com tres pennas de arará laudeado
Des tres flexas, de arco garrote armado.[71]

Not much is known about the majority of the poem or its themes, but it may have possessed certain similarities with more well-known Spanish poems such as <u>La Araucana</u> or the prose account <u>Feliz Cautiverio en Chile</u>.

In contrast, Da Gama's <u>O Uruguai</u> has been preserved. Da Gama was educated as a Jesuit; when the Jesuits were expelled from Portugal he went to Rome and became an Arcadian poet, much in the manner of Ercilla. Upon his return to Portugal, he was forced to denounce violently his Jesuit past. His epic poem, <u>O Uruguai</u>, is noted for its praise of the Portuguese army generals as well as its pro-Indian nature. The poem deals with an Indian war, indirectly instigated by the Jesuits, involving the Spanish and Portuguese. It includes the story of a love triangle similar to Voltaire's <u>Alzire</u>, with which Da Gama was acquainted. Instead of the sudden miraculous happy ending of <u>Alzire</u>, however, Da Gama has his hero, Cacambo (the name probably comes from Voltaire), and his heroine, Lindoya, die since they cannot be united in love due to the Jesuits' perfidy. His descriptions of nature seem to be very Arcadian, while the nature of his attitude toward the Indian has been hotly debated. Perhaps it is best to view Da Gama, whose poem is heavily biased towards Portugal's rulers, as an intermediate figure in the development of the image of the Indian in Brazil, influenced by Anchieta and Ercilla among others. His protagonists are straight from the classical mode, as nobly Lacedaemian as any of the French Jesuits' Canadian Hurons. They accept their fate in the time-honored tragic tradition, while also becoming closer to being "real" Indians. Their habits and colorful customs are described in great detail. Here, although the European laity is presented with great sympathy, the Indian heroes are the real focus of the poem; their moral honesty is in great contrast to Jesuit deviousness.

---

[71] Driver 22.

This poem probably inspired later Brazilian Indianists; but it is not an noble savage poem. Nevertheless, in Da Gama's sonnet on the revolt of Tupac Amaru, the last independent Incan ruler, there is a clear example of Da Gama's intermediate role between Viera and Alencar when he declares:

> Genio da inculta América que inspiras
> A meu peito o furor que me transporta;
> Tu me levantas nas seguras azas,
> Serás em pago ouvido no meu canto.
> E te prometo que pendente um dia
> Adorme a minha lyra os teus altares.[72]

A few other eighteenth-century Brazilian poems make reference to Indians, the most interesting of which is Alvarenga Peixoto's "Sonho" in which he says:

> Eu vi o Pão de Assucar levantar-se
> E no meio das ondas transformar-se
> Na figura de um Indio mais gentil,
> Representou só todo o Brasil.[73]

A clearer prefiguration of the end of José de Alencar's nineteenth-century work Iracema is hard to imagine. Yet this picture of the Indian is incidental to the rest of the poem. The only other Indian poem of any great length or interest is Frei Santa Rita Durão's Caramurá published in 1784. In this poem the innovations of Da Gama are not present. Rather, it is wholly in the spirit of Anchieta, in which the Indian is neither naturally good nor evil, but has a propensity to good which can be realized only through the intervention of the Holy Spirit. Therefore, it has no development of the image of the Indian, it did not receive even the limited popularity of O Uruguai, and it was not influential in the same way as Da Gama's poem was. This was the last Portuguese poem to deal with the Indians in a major way in the eighteenth century.

---

[72] Driver 30.

[73] Driver 33.

The last language group to be dealt with in this study, English-language literature, had some interesting works about Indians appear during this century. Like the French, the English witnessed a struggle of ideas between Libertines (the equivalent of the philosophes and the holders of older notions about religion, government, and society; but whereas societal and political tension was mounting in France and led to the revolution of 1789, in England the process of change begun with the Civil War of the 1640's, the Glorious Revolution of 1688, and the growth of parliamentary power under the Hanoverians had already brought major political, social, and economic developments. This capacity for change and reform in the English was what Montesquieu and Voltaire admired and discussed in several of their works. England herself, of course, had philosophers writing on societal change, the most well-known of whom are Berkeley and Shaftesbury. Unlike in France, these two writers stayed mainly in the realm of non-fiction and did not treat the noble savage in a fictional manner.

Similarly, the great poets and prose-writers did not employ the Indian as protagonist in many works. Swift's Gulliver's Travels[74] and Defoe's Robinson Crusoe[75] can be said to belong to the Rabelais-More school of utopias and distopias. Crusoe also shows certain similarities to Diderot's continuation of Bougainville's travels to Tahiti. In fact Crusoe comes the closest of any major English work to having a noble savage as an important character. However, it is also recognized that even here the European, Crusoe, eventually changes the life of the natives and is never inferior to the natives in any important way.

The one original story dealing with the idea of the noble savage that did come from England was that of Yarico. The story was first written in 1657 by Thomas Ligon in England and was then published by Steele in The Spectator in

[74] Jonathan Swift, Travels into Several Remote Nations of the World by Lemuel Gulliver, First a Surgeon and then Captain of Several Ships, (New York: The MacMillan Company, 1922).

[75] Daniel Defoe, The Life and Adventures of Robinson Crusoe, (London: Oxford University Press, 1910).

1711.[76] In this supposedly true narrative an Indian princess, Yarico, saved a white man from death through her love for him, then they both fled to Barbados where they could be safe from her people. Once safe, Inkle, the white man, sold Yarico as a slave since he could not marry a non-European woman. As Steele remarks, one assumes ironically, Inkle conducts himself as a prudent and frugal man should. Interestingly enough, there are French versions of the Yarico story in which several episodes are added and the ending is changed. The sentimentalism of several, later, English playwrights also forbade such a harsh and unforgiving ending. In some versions, the situations of Inkle and Yarico become reversed, and she has to decide whether to condemn him to slavery or to free him. Of course, she then frees the scoundrel and he promises to make amends. In other versions Inkle sold Yarico into slavery so that she would not interfere with his marriage to a proper English lady. Yarico then discovers his plans and confronts him with his schemes. After a tear-jerking sequence in which she stoically reminds him of her love and her selflessness, he finally comes to his senses and the two then get married in Charleston, South Carolina, and live happily ever after. In this series of plays not only is the image of the Indian interesting, but also the fact that the heroic figure in the English-inspired story is a woman.

Yet compared with France there are few noble savage works in Spain, Portugal, or England. Perhaps the reason for France's use of the savage is due both to the nature of their empire abroad and their society at home. Whereas Portugal and Spain had strong, viable, censorship in force and effective control of both their wealthy empires and the populace at home, France was much less global in its government-controled censorship and less successful in viability of its empire. England, on the other hand, was successful in its empire in the New World, at least until 1776, since it was organizing a new England based upon white European settlement. France's empire did not include much French settlement and consquently depended upon Indian good-will. Thus enobling "French" Indians

---

[76] Chinard 400–402.

made good political sense. Taken with the seventeenth-century Jesuit narratives, the development of the noble savage image there seems logical. So although France was much more involved with noble savage literature than other European countries, perhaps because of its own political and societal interests, it is still important to remember that France was in the center of Europe and its powerful cultural ideals would soon be exported in force along with the armies of the revolution.

In England, we have said that French influence was felt throughout the century and the close ties of some English Libertines and some French philosophes have already been discussed. What is perhaps more interesting, and certainly more ironic, is that after France lost Canada in 1769, France's cultural influence became more widespread throughout the New World than ever before. This would be soon recognized in what would become the United States, since it was recognized as an independent country first by France and became a French ally. It would be true later in Latin America since many of their revolutionary ideals came from France. Elemire Zolla discusses in detail the impact of these enlightenment and revolutionary ideals, originating in both France and England, on North America.He notes that although some Englishmen visiting the New World colonies, such as John Lawson and Cadwallader Colden, wrote paeans on the Indian, the first poetry that one can really label "noble savage" written in North America did not come until the end of the century with the work of Phillip Freneau (in whose name we note his French origins).[77]

The negative image, or the ignoble savage image, also remained strong in the United States. James Madison and other of the founding fathers clearly reflect this image in their writings.[78] Therefore, at the end of the eighteenth century, there remain two portraits of the Indian in the English colonies. One is that of a noble

---

[77] Zolla 61–85.

[78] Zolla 62–84.

Lacedaemian warrior, whose simplicity, strength, virtue, and uncivilized nature give civilized humans a foil against which they can see their own shortcomings. It did not matter whether the savage was perceived as ready to be converted to the Christian religion or as one whose own religion was simpler, clearer, and unambiguous; the savage was still superior in many ways to the European. In contrast, the image of the ignoble savage is one of a brutish animal who knows only that might makes right and has no more sense of compassion, justice, or duty than a wolf might. Indeed, the group behavior of these savages is often described in terms that resemble those used to describe a pack of wolves. This ferocity is somewhat admired, but it is viewed as being ultimately unsuccessful, due to the lack of any sustaining principles or any civilizing influence behind it. In fact neither of these images, as presented in their extreme form, is new when considered in the context of European history. There have always been cultures superior to European ones, either culturally or morally. What is new is the depth to which these images of other cultures influenced the current European philosophy. As the power of Roman Catholic Christianity was declining, the "New" World, filled with persons unknown to the ancients, was being used to fill the void.

In this chapter it has been shown how the two images, both positive and negative, of the native New World man developed from the first sightings of New World inhabitants, and how they were adapted through literary and philosophical conventions to become diametric opposites. With this background presented, it is now necessary to search deeper into European mentality and discover how these images become myths and, then, how the myths relate to the already posited progressive and regressive mentalities. Both the notions of myth and image must be analyzed in greater detail and then related to each other. It will be useful to use certain parts of semiotic theory to discuss the view of the Indian as a sign. Only after having dealt with these issues may we proceed to the nineteenth and twentieth centuries to see how they took these European images of the Indian and modified them for their own literary and cultural ends.

CHAPTER TWO:
THE INDIAN IMAGE AS A LITERARY MYTH

We are always ourselves in the image and unconscious because of it.[1]

Before treating the problem of the image of the Indian in nineteenth- and twentieth-century New-World literature, it is necessary to consider the question of whether the images of the Indian given in the first chapter represent a type of myth in literature. This is necessary, since most literary and historical critics writing about the way the native New World man has been viewed tend to discuss the images ascribed to the Indian as belonging to certain European philosophical tenets and thus, as related to certain mythologies that were important in Europe at one time or another. Other critics, to be discussed later in this chapter, actually call the images of the Indian produced by the eighteenth century amyths, mythic images, or literary myths and relate them to larger European mythologies. Since these critics are important in any attempt to explain the development of the non-Indian view of the native New World inhabitant—both pre-nineteenth century and post-nineteenth century—the problem of how the images and the myths relate to each other and to the text as a whole must be addressed.

After this macro-analysis of Indian images and myths, let us take two specific images from the eighteenth century—the period of transition between the first observations of early explorers and the somewhat complex images of the nineteenth and twentieth centuries—and consider them in light of the previous

---

[1] James Hillman, "An Inquiry into Image", Spring: An Annual of Archetypal Psychology and Jungian Thought, 1977, p. 75.

62

discussion of myth and image. For our purposes let us take two markedly different pictures of the New World native, that of Buffon and that of Rousseau. After a consideration of how these two literary facets are interrelated, we can decide how the literary images of the nineteenth and twentieth centuries differ from what went before.

In any consideration of literary myth and any reflection on how to approach it, it is absolutely necessary to broach the difficult problem of mythology and its connection to the written text. Within the limits of a chapter of a work dealing with a large subject in itself, it is impossible to go into as great detail as one would like. Certain important points can nevertheless still be made.

Myth is a very difficult word to define. It remains highly charged with pejorative connotations, especially in any discussion of modern myth. To many the word "myth" may be defined as a fictitious, spurious story designed to mislead clear thinkers. To others, myth is associated with the maintenance of some sort of reactionary orthodoxy. Many modern thinkers, however, are attempting to free themselves from such prejudices. They understand myth in its broadest sense. It is not a positive or negative story, but rather a narrative, perhaps an ontological or ideological construct dealing with complex symbolic concepts, which must be presented through the use of types of representational signs. These same critics no longer insist upon any didactic or explicitly explanatory function of myth. An early example of such a trend is provided by C. Kerenyi, the associate of Jung, who says that, Ümythology [not myth] is held to explain itself and everything else in the universe, not because it was invented for the purpose of explanation, but because it possesses, among other things, the property of being explanatory."[2] Even this short citation alerts us to another problem that we must consider, that is, the distinction between mythology and myth. The Jungians may be said to think of myth as being the narrative aspect of a broader and ill-defined whole called mythology. In this chapter, this notion will be further defined so that the concept of

2 C.G. Jung and C. Kerenyi, <u>Essays on a Science of Mythology</u>. trans., R.F.C. Hull, (New York: Harper Torch Books, 1949) 4–5.

mythology is the summation of a series of individual myths, whether one is considering the narrative or the functional aspect of myth. Many Jungians or neo-Jungians, of course, do not make this distinction.

This idea seems to be in concordance with what Lévi-Strauss and others posited as the important features of the myth nearly thirty years ago; more recent work, and in particular much literary research on the question, studies individual myths rather than mythology as a whole. As a result, one must infer that a composite of myths (and myth studies) becomes, through a collective summary of individual features, a statement about a mythology relevant to the myths and a statement about the study of mythology in general. Most of the recent writers who deal philosophically with these questions are only interested in non-literary myths, however. When refering to myth itself, they often see it as something created by a non-literate people at an early stage of their history, perhaps as a metaphorical expansion of the successful hunter narrative.

This definition of myth can still be interesting in its discussion of the raison d'être of myths as being that which can satisfy the basic philosphicial needs of a people. The emminent Soviet mythologist M. I. Steblin-Kamenskij even went so far as to assert that myths play an essential role in the development of human beings from non-societal creatures to civilized man.[3] Yet for him myths are expressions of a particular people; they cannot be traced back to some archetype, whether actual or structural.

Claude Lévi-Strauss in his collection of Mythologiques[4] states, however, that all myths, even those from radically different cultures, can and should be compared using a structural methodology. It is his contention that, structurally, all myths embody basic archetypes since all human beings share similar genetic archetypes and many of the same cultural aspirations. Myths do not differ from one people to another, but rather are shared on the level of the species as a whole.

---

[3] M.I. Steblin-Kamenskij, Myths and Literature, (Ann Arbor, Mich.: Karoma Publishers, 1981).

[4] Claude Lévi-Strauss, Myth and Meaning, (New York:Schocken Books, 1979).

This is similar to the position of more scientifically-oriented anthropologists and sociobiologists such as Edmund Wilson.

Even Sir Edmund Leach, although himself not a member of Lévi-Strauss' school of structural anthropology, agrees when he says in his analysis of Lévi-Strauss that it is the act of putting these stories together and asserting that they are simultaneously and equally 'true' which creates a myth-system.[5] Leach does not explain what he means by a myth-system here, but it is probable that he means the intersection of myth-groups from different myth-contexts (or mythologies), or perhaps a unification of myths from a single mythology. He later explains this composite myth by using his controversial example of the four gospels of the New Testament, describing them as being all "true" in their mythic system with their interesting features coming from their divergence and not their convergence.

Other writers think of individual myths as being words, sentences, paragraphs, or even chapters in a mythology. Perhaps we could then use Tadeusz Kowsan's semiotic terminology and think of these passages or segments as being representational signs of the myth which represent either a syntagmatic structure or a symbolic construct, or we could follow Júlio Cezar Melatti's example and say:

> Antes de tudo, os mitos são narrativas. São narrativos de acontecimentos cuja veracidade não é posta em dúvida pelos membros de uma sociedade....Na verdade tudo indica que os mitos têm mais que ver com o presente do que o passado de uma sociedade.[6]

As a result, myth might be a generalized narrative, which if it deals with a past society, must necessarily be seen through the biases of the present. Any observer must recognize this inherent prejudice and constantly be aware of it. Melatti also

---

[5] D. Edmund Leach, Claude Lévi-Strauss, (New York: Viking Press, 1974) 57–94.

[6] Julio Cezar Melatti, Indios do Brasil, Brasília: Coordenada Editora de Brasília Limitada, 1972, p. 125.

says, speaking of Brazilian Indians, that if a myth is related to some kind of rite, then the myth reflects either positively or negatively on the entire social system of the tribe. Nevertheless, this view of myth, as well as those considered previously, tends to ignore, or at least not to deal with, the existence of modern myths, whether literary, social, or both. It seems most anthropologists are more interested in non-literate or non-literary peoples in their ethnological research, perhaps believing that the true nature of man is more accessible in that state, or that primitive peoples represent more of true man untainted by culture in the European sense of the culture/nature split of Lévi-Strauss and his intellectual sources. (Any influence of the eighteenth century and Rousseau in these matters is, of course a given.) As a result the analysis of modern social myths is left to semioticians such as Barthes and more radical anthropologists who work with literate societies. Social myths are also used in research on political beliefs by historians and political scientists. However, these researchers are not often interested in the theory and methodology of myth. Myth, to them, is simply a tool for the consideration of any social question they want to address. Work done by literary critics often tends to avoid any philosophical or anthropological basis yet work done by other researchers who use literary myths, which I define here as mythic material codified in a literary form, feel compelled to dismiss much of the literary nature of these myths and treat them like any other type of myth. Thus those myths with radically different codes and contexts are all studied in the same manner with the same philosophical preconceptions. Perhaps it is thought that a myth is a myth is a myth. Still, even though early literary myths are sometimes used in the study of mythology, as M. I. Steblin-Kamenskij does, modern literary myths, mythic constructs, or mythic images are not generally studied.

One political scientist who proves an exception to this rule, and does recognize the existence of modern myths, is Jean Cazeneuve who writes about what he indeed calls the "modern myth".[7] He believes that the modern myth and

---

[7] See Jean Cazeneuve, Les mythologies à travers le monde, (Paris: Hachette, 1966).

the ancient myth are different and should be considered in different lights, although both relate to their own mythologies or mythic contexts in much the same way. He explains that an ancient myth, such as that of Osiris or Hercules, is a story situated in a vague, timeless past which can be more or less understood through rites and sacred feasts, whereas the modern class-related social myth is a call for change. An example of this social myth would be the anticipations of a group of workers who believe that a general strike of a whole country would lead to immediate social change. Another example is the mythic construct of the whole world uniting peacefully under one central government. These myths have a potential value, and they are projected as being achievable some day in the not-too-distant future. These, of course, are positively-valued myths, just as there are myths, that are negatively-valued or negatively-charged.[8]

A few other modern thinkers discuss myth in the sense of a modern political myth. An interesting critic in any consideration of the European view of the rest of the world is Henri Baudet. In his slim volume, Paradise on Earth,[9] he gives a rather stream-of-consciousness overview of the development of European mythic contsructs of the world outside of Europe. His is an interesting study with important insights, but his terminology and his methodology show little trace of modern anthropological or cultural criticism. He uses, for example, a very unanthropological concept of myth, which he defines as something in opposition to "reality". This rather unhelpful dichotomy is given to the reader as the theoretical underpinning for a European view of the rest of the world as something not only different but also *negatively* different from Europe. In addition, Baudet insists upon using the term "reality" to express what later became a nineteenth-century capitalist's view of the world, as derived from mercantilist theory, placing great

---

[8] The familiar stereotyping present in racial jokes, the popular media, and in the popular wisdom of Americans about other Americans and that of non-Americans about Americans is referred to here.

[9] Henri Baudet, Paradise on Earth: Some Thoughts on European Images of Non-European Man, trans. Elizabeth Wentholt, (New Haven: Yale University Press, 1964).

emphasis upon "concrete" notions such as trade, agriculture, industrial development, markets, and raw materials; in short, reality equating material progress. The other type of <u>Weltanschauung</u> that he describes believes that these supposedly concrete notions hide their true illusory self. Thus, reality as described in terms of material progress is not reality at all. It is an attempt to cover what should be seen as true reality. This view, which Baudet calls myth, is predicated upon a Rousseauist edenic past which occured before the beginning of written history, in which man lived in a type of innocent altruistic fellowship. An example is that described by Lévi-Strauss in his <u>Tristes tropiques</u> in which he describes his excitement about going to Brazil, referring to the glory of "primitive" man as described by Montaigne and Rousseau.[10] Needless to say, the supporters of the "myth" view it as superior to the "reality" of material progress. The myth/reality tension is then given a new signifier by Baudet and discussed under the dichotomal relation of expansionism and regression. Perhaps in contrast to Baudet's intentions, the basis for expansion comes from the part of human nature deemed "base" by many moral philospher's use of Christian doctrine; that is to say, aggressiveness, competitiveness, avarice and greed; whereas the regressive mythology is expressed in the New Testament concept of <u>caritas</u> and certainly is clearly seen in the literary myth of the <u>bon sauvage</u> or the noble savage.

Baudet's reliance on Montaigne, Rousseau, and a host of other philosophers is evident in his expression of the mythology of regression. He comments that these thinkers rely upon visions of a communal and agricultural Golden Age far older than the creation of this image in modern European thought would suggest. To Baudet the strength of this mythic system of regression is clearly seen in the ideal of the <u>bon sauvage</u>, in the writings of Rousseau, Diderot, and Chateaubriand, and in the endless debates on the perfectibility of man. He insists, and probably

---

[10] Claude Lévi-Strauss, <u>Tristes Tropiques</u>, (1955; Paris: Union générale d'éditions, 1965).

68

correctly so, that the tenacity of this mythology indicates the depth of its power and its importance in European, and consequently New World, thought.[11]

Baudet's analysis of what really are two aspects of modern European mythology is indeed enlightening and useful in any consideration of the establishment of the literary myth of the noble savage; it will be equally important in any discussion of the ignoble savage—the image associated with the New England captivity narratives, the U.S. American dime-novels of the nineteenth century (and consequently most of Hollywood's "Western" films), which stands as the basis for much of the similar historical anti-Indian political action of the United States and other New World nations. Unfortunately, although Baudet's work sensitizes us to certain important components of the basically European mythology which created and sustained the concept of the noble savage and its anti-myth, he carries his arguments too far. His work seems to reflect a wistfulness for the period of history in which European civilization was considered the hallmark of all human achievements. Then, not to be European was somehow to be lacking something important. As a result his Eurocentrism, and especially his definition of caritas as a purely European phenomenon, tends to alarm most residents of non-European countries, and probably most anthropologists. Finally, his rather chauvinistic support for and espousal of the cause of the expansionist side of modern European thought seems rather gratuitous.[12]

An inability to understand other perspectives is not unique to European thinkers, however. U.S. American cultural historians can be just as guilty of falling into the expansionism/regression debate. Roy H. Pearce, in his The Savages of America: A Study of the Indian and the Idea of Civilization, goes so far as to deny validity to any early literature which attempts to present the American Indian in a positive light.[13] For him, and many historical ethnographers, the fact that this

---

[11] Baudet.

[12] Baudet 18.

[13] R.H. Pearce, The Savages of America: A Study of the Indian and the Idea of Civilization, (Baltimore: Johns Hopkins Press, 1965).

literature had a strong self-serving aspect, meaning that it served as a linch-pin in European philosophical debates, should prevent it from having any use at all in history, whether it was written as a journal purporting to deal with true events or a literary narrative.[14] While some of Pearce's argument is certainly reasonable, he tips his hand by deciding that the literary myth of the bon sauvage belongs to a philosophy that he calls "primitivism". The iconic connection with Baudet's "regression" should be obvious. Pearce seems also to support Baudet's idea that caritas is a purely European phenomenon that does not occur in the rest of the world. As a result this vision of the European creation of the bon sauvage reflects no reality observable in the New World. Yet one could state just as logically that this literary myth shows the negative side of the European. Since s/he cannot live out the concept of caritas s/he must create a non-European character who can.

It may be argued that we are presenting an overly critical view of this particular use of literary myth and mythology, but other viewpoints can also be criticized in similar ways. Gary Nash's well-respected and popular Red, White, and Black: The Peoples of Early America is just as guilty of failing to see the philosophical difficulties inherent in trying to change mythology into some type of concretized reality.[15] From his perspective, not only are the early European reports of the Indians to be used, but they can be used to ascribe personality traits and social characteristics to the Indian. These early accounts are not taken as exact iconic representations, but they are taken very seriously. Nash is writing revisionist intellectual history, pointing out how the American Indians maintained their role in political struggles through clever policies and skillful manipulation of the English and French until the end of the eighteenth century when the expulsion of the

---

[14] As we have seen, attempts differentiating philosophical, literary, and "factual" accounts are fruitless endeavors. The problem of how to classify journals which purport to be true falls in this category of problem. Let us, for our purposes here, assume that published journals had some philosophical or literary ax to grind and proceed.

[15] Gary B. Nash, Red, White, and Black: The Peoples of Early America, 2nd ed. (Englewood Cliffs, NJ: Prentice Hall, 1982).

European colonial governments, and the combined effects of disease, alcoholism, technological inadequacy, and the sheer weight of numbers forced the natives to withdraw before the white man and start their retreat toward the reservation. From his American revisionist point of view, the European immigrants bear the blame for most of the United States' current cultural and environmental woes; whereas the Indians, and the ideal of their culture, are uplifted to their now familiar role as nature's savior in an adaptation of the <u>bon sauvage</u> image. Nash's revisionist New World view is in direct conflict with Baudet, who seems oblivious to any idea of a New-World perspective. From the viewpoint of mythology, Nash at his most extreme could be said to use Baudet's regressive mythology and assign it as a set of real, positively-valued, characteristics of the American Indian. To Nash the Indian influenced the European to such a degree that a European valuing of the Indian becomes possible.

In this discussion of myth, it should now be obvious that it is necessary to return to the observer of the Indian, whether it be the European, the transplanted European, or the new New World inhabitant, to evaluate the creation of this myth. In fact, philosophically, this is perhaps the only possible way to evaluate a myth and what function it has, that is its importance to its creator, instead of trying, probably futilely, to evaluate its truth-quotient.

If there were some vague need for the existence of a primitive utopia for the extension of European philosophy, as has already been postulated, then the transformation into literature of the <u>Weltangst</u> inherent in this need necessitates an understanding of terminology and concepts. Let us begin this discussion by thinking about myth in general.

If myth is a single complex expression of a mythology, which may be defined as a sort of <u>Weltanschauungspsychologie</u>, associated with either a total or a partial understanding of man and the world, then myth is a microcosm of mythology. Any postulated anti-myth (or the inverse of a myth) could either be regarded as an expression of the inverse of the positive myth and mythology, or conversely as belonging to the same positive mythology but participating in it as an antithesis to the myth which leads to the dialectical synthesis of the mythology that the myth creates. If one considers the chronology of the particular case under study, s/he will realize that the second notion is more probable; that is, the anti-myth belongs to the positive mythology in a dialectical tension with the myth, since it appears in our particular case, historically speaking, that the school of the ignoble savage arose to challenge that of the <u>bon sauvage</u>. Secondly, if we broaden our working concept of the mythology, to include both the regressive mythic system of <u>caritas</u> and the mercantilistic imperialistic mythic system of progress, as Baudet himself does at the end of his work, then it is clear that both mythic systems may be defined as parts of the modern European mythology of the non-European world. Next, if we then consider the levels below that of the mythic systems in their dialectical opposition, the collection of myths of the noble and ignoble savage become metonymic representations of each competing mythic system. Now these notions of myth and mythic systems can be related to specific texts using the notion of the image, "Indian."

In Saussurian terms, if we consider the concept "Indian" as a signifier of a complex sign, then we see that in the eighteenth century, the signifieds fall into two taxonymic categories, one based upon the anti-myth associated with texts such as the captivity narratives and Buffon's treatise on man and nature, and one based upon the semantic attributes of the noble savage myth. Then perhaps we can see more clearly the opposition between the two groups of interpreters of the sign's signifieds. Let us call the noble savage A-1 and ignoble savage myth sign A-2. Since the signifiers of both signs are the same, the signs should share the letter A, but since the signifier "American native" has two different signifieds, which are aspects of the myths associated with them, we should use the numbers 1 and 2. We can also consider the signifieds as being in an iconically-reciprocal relationship. This dialectic, as established here, was kept in tension until the arrival of modern anthropology which tried to suppress value-labeling of cultures and worked diligently to discover the differences between tribes of Indians. Only then, after doing careful ethnological studies, would any anthropologist attempt to make any type of general statement about "Indians" with the idea of a dichotomous noble/

ignoble savage no longer to be discussed.[16] Even the notion of such an image would horrify a modern anthropologist, even though they, too, still worry about their own objectivity or lack of it.[17]

In returning to the literary myths of the Indian common in the eighteenth century, the disagreement shown by the two schools of investigators of historic observations should not obscure the fact that the groups of writers are using the same literary records for their works although most of their sources are themselves polemical and belong to the semantic fields of either the myth or the anti-myth. In fact, we could think of these cultural histories (and their associated cultural manifestations in popular modern culture) as representing new narratives of the myths. From this perspective the myths themselves belong to the general European-influenced mythology already posited, along with their new exempla—the cultural histories. In no way does this indicate that these investigations are without merit. However, any polemicized argument must inevitably expect to suffer from the fault of not realizing that its argument, just as its opponent's, shares the same slippery ground from which it builds its logical structures.

Let us now more fully investigate two eighteenth-century examples of the positive myth of the Indian and the anti-myth in two passages. One is taken from the work of Georges Buffon[18] and the other from that of Jean-Jacques Rousseau.[19] The choice of these two figures as archetypal representatives is, in some ways obvious. The question of the native's nature had been discussed for more than two hundred years by the time these thinkers treated it; but as we have seen, instead of

---

[16] For a very candid expression of how one cultural anthropologist looks at his own problems of subjectivity see the writings of Michael Herzfeld.

[17] See the later discussion of Darcy Ribeiros' Maíra in the fourth chapter.

[18] Georges Louis LeClerc Buffon, A Natural History, General and Particular, Translated by William Smellie, a New Edition Corrected and Edited to which is added a History of Birds, Fishes, Reptiles, and Insects, 2 vols. (London: Henry Augustus Chambers for R. Evans, 1817).

[19] Jean-Jacques Rousseau, Complete Works, trans. John Heaton, 10 vols. (London: Kegan and Paul, 1810).

any consensus being reached, both sides of the question were even further apart in the mid-eighteenth century than they were in 1500. The Indian was becoming the battleground in many larger conceptual and philosophical frameworks. As a result, in order to present their points in a clear and didactic fashion, they wrote about a one-faceted savage. In addition, each of these writers knew of the other, and indeed part of Rousseau's aim was to refute Buffon's theory about nature influencing man in a negative way. A last reason for considering both in detail is that they can serve as a launching pad for discussions on nineteenth- and twentieth-century literature. Although both of these passages are long, they will be given in full below. Both of these passages are given in English in order to facilitate later analysis and are both taken from nineteenth-century translations.

Buffon:

> These extensive regions (of the New World) were thinly inhabited by a few wandering savages, who, instead of acting as masters, had no authority in it: for they had no controul over either animals or elements: they had neither subjected the waves nor directed the motions of rivers, nor even cultivated the earth around them; they were themselves nothing more than animals of the first rank, mere automations, incapable of correcting nature, or seconding her intentions. Nature, indeed, had treated them more as a stepmother than as an indulgent parent, by denying to them the sentiment of love, and the eager desire to propagate their species. The American savage, it is true, is little less in stature than other men, yet that is not sufficient to form an exception to the general remark—that all animated nature is comparatively diminuitive in the new continent. In the savage the organs of generation are small and feeble; he has no hair, no beard, no ardour for the female; though more nimble than the European, from being habituated to running, he is not so strong; possessed of less sensibility, yet he is more timid and dastardly; he has no vivacity, no activity of soul, and that of the body is less a voluntary exercise than a necessary action action occasioned by want. Satisfy his hunger and thirst and you annihilate the active principle of all his

motions; and he will remain for days together in a state of stupid inactivity. Needless is it to search further into the cause for the dispersed life of savages, and their aversion to society. Nature has withheld from them the most precious spark of her torch; they have no ardour for the female, and consequently no love for their fellow creatures. Strangers to an attachment the most lively and tender, their other kindred sensations are cold and languid: to their parents and children they are little more than indifferent; with them the bands of the most intimate of all society, are feeble, nor is there the smallest connexion between one family and another; of course they have no social state among them; cold in temperament, their manners are cruel, their women they treat as drudges born to labour, or rather as beasts of burthen, whom they load with all the produce of the chase, and whom they oblige, without pity or gratitude, to perform offices repugnant to their nature, and frequently beyond their strength. They have few children, and to those they pay little attention. The whole arises from one cause; they are indifferent because they are weak, and this indifference to the female is the original stain which defaces nature, prevents her from expanding, and while it destroys the seeds of life, strikes at the root of society. Man, therefore forms no exception; for Nature, by retrenching the faculty of love, has diminished him more than any other animal.

The passages from Rousseau are taken from several different parts of his work:

The more we reflect upon it, the more we shall find, that this state (of primitive bliss) was the least subject to change; the very best that could be for mankind; and a state, out of which nothing could have drawn him, but some sinister accident which it had been better for the publick good had never happpened. The example of the savages, most of whom have been found in this state, seems indeed to prove that mankind were ever formed to remain in it; that this situation was the real youth and vigour of the world, and that all subsequent improvements have been apparently so many steps toward the perfection of the individual, but in reality to the decrepitude of the species(...)An unbroken horse erects his mane, paws the ground and starts back at the sight of the bridle; while that which is properly trained suffers patiently even the whip and spur; so savage man bends not his neck to that yoke, to which civilized man submits without murmuring; but prefers the most turbulent state of liberty to the most peaceful slavery. It is not therefore, from the servility of nations already enslaved, that we must form our judgment of the natural dispositions of mankind either for or against slavery; but rather from the prodigious efforts of every free people to prevent oppression.(...)when I behold numbers of naked savages; that despite European pleasures, braving hunger, fire, the sword, and even death itself, to preserve their independency; I feel that it belongs not to slaves to argue about liberty.(...)Whatever the moralists pretend, the human understanding is greatly indebted to the passions; which, it is universally allowed, are much indebted also to the understanding. Now savage man, being destitute of every species of knowledge, can have no passions but those of the latter kind (those from the simple impulse of nature); his desires never extend beyond his physical necessities. The only good things in the universe that he covets are food, a female, and sleep: the only evils that he fears are pain and hunger. I say pain, and not death: for no animal can ever know what it is to die;(...)The savage and the civilized man differ so much with regard to their passions and inclinations that those things which constitute the happiness of one, would reduce the other to despair. The first requires nothing but sustenance, liberty and rest; he desires only to live and be exempt from labour; nay the apathy of the stoic falls short of his consummate indifference for every other object. What a sight would the perplexing and envied labours of an European minister of state, present to the eyes of a Caribbean! What a cruel death would not this indolent savage prefer to such a horrid life, the labours of which are seldom ever sweetened by the pleasure of doing good! But, to see into the motives of all this solicitude, it is requisite that the words power and reputation, should have some meaning affixed to them in his mind; it is requisite he should know that there are men who set a value

on the looks of the rest of mankind: who can be
made happy andsatisified with themselves rather on
the testimony of other people than on their own. In
reality, the source of all these differences is, that the
savage lives within himself; while the citizen
constantly lives beside himself.

Let us now proceed to a consideration of the passages.

An obvious first level of analysis of the passages is a search for significant
attributes given to the Indian by each writer. Isolating all these qualities, including
obvious redundancies gives these two lists:

Buffon: few in number, wandering, no control and not capable of
self-mastery, no direction, mere automatons, no love, no desire for propogation,
small stature, small and feeble organs of generation, no hair, no beard, no ardor for
the female, more nimble, lots of running, not as strong, less sensibility, more timid,
more dastardly, no vivacity, no activity of soul, only want causes any bodily
exercise, no effort, mad if hunger and thirst not satisified, remain days in stupid
inactivity, averse to society, no love for fellow creatures, relations little more than
indifferent, no social state, cold temperament, cruel, women treated as drudges and
worked too hard, working beyond strength, few children, children not given much
attention, too indifferent because weak, original stain causes indifference to female,
no expansion of group, love destroyed, man diminished more than any other
animal.

Rousseau: primitive state the happiest state of mankind, youth, vigor,
permanent best state for man, working singly, free, healthy, honest, happy, not
bending neck to yoke, turbulent liberty, no peaceful slavery, rejecting European
pleasures, brave fire and sword, inverse of civilized man—happiness of one
unhappiness of other; sustenance, liberty, and rest only required, only wanting to
live free, exempt from forced labor, more stoic than the stoics, savage lives within
himself.

These lists are obviously not manageable taxonomies. If we then try to eliminate the redunancy we have a much smaller grouping. To make this even more manageable, we can divide our reduced list into three categories of comparison. The first category would include those attributes common to both writers. The second would include the qualities in total opposition. In other words the relation would be such that the attribute in Rousseau's taxonomy would be "q" and Buffon's "~q" (not "q"). The third category is more complex. Whereas in the first and second categories both writers' complex signs are iconic and in the second category they are contrasted with each other as separate opposing signs in a reciprocal negatively iconic relationship, in the third category we come to the case in which the complex signifiers are the same, but the signifieds are different. Thus the attribute described by each writer is very similar at its base; but the language used to signify the attribute has been given either a positive or a negative value. In the revised taxonomies we have the three following categories:

Category 1: Buffon and Rousseau: few Indians, nomadic, few basic physical needs.

Category 2: Buffon: automatons, subjects of life, weak and listless, servile, energyless.
Rousseau (opposite of Buffon): independent, in control of life, healthy, vigorous, free.

Category 3: Buffon: ignore children, cold and cruel, no desire for material advancement, aversion to society.
Rousseau (same signifier, different signified from Buffon): children free to grow, stoic and proud, few things needed, other beings not necessary.

78

Even this can be reduced to Greimassian squares, following the example used by Maria do Carmo Peixoto Pandolfo in her Mito e literatura,[20] so that in this passage if we speak of the opposites upon which the square is created, then we can call the opposites "Nature" and "Culture" in the Lévi-Straussian sense (which of course was influenced by Rousseau). In Rousseau's development as seen in the Greimassian structure profonde, we move from nature to not-nature (which could be defined as Rousseau's intermediate stage in his view of the development of human society). From this stage of not-culture we then proceed to culture.

Rousseau:

Another square could be formed with life taking the place of nature and death taking the place of culture. The direction of movement within the square would not change, however. From life we would go to not-life and then to death.

Rousseau:

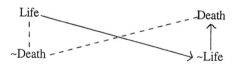

This shows the negative thrust of Rousseau's opinion of what happens when man goes from nature in the Golden Age sense to a state of corruption due to the growth of civilization and culture. In applying the same analysis to Buffon we discover that his square relating life and death is equivalent to Rousseau's.

---

[20] Maria do Carmo Peixoto Pandolfo, Mito e literatura. (Rio de Janeiro: Pluarte, 1981), see especially her discussion of Greimas in chapter two.

Buffon:

However, his square showing the relationship between nature and culture is quite different.

Buffon:

Whereas Buffon believes that the savage goes quickly from life to an extended period of not-life and then death, his use of nature and culture is more complicated, and not well adapted to this type of model. Buffon appears to postulate a static and not a dynamic condition for the savage. The native would suffer from a permanent condition of not-nature and not-culture. It is possible to speak of a movement from nature to non-nature and not-culture in this square, but such a dynamic process is of very limited value. Let us simply say that in a more global sense there seems to be an isotopy (once again I am using Greimas' vocabulary) hypothesizing a static relationship between the savages and their world, since they begin and end in the not-nature/not-culture stasis.

Since this model is not very helpful in an analysis of Buffon, let us discuss a more phenomenological and structural approach. If we use Benjamin Hrushovski's terminology as given in his unpublished work on <u>Integrational Semantics</u>[21], and if we could envision Rousseau and Buffon as two speakers in a contextualized debate, then we can perceive both speakers as belonging to the text

---

[21] Benjamin Hrushovski, <u>Integrational Semantics</u>. Unpublished manuscript.

of this paper using the same Field of Reference; that is, the philosophical discussion of a newly discovered human being. We could also say that both speakers, viewed as characters in this author's text, are talking about "things". Staying with the Hrushovski model of two people engaged in small talk (or perhaps animated debate would be more accurate) about a war (or a "localized response to aggression"), we can identify the fields of reference in our particular case as 1) the debate itself and 2) the concept of the "savage". Quite obviously, the flow of discourse infered from the juxtaposed text, as presented explicity in this specific text, involves a double level of discourse.

This model is also quite useful in that it states that this double structure is a circular "boomerang" structure in that:

> [...] words boomerang and characterize the speakers, themselves, their political and emotional attributes. Indeed, quite often talk 'about' things contributes less to those things themselves than to the characterization and expression of the speakers themselves.[22]

Thus Buffon's textual construct of the "weak servile savage" and Rousseau's "happy, free, and strong savage" say a great deal more about the writers as philosophers than it does about the savages themselves, a point argued earlier. By extension, the constructs say more about the writer's myths and mythology than about the Indian's actual mode of existence. If we keep the idea that this chapter is itself a constructed text composed of smaller texts, then on a macrocosmic level even the discussion of the smaller quoted texts would create a shared Frame of Reference. In a self-referential way this provides another way to prove the interest of the myth in a twentieth-century mythology.

If we now leave the cosmic level and return to the myths, it can be argued that a basis has been made for a discussion of these two writers' binarily-opposite

---

[22] Hrushovski (unnumbered).

descriptions. However if it is true, as many writers on myth believe, that myth is a collection of narratives to be analyzed in a structural manner in order to find the similarities and dissimilarities in groups of related narratives, then these two descriptions of attributes cannot be called myths. They can still function as signs and symbols or as groups of images that can be grouped together to create a myth.

Sign is a confusing term in this context. Each word of a single description can be considered as some sort of linguistic sign à la Saussure, and if several textual descriptions are compared one has to deal with a different level of concepts of the sign or what critics call complex signs, macrosigns, plurisigns, or supersigns. Charles Peirce can help us somewhat in our discussion of how sign relates to the images that become a myth. As Charles Ransdell has written in his unpublished address titled "Peirce: The Conception of a Sign",[23] we should think of myth as being, "iconically rather than symbolically related to its object, the object being that which is exhibited in the form of the story, and which requires being abstracted from it insofar as one is interested in developing a theoretical understanding of the myth as such."[24] In this sense the literary text of a literary myth is the object of the myth's image as sign. The interpretants would then be produced by the text and present us with the sign of the myth, which through the exhibition of the text would be iconically related to the text. The myth does not generate a symbolic text that we call the literary myth, but rather the myth is the text. Neither are the text's interpretants involved through rule generation in the creation of symbol; in fact, the collected literary images are the myth.

Although this is a step forward, the problem of the structure of a literary non-narrative myth remains. Peirce can be of help, again. His concept of the qualisign—that signs, when compared, show shared qualitative properties—will help us with the idea of similar semantic attributes, as will other of his ideas. However, before continuing and perhaps becoming involved in some difficult

---

[23] Charles Ransdell, "Peirce: The Conception of a Sign" unpublished address.

[24] Ransdell (unnumbered).

conceptualizations, it is necessary to investigate how a non-semiotic critic would perform this duty.

Many of these critics would describe the Indian as a "symbol". Then, on the next level of analysis, they deal with "ideas", "images", and "concepts". Needless to say, the referents of these words are rather unclear. Roy Pearce, in his Savages of America, attempts to emerge from the dark when he tries to relate some of these terms to each other. For example to him, "idea is a predication, explicit or implicit which offers a solution of a major problem." Symbol is then a, "vehicle for an idea: a concrete emotionally powerful sign for an abstract proposition." Image then for Pearce is, "a vehicle for a Symbol and the Idea it bodies forth."[25] Although his terms are rather nebulous and too semantically-derived, and although he does not actually use these terms anywhere in his study proper, they can help with our analysis of Indians.

Another approach that can help is that of the new neo-Jungians, and especially James Hillman.[26] In his series of articles on image and archetype, he has proposed certain ideas that can help advance the discussion. He believes that image, not myth, should form the basis for analysis of the individual's subconscious. Myth and archetype are then related to a group's conscious. Thus myth is an ego-connected concept, whereas image is part of the "underworld". In fact, image is the expression of myth, the contextualization of it, according to Hillman. For him myth is the underworld and image (especially as derived from dreams) is the expression of this.[27] He believes that images do not derive from anything. They exist just as the underworld exists. For our purposes his development of the relation between myth and image is useful. For the most part,

---

[25] Pearce, Savages. p xi.

[26] James Hillman, "Further notes on Images." Spring 1978, pp. 171–173.

[27] Hillman, The Dream and the Underworld. (New York: Harper and Row, 1979), pp. 198–199.

we will be dealing with images of the Indians. Only in our conclusion can we say if these images become a myth or myths.

Let us further consider this analysis from a structural viewpoint; since if the text is ultimately the myth, we need not deal with any possible symbolic aspect in the study. However, in order to show exactly how the individual schematized semantic attribute relates to its mythology through the medium of a literary text, certain notions must be made explicit. To begin, the mythology that is the basis of this study is our hypothesized modern European and European-influenced (such as that of the Inter-American writers of the New World) mythology, as it sees itself in relation to the non-European world. This is only one sub-set of the larger set "mythology", but it is the highest level generality that we need work with here since all of the myths to be considered are connected to this particular sub-set of mythology. Going from mythology to myth, it must be remembered that literary myth, as has been described, is a combinational construct built from the collection of literary narratives, episodes, or characterizations in the sense of a summation taken from these texts. As a result the myth is clearly macrotextual and only through its macrotextuality can it be truly seen as a microcosm of the mythology related to it. This concept of macrotextuality may not be equated with a notion of megatextuality, as Hrushovski puts it, since this concept is one of summation, in order to create the iconic relationship between textual summary and myth, and not a sort of interpretative quality.

Returning to the most basic quality of analysis, thinking of the noble savage myth as being a semantic attribute associated with the Indian in a given descriptive context, this can be studied as a sign in the Saussurian sense with a distinct signifiant and signifié. Even though we know that from a Peircean perspective this division is arbitrary and in some senses non-semiotic, it is useful in terms of model analysis. The sign may be a single word, or perhaps a whole sentence, as long as it refers to one explicit semantic attribute. This sign is then a sinsign (a unique occurence of a sign) in the Peircean sense since it is a single printed expression in a unique context. It is also a qualisign in as much as it has a quality that is capable of being in a iconic relationship with other qualisigns. If this concept may be extended to what could be considered a non-Peircean use, then a summation of these aspects of the sign perceived as semantic attributes as taken from the common properties of unique signs in particular passages or microtexts, would create a new category in our analysis. This category could be associated with that of legisigns. The problem with using the Peircean term, however, is that we are talking about a category which is a summation of qualisigns of sinsigns instead of a co-existing aspect of the qualisign and sinsign. It is true that this summation is bound by the rules of its relationship to its textual generation, both in its iconic and indexical basis, and that the legisign is associated with the symbol as mediator, but let us also remember that the legisign summation is still intimately associated with its microtext. Therefore a non-Peircean term for this category must be used; let it be called "Image" using the Pearcean terminology.

The image, however, is still associated with the microtext. It is not necessarily associated with the whole text, which here will be a unique literary work. Thus, it is in association with part of the text and cannot be considered to have any iconic relationship with the whole text. If we want to move to the level of all relevant microtexts of a given text, we must discuss the summation of images as seen from a diachronic perspective. This category could be considered a combined image or a "superimage" in the sense of some semioticians. However let us use the word "construct" instead, since this is indeed what is being done. The construct is the summation of specified images taken from microtexts, considered on one diachronic plane, all of which are part of one specific text and then applied to the texts to create a summary concept.

It is important not to forget that the whole literary text is not always being considered in this analysis of literary myth and image. Such vitally important considerations as plots, sequences, segments, and larger semantic and syntactic features are not being studied specifically in many of the works which will be discussed in chapters three and four. It should be obvious that we are still dealing with series of attributes, albeit in a more complex and global summarial relationship.

The obvious reason for dealing with these attributes is that we are now preparing to relate these proposed ideas to the already established ideas of myths and mythology. If we now speak of the category of the summary of constructs, we realize that we are talking about literary myths. The summary of a series of specific related literary myths would create a mythic system that belongs to the already hypothesized sub-set of mythology. Thus through our step-by-step analysis we have completed our equations, which could be put into algebraic notation:

$$\Sigma S \longrightarrow Q \quad \Sigma Q \longrightarrow I_{M\,T} \quad \Sigma I_{M\,T} \longrightarrow C_T \quad \Sigma C_T \longrightarrow LM$$

$$\Sigma\, L\, M \longrightarrow M\, S \quad \Sigma\, M\, S \longrightarrow M_E$$

To give an example of how these formulas work, let us consider Rousseau's descriptions which have already been compiled. If one goes back to each separate contextualized description as a unique microtext, then we can carry our analysis up to the level of construct as seen in Rousseau's whole Discours. As an example of a combined sign, let us take the words "the savage covets females". The qualisign is the shared concept of heterosexual sexual desire. Other qualisigns of the savage from the same microtext include: requiring food, requiring sleep, fearing pain, and fearing hunger. The composite image then becomes that of a savage who needs only basic material and sexual gratification and fears the lack of them. If we move in the same vein to develop all of the other relevant images as seen in the microtexts, we would emerge with the composite image or construct of the savage as being happy, youthful, vigorous, independent, honest, non-civilized, stoic, requiring only basic mental and physical sustenance, and fearing only the lack of these and the loss of liberty. The composite construct can then be abstracted and given the expected nomenclature of the free noble savage. This is as far as we can go in this chapter. One work can only play a small part in the development of a literary myth, it cannot show the whole myth. This can only be found in a summation of constructs from a summary of relevant texts. Finally, mythology can only be spoken of through the relationships of myths and anti-myths (secondary myths) to mythic systems.

This methodology, although many may feel it to be too detailed and complicated, has several advantages. First of all, it defines in detail the relationships and connections between different levels of texts and different levels of philosophical abstractions. Secondly, not only can these relationships be created from either the point of view of myth and mythology or the point of the attribual qualisign, but they can also be discussed from any point of view in between, such as image or construct, once the algebraically-written methodology is studied and mastered. Thirdly, any group of microtexts with relevant attributes can be studied in texts from different time periods, different languages, and different cultural groups, as long as careful attention is paid when differentiating the qualisigns from the sinsign attribual groups.

Nevertheless, the disadvantages are also immediately apparent. This type of long formula is cumbersome and analyzing all microtexts in terms of it would overtax the rest of the descriptions to be presented in the book. Secondly, most of the analysis will revolve on the types of images that each chapter presents, not on myth or mythology, or even sign. Therefore, two questions may legitimately be asked at the end of this chapter. Why spend so much time on a discussion of myth and methodology, and what good is this since the noble savage should be a clear concept by now?

Myth, especially the myth of the noble savage, is such an incredibly rich and complicated concept with so many meanings of positive and negative value given to it that one must be careful in laying down a theoretical framework to discuss it. Secondly, since this methodology is constructed in detail, it should give an outsider, someone in a different external field of reference, the opportunity to isolate and discuss what s/he feels are unfortunate or untoward generalizations, or what could be theoretical constructs based on an inaccurate reading of the isolated microtextual attributes. As a corollary of this answer, it should also be noted that if the need develops to create additional categories, such as a new category of myth or mythic system based upon unforeseen textually generated ideas, that will also be possible. Finally, although we are primarily dealing with images in chapters three and four, we can come back to the idea of myth in the conclusion having already laid the theoretical foundation.

An additional defense of this method is related to these ideas. Since the notion of literary myth and a methodological consideration have been developed here, these concepts can now be used to describe how different literatures of the New World have used the myths of the savage in the development of their own national or cultural literatures in the nineteenth and twentieth centuries. However, since the structural groundwork in all of its complexity has now been laid, I will try to avoid overuse of most of the complex terminology given in this chapter in the next two chapters. For the most part the concepts of image, myth, and mythology will serve there. However, in the conclusion, it will be necessary to return to some of the terminology and its associated methodology presented here.

Thus, I will not only be considering what is known (or thought to be known) about literary archetypes, but also developing new and useful ideas about the myth of the savage that will help in comparing New World literatures, and in furthering the development of comparative Inter-American or New-World literature.

CHAPTER THREE:
THE NINETEENTH-CENTURY INDIAN

...la novela indianista como toda la literatura romántica de tema indígena, tuvo como esencial estímulo la pasión nacionalista,...[1]

Now that certain basic premises have been established and analyzed, it is possible to move on to a consideration of the literary myth of the Indian in the period after the Napoleonic wars, specifically in the four literatures chosen for study in this work; that is, Brazilian, Peruvian, Québécois, and English Canadian literature. At the same time, however, it will be necessary to bring in some other works beyond these four in order to show the outside influences on them as well as how these four literatures become part of a greater whole.

The early nineteenth century is the period of the first really important works written in the New World. It is a period where nationalism becomes a predominant political and cultural philosophy aided and abetted by the literary school of Romantic individualism whose Indian characters become important national and Romantic symbols, especially in Latin America. The Romantic and nationalist movements began in Europe and not the New World, however, although the New World furnishes important settings and characters for the movement—the most important of which, of course, is the Native American and his environment.

What is most interesting to our analysis is that the mythic image of the bon sauvage is now taken from philosophical discourse and becomes one of the key

---

[1] Concha Melendez, La novela indianista en Hispanoamérica, 1832-1889, Madrid: Imprensa de la Librería y Casa Editorial Hernando, 1934, 12.

focal points of early French Romantic literature. In fact it may be said that the myth of the superior "primitive" man as epitomized by Rousseau becomes a literary commonplace or topos by the middle of the nineteenth century as a result of works by Chateaubriand and other Romantic authors. Whereas Buffon's opposing myth disappears from European literature (if not from popular thinking and philosophy), it is used in some literary works written in the New World. Nevertheless, Chateaubriand's literary myth is adopted by most New-World writers. In fact the importance of Romanticism and Chateaubriand to the way the Indian is utilized in Western Hemisphere literature cannot be overstressed, even though much of the groundwork for Chateaubriand's appropriation of the Indian as literary type had already been laid much earlier, as we have seen. As a result, we will have to give a brief presentation of important Romantic influences on the development of the image of the Indian before treating nationalism and the cultural development of the four literatures and the four novels from each literature specifically, beginning with a discussion of the social background of early nineteenth-century literature and the most important early writers who influenced the development of the images of the Indian. Only then will we understand how the four novels which seemingly vary widely from one another in the portraits they paint of the Indian fit into a larger frame and can be compared as a group.

In the early nineteenth century most of Europe and parts of the New World, (North America in particular), became more populated and more industrialized. All Romantic writers and especially Chateaubriand and the U.S. American, James Fenimore Cooper, reacted to this change by presenting an older, simpler world in a favorable manner. Although the older, more primitive world, whose passing they described and regretted, was somewhat unfamiliar to both personally, the negative aspects of the new order and its seeming inevitability were much too familiar. Indeed from the perspective of the late twentieth century, the reasoning behind Romantic ideals is easily understood. With the future so uncertain and the destruction of older traditions so obvious, the emphasis upon the individual and his relationship to his surroundings as he perceives them has remained a constant preoccupation since the Enlightenment. In the beginning of the Romantic movement it seemed as if the glory of the discovery of the individual was enough of a justification for writing rather egotistical works.

It is in this sense Chateaubriand is often denigrated. It is true that his preoccupation with self, as represented by characters like René, was obsessive. Still his more positive aspects include his "environmental" love of nature, his overwhelming lyricism and his use of Indian characters which initiated an upswelling of interest in the Indian's Romantic potential. Even though his Indians are only a single part of the larger work, Les Natchez, and even though Christianity theoretically wins out as a philosophy over the Indian chief, Chactas', stoic paganism, the very exoticism of the Indian introduced in such a lyrical manner attracted popular interest to the Indian as a literary figure, especially in the newly independent countries of the New World. As Aída Cometta Melendez says in her work on nineteenth-century Latin American writing on the Indian:

> El [Chateaubriand] es, al mismo tiempo, el estímulo mas fuerte de los cultivadores del tema índio en la época romántica [en América Latina]. (...)El entusiasmo por Chateaubriand duró más en la América española que en España y tuvo asimilación mas perfecta.[2]

French influence was also felt in North America—although not to the same extent. In Canada, British political control necessitated some denigration of French culture. In English Canada, Chateaubriand was occasionally read, but his lyrical portrayal of the Indian impressed Canadians less than Latin Americans. In French Canada, British control over French influence reduced Chateaubriand's appeal. At the same time the Québécois' perception that they had been betrayed by the French began to create the feelings of anti-Gaulism, isolation, and alienation which still exist strongly today. In Quebec, although easily identifiable works specifically reflecting Chateaubriand's influence were not written in the nineteenth century,

---

[2] Melendez 55–65.

certain influences can be seen—especially in the poetry of the last part of the century.

While Chateaubriand had a great influence on Latin America and a lesser one on Canada, James Fenimore Cooper had a great influence on Canada and a lesser one on Latin America. Part of this is, no doubt, due to the fact that the images of the Indian that we will see developed in different chronological periods. Latin America, with its legacy of centralized Spanish administrations, urban conclaves, and an intellectual elite had the basic requirements for the creation of a strong indigenous literature much earlier than did North America and especially Canada. Most of the Spanish American countries effectively ended Spanish cultural domination during the late Napoleonic period even though they did not win their independence until the 1820's with the revolts led by Boívar and San Martín. Their interest in nationalistic literature grew correspondingly from this period. Brazil presents a special case; it actually became the capital of the Portuguese empire when the monarch went into exile there during the French occupation of Portugal. Brazil gained its cultural independence with the emperor's one-word decision, "fico" (I will stay), to not return to Portugal. In the 1830's Brazil began its own unique cultural journey into the modern period.

In Canada there was not even any limited independence until the Canadians engineered a small revolt that led to the Durham Report of 1840. Even after this, the emergence of a national culture did not really occur until after the establishment of the Confederation of 1867. Thus Cooper's proximity to Canada in both topography, language, and culture, in addition to his later publication dates, led to his greater influence throughout Anglophone and Francophone North America. Other U.S. Americans will become important in the development of late nineteenth-century Canadian literature with Longfellow's Song of Hiawatha more important in the formation of Canadian poetry's image of the Indian (in French or English) than anything written by Chateaubriand. Nevertheless in the early part of the century both Chateaubriand and Cooper taken together provide the only important influence on the development of the picture of the Indian in any literature of the Americas.

Yet when one compares Chateaubriand and Cooper in terms of the picture of the Indian each presents, there are important differences. If Chateaubriand's Atala seems strongly reminiscent of Marmontel, Voltaire, and even of the distant Ercilla, Cooper seems more a follower of English libertanianism and the Encyclopedists. Atala is a Christian maiden who tries to convert Chactas, and then together they weave their romantic idyll until paganism destroys their dream. Although Chateaubriand did use explorers' reports—especially those of the French Jesuits previously discussed, it is known that he had no direct experience traveling in Louisiana or "Méschassébé". One of his primary philosophical interests was describing the "mal du siècle", the feeling of Sehnsucht (or extreme longing) that could only be dispelled by adherence to Christian moral teachings and a firm belief in the afterlife. Of course, it was his gift of describing that feeling of wistfulness and longing that kept the public reading his works—not his Christian solutions—with his greatest success being the character of the Breton, René. In response, the Indian Chactas is the wise sage, attempting to change René or at least to show him the darkness of the path inspired by emotions alone.

In contrast to Chateaubriand, Cooper is much more intimately acquainted with his New World setting. As an American writer describing the New World, his picture of the Indian is more complicated. Like Chateaubriand his protagonist is European by heritage; but whereas René is a Romantic European being led by the common sense of the noble Indian, Cooper's protagonist, Deerslayer, although not an Indian, acts like many of the Indians also described in his works. He knows how to hunt, how to follow a trail, how to fight, and how to adopt Indian guerrilla tactics when they become necessary. In this sense he is a cultural half-breed, careful to show his belief in the racial and cultural superiority of the white man; but also quite often pointing out the shortcomings of the overly civilized white man. In addition to the perfection and nobility of Deerslayer, combining the best of Europe and the New World, white and red, there are two very different groups of Indian characters, both noble and ignoble savages. Yet, in Cooper's work, nobility will not triumph in the long run. At the end (semantically chronologically-speaking) of his series of works on the Indian, the good Indians have been totally defeated and only the ignoble Indians and white men remain. The white man, not the ignoble Indian, is responsible for this defeat, however. Cooper's importance in presenting both good and bad Indians together in a single work must be seen as significant. Even though some other U.S. American works such as William Gilmore Simm's The Yamasee presented two sides of the same Indians, and certain missionaries such as the Moravian John Blackwelder wrote about the Indian's basic good nature, Cooper was the first really popular writer to present Indians in a Manichean light. His Iroquois are seen as a reflection of the Delaware, but a reflection from a warped or distorted mirror. Whereas each tribe understands nature and how to use nature's tricks to their own advantage, the Iroquois use their knowledge in a different manner. They use their knowledge to expand their confederation and undermine other tribes' holdings. They also stretch, and eventually break, the unwritten Indian code of honor.[3]

Although Cooper and Chateaubriand might be the most influential writers not from the four literatures to influence the use of the Indian in the all of the Americas in the early nineteenth century, a few other writers must be mentioned as well. Sir Walter Scott was extremely influential in the Americas as the most important Romantic propagator of the adventure novel. In North America he was important in popularizing the long novel of romance and adventure, setting the stage for a sub-genre whose popularity remains undiminished in the twentieth century. His specific influence upon Indianist works appears to lie in their stylistic and syntactic aspects—not their semantic ones. In Spain and in Spanish America, however, Scott was also important in reviving interest in the peculiarities of the Spanish past. His importance lay primarily in the area of historical fiction. Writers such as Avallaneda, Larra, and Gil Carrasco attempted to adapt Scott's use of history while writing about Spain's most glorious era—the conquest of America.[4]

---

[3] Melendez 57–63. I also find it quite amusing to see how this Manichean view of Indians has recently resurfaced in Hollywood. Not only do the "Black Robe" and "Dances With Wolves" show Cooper's influence, but Hollywood has also presented a new version of Cooper's own work in the film "The Deerslayer".

[4] Melendez 66–68.

A writer who was more influential in Latin America than in North America was the German explorer Humboldt. Humboldt was one of the first explorers to do a thorough survey of the Western coast of South America. As a natural scientist he served as an inspiration for many new nationalist writers seeking to find a good source of settings for the background for their novels and poems. His descriptions of the physical features of the new countries and the cultures of their populations appealed to the positivist spirit of the times as well as to the need for picturesque details of the landscape. To Humboldt, the Indian was a problem since it appeared that he could not be acclimated to the new and changing social order of the nineteenth century. The Indian was even described as "tímido, misterio, sin confianza, y isolado a su daño."[5] This vision would be most influential during the last part of the nineteenth century, but it was in the background even earlier. Humboldt's new myth could be described as a combination of Buffon's view of the savages as uncivilized, small, and weak beings, and Columbus' description of them as gentle, ineffective, and weak.

Humboldt was perhaps the last important non-New World writer to affect the image of the Indian in nineteenth and twentieth-century literature. Of course, in passing, we might mention Charles Darwin's voyages to South America which took place later in the century. However, his theories were so controversial that he would not have any influence in Latin America before the twentieth century as interpreted indirectly through Social Darwinists and anthropologists.

The reasons for the ending of direct European influence in the creation of Indianist literary myths are simple and historical. By 1830 there were no more European colonies of any consequence in the Western Hemisphere. As a result there was much less reason for European writers to be involved with events in the New World. Secondly, the European progressive mythology dominant in many quarters meant that any interest in the former colonies would focus on their new European-influenced governments and not on the condition of the Indians. Finally, all critically-acclaimed European writers were simply more Eurocentric than ever

---

[5] Melendez 65.

before. They wrote about medieval European history, or the problems of the poor in Paris, Madrid, or London. They were enraptured by the beauty of the Alps, Northern Italy, or the Lake District and disturbed by the growing power of the rather boorish bourgeoisie. America took a back seat to Europe in the most complete way possible since 1492. However, America was beginning to look after itself and discover its own cultural heritage—one associated with the natives of the two continents.

Although literature written in the New World dates from the sixteenth century and a few New World works have already been mentioned that throw light on the development of the image of the Indian, it is only after 1830, throughout the New World of the Western Hemisphere, that this new literature becomes widespread in both North and South America. As a result of rapidly growing populations, urban areas, and through the establishment of new independent governments and intellectual elites throughout the New World, there was a great demand for works that truly reflected the uniqueness of the newly independent countries of the Americas, that is nationalist literature. This was caused by insecurity about the place of these new countries in the world's political, economic, and cultural development. There had to be something unique and important about these countries so they could assert cultural independence from the mother countries and demonstrate the advanced nature of the new New-World inhabitant. At the time of this search, the literary vogue of Romanticism became known and understood in the New World. These two factors combined to create the novels dealing with Indians during the period from 1830 to 1870.

The literary myth of the Native American produced during the Romantic years had to be a colorful one, and provide an excellent example of the extremes of primitive man. In this sense the Indian served as a constant in relation to the new white American. He was either superbly noble or superbly savage, his story was one of either crime or extreme virtue. The nature attributed to him seemed to depend only on whether his author believed in either the progressive or the regressive mythology already discussed. To the regressive writers the Indians were a positive force to emulate and assimilate. The side upholding the progressive mythology re-evaluated the literary myth presented by Buffon and found it rather lacking in drama, and thus the Rousseau-Buffon dispute was altered in the New World. The weak, sexless Indian could not serve as an effective impediment to European advancement. Whereas eighteenth-century Europeans could defend their New World conquests by showing the Indian as naturally unfit to be the dominant human being in new lands, the purposes of nineteenth-century progressive writers were different. They wanted their countrymen to understand how their European heritage had been improved through their conflicts with the natives. Just as ancient Greek writers viewed warfare as a way of improving ethnic character, so did these writers. The battles with the Indians improved the white's relationship with nature as they were forced to be closer to it. At the same time, the skirmishes on the frontier necessarily drew the whites closer together and highlighted, at times, their Christian superiority. Perhaps this philosophy is seen at its height in Cooper and other United States writers. But even in Cooper this view of the Indians is not constant. There are noble Indians in his work, too. Like many other writers of the American Romantic period, his Indians belong to both of the extremes.

We will study the Romantic conflict of noble and ignoble Indians as we delve deeper into the literature of the period, but two points must be clarified before proceeding. One is that the vast majority of nineteenth-century Romantic writers are discussing events far away in time. They are not writing about wars with the Indians fought during their lifetimes, but rather about Indians who have already been defeated. In most instances they are also writing about the first contacts between a specific group of whites and Indians, whether this was on the Atlantic coast or in the interior. This could be due to the European, Romantic, influence of writers such as Scott who delved back into the European past and instilled a desire in American writers to search into their own past; or it could come from the desire to study in more depth the origin of the new American character and consequently assure its superior position on the world stage, in contrast to that of the former mother country.

Another important point of these narratives is that the Indians in these works are almost never rounded characters. They are either as culturally and morally superior as is possible, or as negatively savage as imaginable. They do not often experience tragic conflicts between honor and duty, or even fall in love. They serve as background color, as in the Spanish American costumbrista novels, or they are noble enough to serve as mentors to the whites.

In Latin America, especially, the idea of mentor or guide is at the basis of the concept of the "Indianist" novel, a further permutation of the noble-savage concept which can be defined as a New-World nineteenth-century novel in which Romantic Indians are the main characters and which should be seen as following in a direct line from Montaigne and Ercilla through Rousseau and Chateaubriand. The Indian heroes of these novels often are almost totally mythical and sometimes come from a period before white settlement, such as in the Inca stories. Ercilla's pastoral influence is clear here with many of the Indianist works being independent of white involvement or much in the way of concrete reality. The dramatic contrast of these stories does not come from the conflict of white and Indian, but rather between good Indian and bad Indian. Once again, there are no "gray" Indians. They are either "black" or "white", and once again the work takes place at a time in which Indians were in power and white writers could treat them more as equals. The characters described in these works are Indians, in the sense that Montaigne's "cannibales" were Indians. The veneer of white self-interest remains so strong that any type of verifiable accuracy in the presentation of these Indians is impossible. Instead all early Indian characters seem only to serve to give the new Western Hemisphere countries the basis for creating their own cultural mythos, and although there are both good and bad Indians, the difference between the customs of the good and bad Indians becomes non-existent.

Thus after discussing these two points of general interest, let us return to our four selected literatures and their novels to analyze how each of these literatures created their own images of Indians. After establishing a composite picture for each of the four literatures we can then return to our more general analysis at the end of this chapter based upon a more complete summation of character images. To this end we shall begin with the literature that produced the first important novel with Indian characters in our study of the nineteenth century that of English Canada.

English Canada

One of the first English Canadian[6] works refering to the Indians in Canada is Thomas Cary's Abram's Plains (1789) in which the flavor of the captivity narrative is recalled:

> But oh! a task of more exalted kind,
> To arts of peace, to tame the savage mind;
> The thirst of blood, in human breasts, to shame,
> To wrest from barbarous vice, fair virtue's name;
> Bid tomahawks to ploughshares yield the sway
> And skalping-knives to pruning hooks give way.[7]

Oliver Goldsmith's The Rising Village (1825) presents a clear example of the progressive mythology by calling the new World before the arrival of the Europeans "a land of barbarous darkness" and describing Indians as beasts of prey. Joseph Howe's poem, "Acadia", ends on a similar note although it begins by admitting that the first Europeans arriving in "Acadia" were morally in the wrong in their dealings with the Indians. Catherine Parr Traill's works rely upon dogmatic Christian beliefs to bolster her case against the Indians as savages. In The Canadian Crusoes (1852) two white children are saved from starvation in the forest by a Mohawk girl. But instead of praising the Indian culture which made such a noble act possible, the Mohawk society is ultimately denigrated. Indians are considered to be naturally revengeful and unwilling or incapable of forgiveness. The white hero of the work gives a classic statement portraying the differences between the two societal groups, saying:

---

6 Leslie Monkman, A Native Heritage: Images of the Indian in English-Canadian Literature, Toronto: University of Toronto Press, 1981 8–9.

7 Monkman 8–9.

100

> The wild man and the civilized man do not live well
> together; their habits and dispositions are so contrary
> the one to the other. We are open and they are
> cunning and they suspect our openness to be only a
> greater degree of cunning than their own—they do
> not understand us. They are taught to be revengeful
> and we are taught to forgive our enemies. So you
> see that what is a virtue with the savage is a crime
> with the Christian. If the Indian could be taught the
> Word of God he might be kind, and true, and gentle
> as well as brave.[8]

The result of this belief is the eventual conversion to Christianity of the Mohawk girl—the only Indian chararcter the author feels obliged to redeem.

Other writers of the nineteenth century such as Bishop George Jehosophat Mountain, Egerton Ryerson Young, George Longmore, Charles Mair, and William Kirby all belong to this progressivist school of writers. Kirby's The U.E.: A Tale of Upper Canada (1859) is somewhat different, though, in that the Indian savagery is replaced by white savagery[9]. The United States' opposition to British rule in the War of 1812 is the focus of the story. The Canadian loyalists are nearly canonized in contrast to the white settlers south of the border. The U.S. Americans adopt the worst of Indian ways and murder and scalp innocent Canadians during the war. However, the Loyalists do not react passively to the violence. The hero of the work goes south after a group of marauders, dressing himself as a savage. After finding his enemies he slaughters them all. When he discovers the bloody remains of some Canadians in the knapsacks of one of the slain men, he eats some bread which had soaked up some American blood as an act of ultimate bloodlust and crazed revenge. The contrast between Kirby's white Canadian and Traill's is obvious. Kirby unites white and red men in their capacity for savagery.[10]

---

[8] Monkman 10–11.

[9] Monkman 16.

[10] Monkman 24–26.

This picture of the evil Indian however is not the only one found in nineteenth-century Canadian writers. Frances Brookes' The History of Emily Montague (1769) presents an early example of another point of view. She gives different opinions to different characters; but the character who believes that the Indians, although perhaps naturally noble, fall too easily into alcoholism, seems to most clearly represent the author's opinion.[11]

Standish O'Grady's The Emigrant (1842) and Douglas Huygue's Argimou: A Legend of the Micmac (1847), fall more into the pro-Indian or Indianist school. The Indians in these works fit naturally into their world and are at peace and harmony with it. O'Grady goes so far as to use Enlightenment thought on natural law and reason to support his descriptions. Huygue continues the paeans and sounds a thoroughly modern (and pro-regressive) note when his hero says:

> (...)the Micmacs were finishing their frugal meal, and he thought [a white Canadian is thinking], how little, after all, the advantages of a civilized state of society were capable of ameliorating the moral or physical condition of man. What benefit had art and intellectual culture, after the lapse of thousands of years, conferred upon his nation that these simple children of nature did not receive from their mother's hand, unsolicited? His belief in the progressive improvement of the human race was shaken, as the lamentable truth forced forced itself upon his understanding, that mankind seemed to have journeyed further from the right [path], as they deviated from the plain habits and principles of the primitive ages.[12]

Huygue's Indians are clearly superior to the whites in their adaptation to the environment, and as such represent a viable alternative path for the new white settlers to follow. In this way his novel, as it also describes a time in the past on the

---

[11] Monkman 30.

[12] Monkman 33.

frontier, is the Canadian novel most closely aligned with the Indianist novels of Latin America. One last movement which generates a more positive image of the Indian in English Canada is more associated with poetry than the novel and was influenced by the U.S. Americans, Lewis Henry Morgan and William Wadsworth Longfellow. This is the series of poems associated with "Hiawatha" and "Evangeline" and Indian folk tales. However one Canadian poet assumed to be influenced by these works, Adam Kidd, actually predated Longfellow. Following the long tradition of pastoral Indians in his "The Huron Chief" (1830), he describes the early Huron's world in terms of pastoral perfection, the Indian women as "Eden's daughters", and of their land as "Calypso's paradisial retreat." Even Arcadian love songs are sung between Huron lovers. The image of peace and perfection is only destroyed by the arrival of the first whites in the area.

Although Kidd's pre-Hiawatha poem has a happy ending, Charles Sangster and Rosanna Leprohon sound the Romantic refrain by having their heroines sent over roaring waterfalls or leaping from cliffs in acts of ultimate sacrifice to end impossible love relationships. Other Romantic Indianist poets include Charles Mair, who became interested in the myths and legends of Indians before European contact, and Charles G.D. Roberts who attempted to write Longfellow-inspired poetry in "The Succour of Gluskûp", "The Vengeance of Gluskûp", and "The Departing of Gluskûp". This trilogy is about the Malechite chief god and his intervention in the world to save his people. There is yet another set of poems associated with this school that deal with Algonquin and Iroquois maidens doomed to perdition in the same way as Charles Sanger's previously described Indian maidens. However, we do not need to provide additional details of them here.[13]

All of the proceeding demonstrate three basic literary myths in writing on the Indian in nineteenth-century English Canada, and although this is not our purpose here, they probably could function as summary groupings of the view of the Indian in nineteenth-century U.S. American literature. The first group, the

---

[13] Monkman 127–130.

Longfellow school, deals with the Indian of a shadowy mystic past, much like the inhabitants of the Golden Age of ancient Greece or the Christian Eden. Only the advent of the white Europeans can disrupt the natural harmony inherent in this world. The second group deals with early Indian-white relationships and gives the Indian side the most credit following in a clear line from Rousseau and Chateaubriand, with its didactic purpose being to provide white civilization with a clear path to follow in opposition to the dominant progressive philosophy. Late in the century and early in the next century, as epitomized by Pauline Johnson, this school loses its impetus with the disappearance of a separate Indian civilization in Canada. A note of tragedy and bitterness appears more frequently which will be explored in more depth later.

The final grouping is that of the "progressives" (using Henri Baudet's terminology) who identify the Indian with all types of savagery and insist that s/he must be defeated and eliminated. This is perhaps the most popular image in nineteenth-century Canada since it provides a way of assuaging the guilt of conquest. It is also extremely strong in the United States and has been thoroughly explored in Louise K. Barnett's study of nineteenth century U.S. American frontier novels The Ignoble Savage.[14]

In Canada, the most popular representation of the frontier novel and perhaps even the earliest English Canadian novel written is Major John Richardson's Wacousta (1832).[15] Since Wacousta was a very popular novel, since it is perhaps the most important English Canadian novel with Indian characters written in the nineteenth century, and since it presents the Indian in two very different lights, let us analyze it in more detail as our chosen nineteenth-century English Canadian novel.

[14] Louise K. Barnett, The Ignoble Savage: American Literary Racism 1790–1890, Westport, Conn: Greenwood Press, 1975.

[15] John Richardson, Wacousta; or The Prophecy, a Tale of the Canadas, Philadelphia: Key and Biddle, 1833.

104

Wacousta is a novel based upon a true incident—the Indian chief, Ponteach's (Pontiac's), attack on the isolated English Great Lake forts in 1763. Its author, John Richardson, was himself an officer in the British army during the war of 1812 (or the Canadian War for Independence) and thus had first-hand acquaintance with the battle tactics of both Indians and whites, as well as the knowledge of the country that he describes. The story is one of a civilized man reduced to blood lust through the loss to his best friend of the woman he loves. As Leslie Monkman suggests, the real tragedy of the work (such tragedy as exists) is the reduction to savagery of its protagonist Scottish noble, Sir Reginald Morton.[16] The two worlds of the whites and the natives are compared in what appears a violent contrast. This becomes apparent when the plot is viewed in its chronological order, if not in its order of presentation.

Sir Reginald is a son of the Scottish Highlands. He grows up hunting, fishing, swimming, and developing his physique in an impressive manner. Nothing is too difficult for him to achieve in this pastoral wilderness. One day while chasing a wounded stag into particularly rough country, he leaves his hunting companions behind and finds himself in a completely unknown territory. Still he pursues the stag and follows its trail of blood through extremely perilous defiles until he finds himself in a pocket paradise. There in the middle of a lush meadow stands a beautiful girl clad in white who was quite surprised to see the tall handsome warrior (any comparison to European legends and mythic stories appears to be intentional). After gradually befriending the girl, he uncovers her history. Her father, having seen the fall of the old order after the defeat of the Jacobites, decided to sequester his family from the ravages of civilized life. Morton, at last, has disturbed this pastoral idyll in which all is described in terms of natural perfection. Clara, the "maiden resident" of this Eden, finally agrees to leave it with Morton giving no word to her father as to where she intends to go. After a dangerous journey they both leave "Eden" and return to Morton's camp. Morton,

---

[16] Monkman 22–24.

however, is soon imprisoned for a short period after Clara comes to his camp since he cannot bear to be parted from Clara, even for guard duty. Before he is put in prison he commends Clara to Sir Charles DeHaldimar as protector. DeHaldimar, faced with the temptation of the defenseless goddess, decides to marry her himself and have her believe Morton has abandoned her. She sees no reason to disbelieve DeHaldimar and after much grieving finally agrees to marry him to save her honor and to survive in this unfamiliar world of civilization.

After his release from prison Morton goes temporarily insane when he discovers his friend's treachery and he cannot convince Clara that he, Morton, is blameless. After a series of adventures in which he attempts to kill DeHaldimar in battle, Morton comes to the New World when DeHaldimar's regiment does. Still trying to kill DeHaldimar honorably he joins the force opposed to the British, that of the Native Americans. His fierce hatred of the British, civilized European ways, and his enormous physical prowess make him a natural leader of the natives. He finally comes to the Great Lake region, becomes associated with Ponteach, and takes the name Wacousta. As Wacousta he pledges undying emnity to the British, especially DeHaldimar.

In the novel's presented order of events this story of treachery, perfidy, and violent hatred only becomes clear near the end of the novel after Wacousta has captured one of DeHaldimar's sons, DeHaldimar's only daughter, and two other young Britons. Thus until then in ignorance of Wacousta's European heritage, he seems to embody the evil of the most unreasoning New-World savage in his incarnation of the diabolic. The young DeHaldimars, the children from the marriage of Charles and Clara, are presented in contrast to both Wacousta and their father. It must be assumed that they favor their mother and not their father because of their innocence and purity. Even though many critics seem not to notice it, the father, DeHaldimar, is painted in a most unsympathetic light. Not only is he harsh and unloving to his children; but he eventually has a man executed under highly suspicious circumstances. This execution was carried out in spite of entreaties from the other officers, the man's wife (who later joins Wacousta), and the imminent arrival of the one man who could clear the man's name, Frederick

DeHaldimar. In fact, Frederick is even seen in the distance riding towards the camp as his father hurries to have the "criminal" executed. As we learn later this unworthy act took place to safeguard the fictive past created by DeHaldimar, since the prisoner threatened to reveal the truth about DeHaldimar's treachery to Morton/Wacousta. As a result of this incident and others, it appears Wacousta's total ruthlessness is well-balanced by DeHaldimar's lying and treachery. Indeed one may even argue that Wacousta is better justified in his actions by Richardson than DeHaldimar, although few Canadian critics have ventured so far.

The real (not Scottish) Indians in the work are relegated to the role of supporting characters. Ponteach is the only bad Indian given any major role, and his evilness and savageness both pale before those of Wacousta, indeed one could say that in this Wacousta is his inspiration. In essence Richardson defines Ponteach as evil due to his opposition to the whites although Richardson also makes it clear that Ponteach is also treacherous. Ponteach's ruse of a false lacrosse match enables him to destroy the garrison at Michimilinac (Macinaw), even though the same trick did not succeed at Detroit (where the DeHaldimars are living). Nevertheless, he is shown to subscribe to a fiercely legalistic code of honor which is not unlike DeHaldimar's own. Outside of that code anything is permitted, but the code still does exist. It is this same code that enables Ponteach to become the friend of the whites after Wacousta is killed at the end of the novel. On the whole the Indians, as a group in the novel, are nothing more than a savage rabble ready to follow the bidding of any strong leader. They have no independent mind, and as a result, no individuals can be detected in their midst.

There is another picture to be presented, however. Wacousta contains two very important noble savages who actually become a sort of Deus ex persona and save the Europeans from annihilation. Oucanasta is an Indian woman who falls in love with Frederick DeHaldimar after he saves her from drowning, and with her brother she helps the whites. Both of them are described in terms that vary widely from the other Indians. In fact, they are almost white European and remind us of Clara in their goodness and selflessness. Still any thought of consummated love between Frederick and Oucanasta is impossible here. They belong to different orders and there they must remain.

Richardson presents an Edenic Scotland in opposition to a savage New World, two noble Indians versus a tribe of savages, and a good white who turns evil savage against a bad white. The resultant picture is much more complicated than might first appear in a simple frontier novel. However, the three types of Indian literary myths we have discussed in North America are not negated by this greater complexity of image. Richardson does not use the mythical pre-Europoean Hiawatha Indian, but both the ignoble savage and the good Indian are present and important to the novel as a whole. The ignoble savage dominates in the novel but the noble savages provide the turning point of the work's resolution. We cannot say, however, that the good Indians here are simple Rousseauesque figures; they are aware of the evil caused by their brethren. Yet they become Rousseauesque since they view their own actions toward the DeHaldimars as a way of alleviating this evil. Thus this novel, and all of the Canadian works we have discussed, fit in with the three schools of early nineteenth-century literature with Indian characters presented earlier. Let us now examine the other three literatures, beginning with Quebec, to see if they differ in their images of literary Native Americans.

Quebec

Let us now move to the French part of Canada which we will identify here by the name, Quebec. This is not a misnomer since extremely little literature written in French in Canada comes from any other province. One would suspect the influence of European French culture would be stronger in Quebec than in the rest of Canada, and early attempts at defining the history of Quebec, such as François-Xavier Garneau's Histoire du Canada (1845), show this tendency when discussing Indians. The French Jesuit accounts of the seventeenth and eighteenth century are often cited as the sources which influence Québécois thought about Indians. As Margot Northey notes in her Haunted Wilderness: The Gothic and

Grotesque in Canadian Fiction [17], there was a nineteenth-century French Canadian tendency to idealize the period before English conquest and, as a result, there was also a clear regressive impulse in Quebec writing during this period. The image of the Indian employed in such works was consequently often idealized.

However, the complete picture is not quite so simple. Three other factors must be considered. First, Quebec was a conquered nation during the nineteenth century, and in some ways was treated as one. Quebec was perhaps the first colony which the British treated well, perhaps because of their respect for the European culture of the settlers (even if it was based upon Catholicism and absolutism), or more likely because of their fear of the effect the French or the Americans could have had, trying to spearhead a revolution in an unhappy people. As a result of their status and their relatively small number, the Québécois did not publish many works of literature in French until the 1840's. Even then there was some English concern about the effect of Canadian literature published in French and efforts made to limit publication of such works. Secondly, direct contact between Quebec and France was interrupted in 1763. Thus France's cultural influence became more indirect; it was replaced by British influence, to some extent U.S. American influence, and by retreating into Quebec's own history and cultural heritage. Thirdly, by mid-century there was little in the way of a separate Indian culture left in Quebec—especially in the more heavily populated south. Unlike in Peru, Brazil, or even English Canada, the presence of the Indian soon became relatively unimportant (at least until very recently!). Thus the use of Indians in Québécois literature is even more clearly a reflection of foreign cultural influence than in any of the other three literatures. As a result of these factors, there are few nineteenth-century Québécois literary works that treat the Indian and even fewer in which s/he is an important character.[18]

---

[17] Margot Northey, The Haunted Wilderness : The Gothic and Grotesque in Canadian Fiction, Toronto: University of Toronto Press, 1976, 76.

[18] See Jack Warwick, The Long Journey, Literary Themes of French Canada, Toronto: University of Toronto Press, 1968 for a discussion.

One of the first novels that does contain some reference to Indians is Aubert de Gaspé's Les Anciens Canadiens (1847).[19] It has two chapters in which differing faces of the Indian are presented and as such it will be analyzed later much in the same way as Wacousta was earlier.

Another early Quebec novel that deals with Indians is Charles-Louis Taché's Forestiers et Voyageurs (1862). It is composed of three short stories bound together in the form of a novel. These stories remind us of the Catholic missionary background of many of Quebec's nineteenth century novels. Like the earlier Father Gabriel Sagard and the later Father Alexandre-Antonin Taché, Charles-Louis Taché's work contains references to converting the Indians. Charles-Louis also introduces an important Canadian literary figure, the voyageur. The voyageur is a Québécois who has in some senses become assimilated into the Indians' life, sometimes with results that led to the establishment of the Métis as a new racial group. He (the voyageur is never female!) has much in common with the Indians, and like them owns the land in a non-physical sense. With the Indians he shares a feeling of kinship with each other in a way the more class-conscious English cannot understand. In his lavish praise for the voyageurs, Charles-Louis Taché has taken many adjectives formerly given to the noble savage and applied them to his French Canadian hero. This hero may even be called the "new happy savage" as Jack Warwick does in his The Long Journey: Pays d'en haut.[20]

Many other writers wrote about "happy savages" although Indians here function mainly as background decor. Adario (the name more than likely comes from the eighteenth-century play) in Les Deux Anneaux (1853) by James J.T. Phénan, is a young Indian who befriends the hero, Claude Bronsy, during Bronsy's captivity. Adario functions as a noble friend even though his people have carried Bronsy away from the French. His nobility reminds us of Wacousta's Oucanasta. In Les fiancés de 1812 (1844) by Joseph Doutre, one of the French Canadians in

---

[19] Aubert de Gaspé, Les Anciens Canadiens, Montreal: Fides, 1967.

[20] Warwick 110.

110

the work, Alphonse de P....., a rich baron's son, saves an Indian maiden, Ithona, from death and later marries her. This is one of the few explicit Indian-white love matches in nineteenth century Québécois or Canadian literature. It and the publication date of Les fiancés are worth noting.

The literary myth of the "Iroquoise" illustrates the other tendency of writers who use bons sauvages in nineteenth century Quebec. The first version of the story was published in 1844 by C.V. Dupont and given the name, Françoise Brunon. Françoise is an Indian who marries a French Canadian but who cannot adapt to civilized life. She starts to wander, rather aimlessly, noting only the beauty of the nature all around her. Eugene, her husband, in vain tries to persuade her of the advantages of civilized life. Perhaps ironically, warring Indians eventually capture her and put her to death. At the end of the story the moral appears to be that although the Europeans believe that they are bringing all of the benefits of Christianity and civilization, the truth is that they have corrupted an Indian population which was, until then, happy and healthy.[21] There are other writers who use the legend such as Charles de Guise in his Hélika (1871), Rudolphe Girard's L'Algonquine (an urban bourgeois version) (1912). In the twentieth century Arthur Bouchard's Les Chasseurs de noix and G. de Montreuil's Fleur des ondes (1912) continue the tradition.[22]

However, it is Henri-Emile Chevalier who best exemplifies the legend of the Iroquoise. Chevalier was a fan of Cooper and read the Leatherstocking Tales in English. He even translated J.H. Robinson's The Hudson Bay Trappers (1858) and The Dark Hunter (1859). This anglophilia led to his narrative series called Drames de l'Amérique du Nord, with La Huronne de Lorette, L'Iroquoise de Caughnawaga, la Tête-Plate, les Nez-Percés, les Derniers Iroquois, and Poignet d'acier. All of these works contain the story of an Indian woman who is supposed

---

[21] Jeanne LaFrance, Les personnages dans le roman Canadien-français, Sherbrooke: Editions Naaman, 1977.

[22] Maurice Lemire, Les grands thèmes nationalistes du roman historique canadien-français, Quebec: Les presses de l'Université de Laval, 1970.

to be abducted by one Indian chief, following which another Indian chief rescues her. The events take place in such diverse locales as the Western prairies of Canada and Greenland, yet the botanical setting always reflects Cooper's eastern United States.[23] None of these writers breaks new ground. All of the writers associated with the Iroquoise legend belong in our historical myth (the faraway noble native such as Hiawatha) category, in which the events described that reveal a superior Indian occured long before and had little to do with the Indians of the then present day.

Alexandre-Antonin Taché's Esquisse sur le Nord-Ouest (1869) and Vingt années de missions dans le Nord-Ouest et de l'Amérique (1866), while not exactly novels, have important Indian content. Taché believed that the white Canadians mistreated and discriminated against the Métis (half-breeds normally from an Indian mother and a Canadian or Québécois father). As a priest he was a believer, still, in the progressive mythology and wished to bring the Indians into the mainstream of Western civilization. He called them "les excellents sauvages"[24] and used the familiar pastoral images to describe their lives. In one passage he describes the setting of the Indians:

> [...au chasseur de bison, la prairie est un pays à nul autre pareil, c'est là qu'est son empire d'hiver comme d'été; c'est là qu'il éprouve un bonheur véritable à lancer son rapide coursier à la poursuite d'une proie nagure si abondante et si facile. C'est là que, sans obstacle, pour ainsi dire et sans travail, il trace des routes, franchit des espaces, et jouit d'un spectacle souvent grandiose, quoiqu'un peu monotone.[25]

Taché requires us to stretch our categories of literary myths a bit.

---

[23] Lemire 29–31.

[24] Warwick 51.

[25] Warwick 51–52.

112

The section on English Canadian literature writers mentioned authors who regretted the passing of superior Indian traits. They wrote about the inevitability of the decline of the noble red man, but tended to describe a period in which eventual defeat might be anticipated, although it was far in the future. Antonin Taché, certain other later English Canadian writers, and as we will see, other New World authors, also wrote about the decline and the defeats of the Indians in the nineteenth century. Their writing emphasized the tragic nature of the defeat and combined a feeling of resentment with anger at the way the Indians wre treated. Taché is not the only French Canadian writer to have these opinions. Louis Frechette's La Légende d'un peuple (1887) also details the ideal voyageurs or the coureurs de bois and their decline. His Dictionnaire historique des Canadiens et des Métis Français de l'Ouest (1908) speaks of these groups' innate nobility. In this he may also be linked to Charles-Louis Taché.[26]

Joseph Marmette's François de Bienville (1870) provides an exception to this pro-Indian representation in Quebec, whether it be with Indian characters or by ascribing his good characteristics to the frontier voyageur. It resembles the already discussed U.S. American frontier novels and certain English Canadian works; it contains an evil Indian anti-hero, Dent de Loup, who, at home in the dark, brooding, mysterious world of the primeval forest, becomes a sort of satanic anti-Christ. The work presents a view comparable to the most negative uses of the Indian in Richardson's Wacousta. It shows clearly the English and the U.S. American influence—especially that of Cooper—upon Québécois literature. His Le Tomahawk et l'epée (1877) also touches on historical themes, putting the Indian in an unfavorable light.[27] Henri-Emile Chevalier also wrote a novel that was anti-Indian in addition to his pro-Indian ones. His L'Héroine de Chateauguay, Episode de la guerre de 1813 (1858) presents Indians in a savage light—especially the ones who fought on the side of the U.S. Americans in that war. Since this is in

---

[26] Warwick 58, 111.

[27] Lemire 77–83.

marked contrast to his other novels we must assume that it results from these Indians being too closely allied with the Americans, similar to the Indians of William Kirby. However, although the ignoble savage image is present in Quebec, it still is in a definite minority in the works that treat the Indian in nineteenth-century French Canada. The positive image related to that of the bon sauvage is dominant. Let us consider now, in detail, a novel to examine this assumption.

The novel that I have chosen for analysis in detail here is representative of all of the images that have been isolated so far. Aubert de Gaspé's Les anciens Canadiens is one of Quebec's earliest novels (1847) although it was first published in 1863. In terms of its themes and the actual date that it was written, it follows Wacousta as the second written of the nineteenth-century novels selected for special attention in this book. Les anciens Canadiens is basically the story of one noble habitant family and a young Scot (once again!), Archibald DeLocheill, whom the oldest son, Jules, befriends. It describes the last years of the French presence in Canada, the war in which the French were defeated and the early adjustments to British control over Quebec. In a sense, it is not a unified novel; rather a series of anecdotes and short stories involving many different characters, tied together by a single thread. The thread, as such, revolves around Archie. His family, like the Beverlys in Wacousta, had been Jacobite and was defeated after the downfall of the pretenders to the throne. Being younger than Wacousta or Reginald Morton, the Archie of Les anciens Canadiens was eventually sent to school in Canada where he met Jules and his family. They become good friends and Archie fell in love with Jules' younger sister, Catherine. During their school years Archie, like Morton, was well-known for his great physical prowess and his endurance. In one especially dramatic incident, he jumped into an ice-choked river and saved a simple habitant's life.

One day during a visit to an old friend of the family, after having finished school and having been to Europe, Jules was told the ways of the world. A friend of Jules' family, a former nobleman had ruined his fortune by loaning money to friends who had no intention of repaying him. In fact, the only man who repaid a kindness to him was an Indian. The bon monsieur had mercy on a dying Indian one winter and saved his life. Much to the Frenchman's surprise, a few years later a handsome, dignified Indian chief showed up on the doorstep with a sled full of rich furs and other valuable items. The Indian insisted that all of these items were not his, but in fact belonged to his French benefactor for whom the Indian had merely kept them in safekeeping. This is one good example of a truly noble Indian in a French Canadian work. It is especially interesting, as the Indian is put in contrast with the noble habitants of Quebec City. True nobility, seemingly, belongs only to the bon monsieur and the Indian. Nevertheless, this is not the only side of the Indian presented here.

After Archie and Jules go off to Europe, Archie makes a fateful decision. Instead of serving in the army under the fleur de lys with Jules and his French friends, he returns to Scotland to make his peace with the government and to attempt to recover his claim to his ancestral lands. There he discovers that in mid-eighteenth-century Scotland the only honorable path open to him is that of a soldier. Somewhat reluctantly he enlists in the British army, but serves with distinction, and rises to become an officer. Much to his dismay, however, war between Britain and France breaks out and his regiment is called to serve in Canada. There he is ordered by his evil commander, Montgomery, to set fire to the farms of his former friends. After obeying orders only when faced with court martial and possible execution, he is watching his friend Jules' house burn when he is captured by Indians allied with the French. These Indians appear real savages at first. Their code of war does not comprehend the notion of prisoners, and after discovering Archie's low rank, they prepare to burn him at the stake, a death befitting a brave warrior. Archie is rescued in the nick of time when an unidentified Québécois takes an interest in him. This man gets all of Archie's guards drunk except for the chief of the small band. The chief refuses to drink and at first refuses to yield to the Frenchman's pleas. Finally, the man asks the Indian if they are not good friends and would they not do absolutely anything for one another. The Indian warily agrees and then the habitant reveals himself as the man Archie had earlier saved from the river and tells the chief that his honor requires saving Archie's life. Finally the savage relents and covering his eyes so as not to see what was going to happen, he allows the release of the terrified Archie. This is the last Indian incident in the work. After the war Archie and his Canadian friends make peace, and he helps them maintain their position in the new Canada. Catherine, however, becomes a nun and both she and Archie remain unmarried.

The Indian, on the whole, plays a minor role in the plot of <u>Les anciens Canadiens</u>, but not an insignificant one. At the same time the role played is a totally traditional one. These Indians are indeed savages, capable of exercising a harsh penalty on enemies and wrongdoers and prone to alcoholism, but they are for the most part noble savages who listen to reason and are honorable in their relationships with the Europeans; as such they emerge as an object lesson for the white settlers.

Brazil

Brazil, as already indicated, first had a taste of independence with the decision of Emperor Dom Pedro I to stay in Brazil after the end of the Napoleonic era. Ultimate independence, and the first attempt at democracy, did not come until 1888. As a result, ties with Portugal remained close throughout the nineteenth century. The new Brazilian <u>literati</u> felt an especially strong need to proclaim their cultural independence from Portuguese influence. After Dom Pedro abdicated in 1831 in favor of his infant son, Brazilians began to look inward to find that part of them which was not Portuguese and yet was still positive and worthy of description. The whole feeling of "cá e lá" ("here" and "there", with "here" being Brazil and "there" Portugal and/or Europe) so important in modern Brazilian poetry was also important in the novel. As indicated earlier, one of the most important parts of the "cá" was the Indian. As José Veríssimo de Mattos in his <u>Historia da Literatura Brasileira</u> (1916) himself indicated, there was

> a simpatía com o indio, a intenção de o habilitar do
> juízo dos conquistadores e dos mesmos políticos
> coloniães, o errado presupôsto dêle ser o nosso

116

> antepassado histórico, o amor da natureza e da
> historia do paíz encaradas ambas com sentimentos e
> intenções estreitamente nativistas; o conceito
> sentimentalista da vida, o propósito manifesto, de
> fazer uma literatura nacional, e até uma cultura
> brasileira[28].

The importance of the Indian is perhaps the greatest in Brazilian literature of any of the nineteenth-century literatures due to Brazil's unique method of establishing its independence. Although the Indian plays an important role in both English Canadian and Québécois literature, he is not the central character that he is in Brazilian or most Spanish American literatures. In Latin America the Indian becomes the major focus of a school of literary creativity. This Indianist school is central to an understanding of Latin-American romanticism. In the Indianist school the Indian is rescued from early Jesuit criticism and restored to the picture created by Jean de Léry and Montaigne. This picture of the Indian is not unlike that which we saw in some of the seventeenth- and eighteenth-century works earlier discussed. The difference is that the ennobling poetic aspects are even stronger, and the Indian emerges as the superior hero of the work. The other main difference is not so great in the works themselves as it is in the societal attitudes of the times.

Brazilians have generally had a relaxed attitude about interracial relationships; mid-nineteenth century provides examples of this. As the Indian rescued from the conquistadores became the "real" Brazilian, the leading families of the country took pains to point out their Indian blood—no matter what the percentage was. Leading Brazilian scholars even pushed for the replacement of Portuguese as the national language with Tupi (Tupy), an Indian language. This type of pro-Indian emotional enthusiasm was not often duplicated in other New World or Western Hemisphere countries. In its strength it will also help explain the paucity of Indian works written in twentieth-century Brazil and their type. Yet

---

[28] David Driver, The Indian in Brazilian Literature, New York: The Hispanic Institute, 1942, 41.

at the same time, the similarities between the Brazilian Indianist nineteenth-century works and other New World works are striking. First of all, the Indian hero is never a contemporary nineteenth-century Indian. He comes nearly exclusively from the earliest period of Portuguese colonization and his environment is minutely described in a manner acceptable to fans of Chateaubriand. His position in the then current society of the nineteenth century is never discussed. In most of the works the misty obscurity of the past clouds over any attempt at realistic portrayal. Indianist authors portray Indians either as developed completely good or evil characters or as underdeveloped stick figures to whom events simply occur. Their works have the same air of tragedy and wistfulness noted earlier in English Canadian literature more than likely since the author cannot forget the current position of the Indian, that is that Indians are now controlled by European descendants. However, the earliest Indian literature is more a celebration of the new Brazilian and anti-Portuguese spirit than anything else.

In summary, then, we can say that Indianist works contain a colorful, romantic, pro-Indian bias as their central feature and make no attempt to portray the actual political or social condition of the Indian. We can also say that these Romantic characters reflect their creators' ideals of what the cultures of the newly independent New World countries should reflect.

António Gonçalves Días is the first important Indianist writer in Brazil who known for his Indianist poetry rather than his novels. His <u>Poesias Americanas</u> (1846) include poems such as "O Canto do Guerreiro", "O Canto do Piaga" (which contains the word "Manitou" and shows his North American influence), "O Canto do Indio", "Deprecação", "Tabyra", "Leito de Folhos Verdes", and "Y Juca-Pyrama" which Días translated as "that which is worthy to, or must die"[29]. In this poem, perhaps the best of all Indianist poems, a group of Indians, the

---

[29] Driver 52. Driver consistently spells certain Indian names with a "y" instead of the "i" that modern Brazilian critics use. I shall show my twentieth century influence and use the "i" more often than the "y", especially where modern readers would be more accustomed to the "i".

Tymbira, prepares to sacrifice an unknown Indian prisoner. In it the prisoner pleads for his life so he may succor his father in the last days of the aged man's life. The Tymbira chief, astounded at the young man's audacity in asking for a shameful reprieve; lets him go out of contempt. The young man then returns to his father and relates the story. His father, angered by the shame brought upon his tribe, demands that his son return and surrender. This he does but the Tymbira refuse to sacrifice one so unworthy. Suddenly and unexpectedly, the son has to defend his father and the Tymbira from a new menace. He does so with great valor and the Tymbira then grant the father's request for his son's sacrifice. The tribal honor is salvaged. Although some critics, including David Driver[30] feel that this is a truly Indian story, it reminds one more of Corneille, Camões or Lope de Vega than the Tymbira. It is also important to note that there are no European characters in the poem.

Other Días works dealing with the Indians include an epic poem called Os Tymbiras. Días could not resist attempting to write a poem as great as Os Lusiadas by Camões, perhaps the greatest literary work written in Portuguese. Although Os Tymbiras holds promise, Días never completed it. It tells a story of Indian battles and heroism in the epoch of the conquest. The only mention of Europeans occurs in the third canto's metaphor relating America to a beautiful virgin who is duped into marrying Europe, an avaricious old guardian.

Gonçalves de Magalhães in A Confederação dos Timoyos (1856), Junqueira Freire in Deltinka, O Hymno da Cabocla (1854), Fagundes Varella in Vozes da America (1861), Araujo Porto Alegre in Colombo (1866), Luis Guimarães in Noturnos (1872), Machado de Assís in Poesias Americanas (1875), and Olavo Bilac in "Morte do Tapir" (1888) also wrote works similar to those of Días. Some minor works, involving the Indians include Adolpho de Vernhagem's fiction such as Sumé (1855), an Indian myth transposed into fiction, Escragnole Taunay's Ceus e Terras de Brasil (1882), Luis Carlos Martins Penna's Itamindá ou

---

[30] Driver 56.

O Guerreiro de Tupán, and José Bernardino dos Santos' I-Juca-Pyrama. All of these works are Indianist to the extreme. One work, however, which does not fit in with the Indianist stereotypes is Franklin de Silveira Tavora's Os Indios do Jaguaribé (1862). Tavora writes about noble Indians, but also describes other Indians' savagery, violence, and unruliness[31].

Some works written in the last fifteen years of the century in Brazil gave a new view of the Indian, one very similar to that which we will examine in detail in Peruvian Clorinda Matto de Turner's work and the school which Spanish American critics call indigenist (indigenista). As such we will consider them later in our section on Peruvian (and Spanish American) literature. The interesting thing about all of the earlier Brazilian Indianist works, however, is how similarly they describe the image of the Indian presented. It is also surprising that all of the great literary figures of nineteenth-century Brazil participated in this movement, even the sceptical and cynical Machado de Assís. Thus in its wide range and scope, the Indianist movement in Brazil is unique in the Western Hemisphere, although in terms of the actual picture of the Indian presented in the works, the movement is not unique in the slightest. The uniformity of opinion on the Indian in nineteenth-century Brazil shows itself, in fact, less relevant to our purpose of cataloging and discussing Indian images than English Canadian literature. Before going on to Peru, however, it is necessary to discuss the author best known for Brazilian Indianism and to present the best-known novel of Brazilian Indianism.

This last great remaining Brazilian Indianist author is José de Alencar. As Gonçalves Días is the most important Indianist poet in Brazil, Alencar is the most important Indianist novelist, essayist, and critic. Alencar's best and most influential works are his three Indianist novels: O Guaraní (1856), Ubirajará (1875), and Iracema (1865)[32]. O Guaraní is the first good Indianist novel written in Portuguese and reflects Alencar's historical and cultural research on the early period of

---

[31] Driver 57.

[32] Driver 83–86.

Portuguese colonizers. The novel's plot is much more romantic than historical, however. It tells the story of a noble Indian, Pery, who saved the life of a beautiful white girl, Cecília, became her servant, and who through his tireless nobility and devotion finally convinced her to fall in love with him. The story originally took four volumes to tell, as the pair suffered through pages of adventures and difficulties. Pery is the only Indian character treated at length in the work, and no reader could ever question his perfection of character. At the end of the novel he finally becomes a Christian, perfect in every way. The only other Indians in the work, a tribe called the Aymores, attack Cecília's family to avenge a murder committed by Cecília's brother. Therefore, bloodthirsty savages are present just as in works in other literatures, but here they have very good reasons for seeking revenge. Finally, after hundreds of pages, Pery and Cecília find themselves alone on a palm tree heading over a waterfall, preparing for their first kiss, when the novel ends. One, however, probably should believe Pery's earlier assertion that they would survive the storm and the trip over the fall.

This survival and the consequent sexual relationship between the characters would contain a new beginning for Brazil, through the fusion of Pery and Cecília, even if Alencar could not describe it in this novel. However he is not so coy in his Iracema, as we will soon see. Perhaps Alencar did not feel the need for caution when he was writing about a white man and an Indian woman and not an Indian man and a white woman. Considering the avoidance of consummation in O Guaraní and the emphasis placed on it in Iracema, it is hard to agree with David Haberly that these couplings are only of symbolic and not anthropological or social importance[33].

In Ubirajará Alencar did not have to face the problem of deciding whether to have the white-Indian fusion occur in the work. He avoids the whole question by eliminating whites from his work. His protagonist, Jaguarê, an Araguaya was betrothed to a maiden named Jandira. One day, however, he met a Tocatín maiden,

---

[33] David Haberly, Three Sad Races: Racial Identity and National Consciousness in Brazilian Literature, New York: Cambridge University Press, 1983 47–50.

Aracy, and fell in love, forgetting Jandira. After a long combat in which he defeated the Tocanín champion and Aracy's other suitor, Pojucán, Jaguarê became chief of the Araguay and took the name Ubirajará. After a long series of adventures involving personal honor and customs similar to those in Días' "Y-Juca-Pyrama", Ubirajará emerged as the only man capable of leading both tribes and bound both the Araguaya and Tocantín nations together, founding the Ubirajará nation. As a result of the union of nations he had to take a wife from each nation to render the union perfect. Therefore he married both Aracy and Jandira and made them equal to each other in love.

No matter how entertaining his other novels might be, Alencar's Iracema is probably the best work[34]. Again there is a story of white and Indian contact, but here the sexual contact between the two sides was much more explicit as we have indicated. Martim Soares Mereno, a full-blooded Portuguese became involved with Iracema, a Indian "Vestal virgin". Martim's name (as is clearly indicated) means "martial", although it could come from the Portuguese word "mar" which means sea (refering to Martim's Portuguese origin and his manner of arrival and departure).

In this novel, Alencar begins by showing how Martim, the protagonist, lost his way in the forest and was surprised by Iracema (whose name means "honey lips" in her Indian language). She was obliged to honor the custom of hospitality and took him to her father, the high priest (or pajé) Araquém's, camp. There they began to fall in love. She tried to resist her passionate inclinations; she was supposed to devote her life to being a priestess of Tupá with the attendant position of being the virginal keeper of the sacred wine, the "jurema". She therefore had to remain a virgin. Although Martim was also immediately attracted to Iracema, he was already betrothed to a European woman with blond hair (as the author emphasizes), and understanding the customs of the Indians, he knew that falling in love with Iracema would be an excellent way to dishonor the hospitality laws of the

---

[34] José de Alencar, Iracema, Lenda do Cear , Rio de Janeiro: Edições de Ouro, 1969.

tribe he was visiting as well as put him in imminent danger of death. Nevertheless, the two became closer and closer while attempting to restrain themselves. Irapuá, another suitor trying to claim Iracema, became jealous of their growing intimacy and attempted to rouse the whole Tabajara tribe against Martim, who was discovered to be an ally of the enemy Potiguaras. Finally Araquém had to step in and make Martim a virtual prisioner to rescue him from Irapuá and the other Tabajaras. Martim grew more and more passive in his captivity, drugged by Iracema's presence. Only when Potí, his best friend from the Potiguaras, came looking for him could he prepare to leave. Even then all of the preparations had to be made by Iracema in league with Potí, as Martim could not leave Araquém's dwelling. Helping Martim, Iracema broke her tie of loyalty to her own people. The next night, the night before Potí could ready the escape, Martim made matters infinitely worse. He drank some of the jurema. The wine of dreams caused him to dream about Iracema and making love to her. Hearing him call out, she appeared and assented to his amorous overtures, thus breaking her last tie to her people. The next evening, she gave the jurema to all of her tribe's warriors, preparing their escape. She then told Martim the truth that what he had believed to be only a dream had happened in actuality and then convinced him to flee with her and the stoic Potí to the Potiguaras. When almost safe, a war party of Tobijaras caught them and Martim and Potí fought against overwhelming odds. When all looked blackest, Potí's faithful dog, who had been sent ahead for help, arrived with reinforcements and all the Potiguaras were saved.

For a brief period after the battle, the two lovers were happy living with Potí in his father's camp, but Iracema could not bear the constant reminders of living in the camp of her enemies. The couple, together with the faithful Potí, left the Potiguaras and built a romantic, isolated, home on the strand. All seemed well at first. Martim and Potí hunted together; there were friendly neighbors, and a child was expected, which Iracema informed Martim would be a son.

Then, in a series of scenes strikingly familiar to readers of medieval chivalric romances[35], Martim became vaguely restive, then increasingly unhappy. He longed for adventures, for his past life, and his own people. Always the call of the sea beckoned him and any white sail in the distance was watched avidly. Finally news came that Potí's tribe was to be attacked by the French and their Indian allies. With great relief the two warriors, white and Indian, strode off together to war. There they had great personal success and repulsed the French and the enemy Indians. Iracema, alone, gave birth to a son, Moacir, or "child of pain". The pain expressed is physical due to the rigors of childbirth and emotional because of Martim's desertion and his falling out of love. Only after Moacir was born and Martim did not return, did Iracema completely lose hope. She slowly began to fade away, not eating or doing anything to stay alive. Not even the visit of her brother, Caubí, and his forgiveness could rescue her. She stayed alive only long enough to hand the infant son into Martim's arms while requesting burial beneath a palm tree, where she could hear the sound of the sea. The work ends with Martim, now a successful and famous Portuguese settler, coming back to her grave, driven by the sound "Iracema" heard in the rushing of the waves. At last Martim and his son make their peace and are adopted by "America" (the letters rearranged spell Iracema).

Although in some respects the plot is one of the least important elements in this work (the poetic language being the most important), one must still examine it since this was the most important Indianist novel in Brazil. The two key Indian figures, Iracema and Potí, are just as good and as noble as Pery or Cecília. Potí is perhaps the only completely perfect chararcter, since Iracema finally broke her sacred vows to her people through her love for Martim. She can thus be considered a type of Edenic Eve, imperfect, but extremely desirable and loyal to what she considers her highest calling. The other Indians do not differ greatly from figures in any novel which contains dramatic action. They serve merely as devices

---

[35] I am thinking especially of the romances similiar to the medieval French story of Yvain.

to advance the plot and create dramatic interest. There is no hostility toward the enemy because of different customs, language or morality. They simply represent the wrong side. Irapuá comes closest to being an evil character. But his actions remain understandable, since his motivation is exactly the same as Martim's.

The picture of the Indian that Alencar presents resembles those of other Brazilian Indianist works. The Indian characters described are not real human beings. Iracema comes closest, being mastered by an overwhelming love and then dying from neglect, but the romantic aspects of her history are too extreme and improbable. She simply becomes an essential part of the allegory of Iracema, representing the Indian aspect of the new nation of Brazil's symbolic genesis, just as the Biblical Eve is the symbolic feminine aspect of all humankind's genesis. The Indians in these novels become tools of a novelistic purpose and not accurate representations of any human. As such these novels belong to the group of works which deal with faraway and often legendary Indians, whose real importance is linked with didactic intent, the historically distant literary myth already discussed in Canadian literature. By extension, then, almost all of nineteenth-century Brazil's works containing Indians can be considered to be part of this historical, "mythical" Indian. Only in the very last part of the century, influenced by other literatures' works, especially Spanish American ones, will a new type of Indian novel appear in Brazil.

Peru

Before arriving at the last literature to be considered here, that of Peru, let us treat, briefly, some works in other Spanish American literatures since Peruvian literature is not well-known for its literature dealing with the Indian before Clorinda Matto de Turner's startling work, Aves sin nido (1889)[36]. Only after considering

---

[36] Clorinda Matto de Turner, Aves sin nido, Cuzco: Universidad Nacional de Cuzco, 1949.

these other Spanish-American works can the early Peruvian ones can be put into their proper context.

Some of the first important novels in other Spanish-American literatures deal with Indians for many of the same reasons we have seen in the other literatures already considered. The first Argentinian works printed in the nineteenth century use Indian characters, albeit in a negative manner, similar to some English Canadian works. Esteban Echeverría's poem La Cautiva (1837) is a case in point[37]. In it the defeated savages decide to rise up aginst the good whites in a fury, "Los salvajes pasan a caballo, hendiendo el espaso, atronado el desierto, con sus alaridos, levantando sus lanzas, donde van clavadas las cabezas de sus víctimas"[38]. The Indians in Sarmiento's Martin Fierro are similar. Interestingly, this negative picture is almost unique to Argentinian literature. Ignoble savages, while common in Argentina, are extremely uncommon in other Spanish American literatures. The reason for this particular type of Indian image in Argentina may be for the same historical reasons as that of English Canada or the United States. At the time these early works were being written the Indian in Argenina was still being conquered by the gaucho or the cowboy. Thus this ignoble savage literature serves to build up the Indian as an evil, violent figure and creates a marked contrast with the gaucho who becomes the real national hero.

The Argentinian (and later general Latin American) legend of Lucía de Miranda also continued this trend, up to a point. This is the story of a white woman, Lucía, who was kidnapped from a Spanish fort by an Indian tribe after a successful attack. She soon feared for her "honor" since the tribe's chief, Mangoré, was attracted to her. That threat was soon addressed, however, since Mangoré later died in the attack. A new threat developed, though, when she became the spouse of the new chief, Siripo. Her white husband, who had been hunting while the attack occured, searched for Lucía. When he found her he took

---

[37] Melendez 76.

[38] Augusto Raúl Cortázar, Indios y gauchos en la literatura argentina, Buenos Aires: Instituto Amigos del Libro Argentino, 1952.

the surprising action of enlisting in the service of her new husband in order to be near her. Finally their feelings toward each other became too obvious and Lucía was condemned to be burned to death for treason to "her" tribe while her former husband was forced to watch. This is the original, rather anti-Indian story told in Lebardén's Siripo. However legend soon changes, even in Argentina. Rosa Guerra's novel Lucía de Miranda (written by 1858) describes the Indian attacker of the fort in these terms:

> Mangoré, cacique de los tímues, a pesar de ser bárbaro, reunía en su persona toda la arrogencia de su raza, las bellas prendas de un caballero, y en su corazón, educado y cultivado espíritu por el trato de los españoles, había adquirido casi todas sus caballerescas maneras y fino arte de agradar. Tenía alta talla, y era de fuerte y nerviosa musculatura, sus formas esbeltas. Era Mangoré uno de esos tipos especiales entre los indios descritos por el celebre Ercilla en su Araucana[39]

Thus Mangoré becomes a noble, chivalric hero in what has become a familiar mode to us. In Eduardo Mansilla de García's version (1860), Mangoré is also noble. He is defeated by Siripo in combat after one of Siripo's men interferes in the fight[40].

Other countries and other literatures created large numbers of noble Indian heroes similar to Mangoré. Gertrudio Gómez de Avallaneda's Guatimozín, although written and published in Spain in 1846, was created by a Cuban-born author. In its story it brings back another hero from the past, telling the story of Cortés' conquest of Mexico and the heroic although ultimately unsuccessful defense led by Guatimozín. Even though Avallaneda describes Cortés in not uncongenial terms, the defeated Indians receive Avallaneda's most lavish praise

---

[39] Melendez 97.

[40] Melendez 97–99.

and her tears. Once again the Indians are described in terms reminiscent of Ercilla's <u>Araucana</u> as refined "caballero-pastores".

In spite of what may seem to be a lack of originality to the modern reader, this novel went through more editions than any other Indianist novel in the nineteenth century. This may be entirely due to its Madrid publication, but its consequent influence cannot be denied[41]. Several other authors wrote their own version of the tale. One of them is Eligio Ancona, a Mexican, who wrote <u>Los Martires del Anahuac</u> (1870) and was the first to write a good Mexican novel on these themes. His version of the conquest was much more violently anti-Spanish, however. Cortés becomes a character filled with greed and injustice. Only the Aztecs are drawn in a favorable light in Ancona's novel.

Other writers who attempted to write Aztec novels include Mariano Melendez Muñoz's <u>El Misterioso</u> (1836), but it was not as successful as the later <u>Los Martires del Anahuac</u> or Ancona's other major historical novel, <u>La cruz y la espada</u>. Another interesting novel which should be mentioned here is J.R. Hernandez's <u>Azcaxochitl o la flecha de oro</u> (1878), which omits the whites altogether and gives a fictional account of certain Aztec battles[42].

In addition to <u>Guatimozín</u>, one of the other most important Indianist novels is Manuel de Jesús Galván's <u>Enriquillo</u> (1879–1882); it relies upon Las Casas' descriptions of Santo Domingo at the turn of the sixteenth century[43]. It tells the story of Enriquillo's life as he grows up, the son of the deposed chief. With his coming of age, he fully understands the subjugation of his people and he tries to free them. He ends up fighting many battles from an ancestral stronghold in the mountains. Finally, after thirteen years of maintaining his independence, Charles the Fifth of Spain sends a decree granting Enrique's freedom. Here the pro-Indian

---

[41] Melendez 87–89.

[42] Melendez 107–115.

[43] Melendez 123–144.

attitude is quite obvious and the equation of Indian and "caballero" continues. Enriquillo became a Santo Domingan national symbol. A new attitude begins to appear. At one point Galván himself said:

> Enriquillo no quiere matanza ni crímines.
> Quiere tán solo, pero quiere firme y amorosamente,
> su libertad y la de todos los de su raza. Quiere llevar
> consigo el mayor número de índios armados,
> dispuesto a combatir en defensa de sus derechos; de
> derechos que los mas de ellos no han conocido
> jamás y que es preciso ante todo hacerles concibir y
> enseñarlos a definir[44].

Although the action still occurs in the distant past, there is a note of patriotism and liberty applicable to the present. This novel still represents the Indianist literary myth, however, since it does not deal with the present-day problems of the Indians, nor does it introduce a more realistic appraisal of the Indian.

In the same year as Rosa Guerra's Lucía de Miranda, the Venezuelan, José Ramón Yepes' Anaída appeared. Later he published another novel, Iguaraya[45]. Yepes' works, in contrast to those discussed earlier were more poetic and less historic. In Anaída there are no white men. An Indian maiden becomes lost in the forest and has to be protected throughout a long night by a young Indian warrior, from whom she had fled in the past. During the night the warrior must save her from such dangers as an attack by a jaguar. She consequently falls in love with him, but before their union can be finalized, Iurupén must defeat two powerful warriors in succession. This he does, leading to the final hymns of praise. Iguaraya (1872) is even more mythic than Anaída. When Iguaraya, an Indian princess, was born, the tribe's soothsayers forecast a terrible future unless her husband could launch an arrow into the air and have it stay stuck there. One of Iguaraya's suitors despairing of not being able to fulfill the precondition for

---

[44] Melendez 137.

[45] Melendez 151–157.

marriage attempts to drown himself one night, and as he was sinking, he suddenly realized how to fulfill the prophecy and managed to save himself. The next night he gathered the tribe together and shot an arrow into the air, with the result that it landed in the lake near the shore. All of the tribe was astounded at his evident failure until a soothsayer explained his attempt. When the tribe was brought to look in the lake then during the night of the full moon, they saw the arrow stuck in a shallow part of the lake. Looking down at it they realized that it was stuck in the image or reflection of the sky. Thus it appeared to be truly stuck in the sky. When the tribe realized that Taíca won, Iguaraya's father killed himself, and Iguaraya went mad. Taíca then became the new chief who never smiled, laughed, or cried. When Iguaraya left reality she took his spirit with her. As in Chateaubriand's Atala, there is evidence of a "voto" which brings about a catastrophe. The peculiar type of romanticism in both poetic novels also brings Chateaubriand to mind. At the same time, the lyricism in them is similiar to that of José de Alencar's Brazilian Indianist novels. Even the plots, so simple in their structure, remind us of romantic tales in which the work's emphasis resides in the character's emotions and their development. Yepes' novels are clearly strongly Indianist and Romantic and must be viewed this way[46].

Other Venezuelans influenced by Yepes include Fermín Toro and Francisco Guaycapuro Pardo. Venezuela was not the only Spanish-American country to have poetic Indianist novels however. In Mexico José María La Fragua wrote Netzula nearly fifty years before Yepes' Iguaraya. Once again Chateaubriand's influence is evident in the passage "la hija de Ixolou sentía arder sobre su frente la fiebre que la conducía a la tumba; pero no queriendo afligir a su padre, callaba y miraba la muerte como el lecho de su descanso, el asilo contra la tormenta"[47]. Father Crescencio Carillo y Ancona's Historia de Welinna is similar to Netzuela in terms of its language but its plot is one of Christianity triumphing over pagan fears. The

---

[46] Melendez 156.

[47] Melendez 160.

130

real hero of this work is not really the valiant Yibán nor the fearful Welinna, but rather the priest Fray Pedro de Landa who converts Yibán and saves both Yibán and Welinna at the last minute from being sacrificed. After such a noble and powerful gesture, Welinna finally converts to Christianity. Father Landa then baptizes them and marries them to end the story. Juan Luís Tercero's <u>Nezaualpilli o el catolícismo en México</u> (1875) follows the same line, praising the Catholic faith incessantly and praising the Indian characters only when they are upholding it.

These two works are rather different from most other works which are properly Indianist. Indianist works praise the Indian's pagan culture and his innate nobility. Even though Alencar does talk about "o Dios dos brancos" in <u>Iracema</u>, there are no great paeans to the Catholic faith, nor is it deemed necessary for Iracema to convert. In some senses these two Mexican novels are more similiar to pro-Catholic French Canadian novels such as <u>Les anciens Canadiens</u> than Spanish American Indianist novels, and the mutual Jesuit heritage is obvious. In <u>Nezahualpilli</u> as in <u>Les anciens Canadiens</u>, the Indians are not savage beasts, but neither can they become really good perfect human beings until they embrace Catholic Christianity[48].

Let us move from Mexico to a country closer to Peru, the Ecuador of Juan León Mera. In 1858 the first volume of his poetry <u>Las Melodías Indígenas</u> appeared, and in 1861 his first full-length poem <u>La Virgen del Sol</u>. Both of these works are more properly Indianist in their descriptions of the natives than his best-known work <u>Cumandá</u> (1872 or 1879) which was one of the most important nineteenth-century Spanish American novels in which an Indian appeared. In contrast to his poetry however, <u>Cumandá</u> is clearly not a typical Indianist work[49]. It contains the story of a group of Indians partially civilized by the Jesuits and then left to their own ways after the eviction of the Jesuits in the eighteenth century. In a scene reminiscent of ignoble savagery these Indians then became restive and eventually attack whites in a series of uprisings.

---

[48] Melendez 169–170.

[49] Melendez 180–190.

Within this framework a Spanish gentleman's son, Carlos, meets a beautiful Indian princess, Cumandá, and they fall in love. Carlos' parents object to the match but Cumandá's parents take violent exception to it and marry Cumandá off to an old chief. Fortunately the chief dies the night of the ceremony and Cumandá flees. She consequently saves Carlos' life on three occasions, the last being at the cost of her own life. When it is too late to save her life, Carlos' father arrives, saves him, and after looking at a locket which Cumandá had given to Carlos, they all finally realize that Cumandá was actually Carlos' sister who had been carried off by the Jíbaro tribe while only an infant. Thus Cumandá herself, easily the noblest and the strongest character in the work, is actually white beneath her Indian veneer. The ultimate nobility in this story then actually resides in its white characters. In contrast the Indians are harsh, Old Testament figures whose lack of kindness and flexibility make them unsympathetic. Even a relatively good Indian, the old chief Yuhuarmaqui, whom Cumandá marries is characterized thusly:

> (...)se acercaba(...)a los setenta años y sin embargo tenía el cuerpo erguido y fuerte como el tronco de la (chonta); su vista y oído, eran persipaces y firmísimo su pulso; jamás erraba el flechazo asestado el colibrí y percibía como ninguno el son del (tonduli) tocado a cuatro leguas de distancia. En su diestra, la pesada maza era como un bastón de mimbre, que batía con la velocidad del relámpago. Nunca se le vó sonreír ni dirigío jamás, ni a aun de sus hijos, una palabra de cariño[50].

Such a description seems more worthy of Cooper than José de Alencar, or than even José Ramón Yepes. This type of severe, unfeeling patriarch could come from The Leatherstocking Tales. Other parts of Cumandá, including Cumandá's white background, could reflect influences from Cooper, but the weak and ineffectual Carlos reminds us of Chateaubriand's René. Mera's assumption appears to be that

---

[50] Melendez 183.

132

Indians are inferior to white men and need to be assimilated into white society. In this sense Mera is more closely related to the Victorian, the Whig, and progressive mythology than he is to the regressive Indianist.

This brings us back to Peru and its own tradition of Indian literature. As early as 1839 Manuel Asensio Segura published a work, Gánzalo Pizarro, which dealt with the conquest of the Incas. In Ricardo Palma's Tradiciones Peruanas (1860–1899) he has several stories relating to the native Peruvians, most of which were written about events which occured before Pizarro's invasion. Palla-Huarcana (1860) deals with the victory of Tupac-Yupanqui, "the one who is rich in all virtues"[51], over the pachis. La achirana del Inca, La gruta de las maravillas, and Just cia mayor de Layeacota detail stories of the conquest in which the Incas appear much the same as the Spaniards. Many of these stories are more similiar to English Canadian Indian legends than to the Indianist school. There is no overt superiority assigned to the Indian characters although they are often given a sense of nobility. The stories occur in the far distant past and as such give a sense of history and tradition to what had become Peru. They are nationalist, and help give roots to a new country looking for its past.

In summary, all of the above works give examples of the importance of Indian elements as presented in Spanish-American literature. Yet even though they come from a very different series of cultures, the picture that they draw of the Indian does not vary from the three literary myths that we have analyzed in the section on English Canadian literature. A few of these works, especially early Argentinian ones and Cumandá, use Indian characters to highlight the superiority of the white man when faced with the powerful yet ignoble red savage. This savage must be defeated and eventually civilized. Several works discussed in this section deal with the legendary or allegoric Indian who lives in a mythicized past, who has problems with other Indians, and only occasionally must deal with any white Europeans. The majority of the works discussed here, though, deal with the

---

[51] Melendez 197.

noble Indian whose shining virtues are an example to all of the new patriots to follow while gaining their independence from Spain. In Spanish-American literature, these categories are often seen in the same work, and while the use of Indians is somewhat more complex than these categories may be able to indicate, on the whole they serve as a good summary of this literature's use of the Indian. They demonstrate how unimportant the "real" flesh and blood Indian was to nineteenth-century New-World writers even in areas where his numbers were extremely significant. It took until 1890 andthe Peruvian writer Clorinda Matto de Turner's Aves sin nido[52] to begin the change toward a new literary use of the Indian. Just as Uncle Tom's Cabin was shocking to the literate public of the United States through its advocacy of reform for the black slaves of the South, Aves sin nido was shocking to the Peruvian public of the coast since it described conditions and a way of life in the mountains which was almost unknown to them. In her novel, Matto de Turner also broke with the traditional Romantic uses of the Indian already described, in much the same way Emile Zola did in his discussions of the French working class during the same period. Turner dared to describe the Peru of twenty-five years past, not two hundredand fifty years past. At the same time she wrote about Indians as modern-day flesh and blood beings, as if they were just another group resident in Peru. While doing so she detailed the problems Indians in Peru had to face in white-dominated society. Thus this novel, while still Romantic in tone and even in plot, became the first of what we will call the indigenist or indigenista novel in which modern Indians are described with all of their concrete problems and where some type of social reform is proposed. This trend may be associated with "naturalism" in Europe or, perhaps more accurately, the reform novel of the late nineteenth century. In fact many indigenist novels are written in a manner analagous to both Dickens and Zola. The worst features of the Indians' life are brought forth in a melodramatic manner calculated to inspire tears and sympathy. As a result some of the early novels, especially Matto de Turner's

---

[52] Turner and Melendez 197–205.

Aves sin nido, are not "naturalist" in the sense of painting a bleak background and trying to write down as many details of a particular type of life as possible or giving a central role to a social Darwinist predestination. Rather they paint with broad strokes and are more "Romantic" in their presentation than almost any Naturalist novel.

Aves sin nido is a particularly good example of the transition in the literary image of the native New World human from the nineteenth century to the twentieth century. It tells the story of the problems an aristocratic white family and an Indian family face in a small mountain town, attempting to obtain justice. Don Fernando Marín and his wife, Lucía, had just moved into Killac from Lima since Don Marín had become one of the large mineowners. Both of them apparently had been raised in a very protected society where they believed that helping other people was their Christian duty. One day, because of their utter poverty, Juan Yupanqui and his wife, Marcela, discover he is to be sent away to work to pay for an offense he did not commit. Marcela goes to Lucía to pray for help. Lucía and her husband try to help and thereby encourage the displeasure of the town's real rulers: Don Sebastián,the governor of the region; Father Pascal, the village priest; and the supposed Indian chief. They and their easily swayed minions become convinced that the Maríns are dangerous and have to be dealt with decisively. They arrange for a mob to attack the Marín house with the expectation that both of them will be killed in the tumult. Thanks to Juan and Marcela and others, the Maríns escape the mob. Juan and Marcela are not so fortunate, however. Juan is killed by a stray bullet and Marcela dies from grief and shock, but not before confiding a deathbed secret to Lucía and asking Lucía to look after her two soon-to-be orphaned daughters. When the people who comprised the mob discover Juan and Marcela have died and that Lucía and Fernando have taken in their daughters, the town's attitudes towards the Maríns change. The rest of the work's plot becomes apparent when the governor's son comes home from Lima and quickly discovers how lovely Marguerita Yupanqui is. Marguerita, by this time, has become "white" in terms of her appearance and manner so that there is no real shock for the reader in this possible pairing.

During the last part of the book, one of Don Sebastián's plots is uncovered and he is finally deposed from power. His son Manuel then is able to forgive his father and restore unity to his family. As this is happening Father Pascual nearly dies from an illness and goes away to a monastery where it appears that he confesses his crimes silently to God on his deathbed, although his redemption remains ambiguous.

By the end of the book the old power block has been overthrown and the new rulers seem to be more generous and accepting of all of their subjects. However Don Fernando and Lucía have already decided to move back to Lima, taking the two Indian girls with them. Manuel, has to stay behind in order to make sure that another Indian, Champí, who was imprisoned unjustly under the old regime is freed. Finally at the end of the work both secrets of the lovers' heritage come out in Lima. Manuel discovers from his mother that he is actually the son of Father Pascual and not Don Sebastián. Then, when this secret is let out and Don Fernando and Lucía become aware of it, they decide to tell Manuel Marguerita's secret before the two of them could go any farther in their relationship. Much to the lovers' dismay, they discover that they are half-brother and half-sister—Father Pascual fathered both of them. The work ends describing both Manuel and Marguerita as "aves sin nido" (birds without a nest).

From the plot summary alone the melodramatic import of the work is manifest. It is much closer to Uncle Tom's Cabin or even Le père Goriot than to Germinal or Hard Times. Juan describes his feelings about his wife in a speech that could come from Harriet Beecher Stowe when he says:

> Pobre flor del desierto, Marluca; tu corazón
> es como las frutas de la penca: se arranca uno, brota
> otro sin necesidad de cultivo. Yo soy mas viejo que
> tú y yo he llorado sin esperanza![53]

---

[53] Melendez 53.

136

Matto de Turner's own attitude towards the gentle innocent Indians is expressed when she says, "Amo con amor de ternura a la raza indígena por lo mismo que he observado de cerca sus costumbres encantadoras por su sencillez y la abyección a que someten a esa raza aquellos mandones del villorío que si varían de nombre, no degeneran siquiera del epíteto del tírano"[54]. Even the strongest speech made by the Indian Champí when speaking to his wife after being released from prison, sounds rather flowery:

> ¡La tumba debe ser tranquilo como la noche de luna en que se oye la quena del pastor! Nacimos indios, esclavos del governador, esclavos del cacique, esclavos de todos los que agarran la vara del mandón. ¡Indios, sí! ¡La muerte es nuestra dulce esperanza de libertad![55]

Other than the incidents involving Champí and the Yupanquis, there are no descriptions of Indian families or lives. The reasons given for their problems are based solely on personal animosity and the problems of clerical celibacy, not economic injustice or even prejudice. The Indians presented here are closely related to Rousseau's children of nature or his socially unaware Emile. They are so trusting and naïve that they have to be protected by good whites from bad whites who abuse their good nature. Matto de Turner proposes no solution to this problem, prefering to outline it the way she observed it. However, in spite of the work's limitations it still represents an important turning-point in the image of the Indian.

Before going on to the culmination of the indigenist novel in the twentieth century and the other changes the literary image of the Indian has undergone up to the present day, it is important to consider how nineteenth-century literature in the New World took the existing European-based view of the Indian and altered it.

---

[54] Melendez 202.

[55] Melendez 202.

Even before 1830 the philosophical debates about the worthiness of the savage, whether s/he was to be considered superior or inferior in his/her noble isoloation and simplicity, had become largely an argument confined to scholars in what would later be called "anthropology". Ercilla's and others' representations of superior pastoral figures would eventually give way to an attempt to write down the ways in which Indians actually lived in any "scientific" consideration of "primitive" peoples. However, as we have seen in the second chapter, the argument quickly became polemical with ultimate philosophical truth being bound up in proving the native New World man's ultimate sinfulness or sinlessness.

In some senses literature parallels the "scientific" considerations on Indian, especially by the end of the century. In the early part of the century, however, the noble savage and ignoble savage myths reign supreme and any type of "anthropological" interest gives way to literary and cultural self-awareness. The Indian as an important participant in the new country's society and economy disappears from sight, since the Indian taken from the period of the conquest becomes essential to the Western Hemisphere's created cultural self-confidence. Indeed, it seems that philosophers in the nineteenth century dropped primitive peoples from the list of their concerns, just as literary writers picked them up. But at the same time as the Indian disappears as a source for questioning philosophical truths s/he also disappears as contemporary being. In all four of the literatures chosen for this study, there are no novels which deal with Indians who lived after 1830 before <u>Aves sin nido</u>. The characters, whether good or bad, are historical Indians, and as such they exist to guide the white European into becoming the new, white, native of the New World. As good Indians they exist to serve as an inspiration of the virtues of the New World, and as bad Indians they show the white human the practices s/he must not adopt, or the savagery into which s/he must not sink, but must fight and conquer. As guide, these Indians appear to be adhering to many of the extremes posited by Rousseau or Buffon with the exception that they are no longer lethargic or weak, whether good or bad.

In conclusion we must say that it is during the nineteenth century, writers strayed the farthest from considering the Indians as normal flesh and blood human beings of any group of writers since the 1600's, with the culmination of this trend being represented by the Indianist novels of Latin America. Interestingly, it was also Latin America that presented the first major shift in writing on the Indians. Still the three literary myths discussed in the section on English Canadian literature appear to serve as viable summaries of the different images we have seen in all four literatures' nineteenth century works dealing with Indians. We will come back to these images and myths in the fifth chapter after discussing the twentieth century's own peculiar literary myths about Indians.

CHAPTER FOUR:
THE TWENTIETH-CENTURY INDIAN

After the appearence of Clorinda Matto de Turner's <u>Aves sin nido</u> in 1889, many other authors throughout the New World wrote works that were similar to those of Matto de Turner. It cannot be said that she influenced all of these other writers; instead, it is like the period in which Einstein discovered his theory of relativity. Many other researchers had similiar ideas and wrote them down very soon after Einstein. The time was simply ripe for researchers to come to the same conclusions as Einstein. The <u>Zeitgeist</u> of Matto de Turner's period induced literary writers to discuss the problems of contemporary Indians. They would no longer be removed from any discussion of the world as they were experiencing it. In fact, the key difference between those works written between 1830 and 1890 and works written after 1890 is the paucity of occasions in novels written before 1890 in which Indians were treated as human beings with human concerns and problems similar to those of whites. In part this is due to the fact that very few works dealt with real human beings during the Romantic period. Nevertheless, there is no well-developed René, Werther, or even Jean Valjean among the Indian characters figured in most of nineteenth-century literature. The vast majority of the Indians presented were as wooden as an old dime-store chief with his cigars in hand. One of the few Indians who acted like a real flesh and blood human being in the works we treated in the last chapter was the Indian who repaid a favor done for him by the <u>habitant</u> in de Gaspé's <u>Les anciens Canadiens</u>, but even this character seemed to owe more to Aesop or the Bible than to nineteenth-century Quebec. In 1890, however, all of this changed. If one of the recurrent nineteenth-century images of the Indian could be labeled as that of a "National Unifier" or "National Symbol", then the image of the Indian presented in many texts after 1880 might be labeled "In Search of the Most Human Human".

This search started for a variety of reasons. By 1890 romanticism had been dead in Europe for some time. Realism and Naturalism, with their emphasis on the concrete details of existence, had replaced Romanticism. Even the Parnassian poets had given way, in France at least, to the new wave of Symbolism. In the New World these changes had occurred to some degree. Before 1890 however, Indians did not serve as a suitable subject for a naturalist or realist novel, for several reasons. From a literary standpoint, the Indian could not be supplanted as a Romantic tool in New World literature until Romanticism itself had completely died out since the Indian had been *the* Romantic character in the New World—especially the New World of Latin America. The Indian of feathered savage nobility remained a literary topos until Romantic nationalism itself was no longer the fashion for sophisticated writers.[1] Only after 1890 was the need expressed that works different from those written in the past dealing with the Indian, with different themes, plots, and characters should be written. In addition to these purely literary reasons for a change in the types of Indian characters used after 1890 there are other compelling social and economic factors. By 1890 there were no Indians not subject to some type of white control. This is most evident in North America with the end of Indian uprisings and the subjugation of the last plains Indian tribes. It is no less true in most of South America, although some Amazonian tribes have managed to avoid white men throughout the twentieth century[2]. Still, the notion of the free, wide-ranging, independent Indian was a dead

---

[1] Let us not forget to note that the way the Indian was written about in the nineteenth century is also the way that many of the popular arts chose to use him—even in the late twentieth century.

[2] A newspaper in January 1985 (The Sumter S.C. Daily Item, 20 January 1985) noted a recent battle between Indians and white settlers in Brazil in which the Indians used poison arrows, thus showing that all Indians have not been conquered in the Western Hemisphere. This is also the case in Maíra, a work we will discuss later.

one by 1890. The Indian had been conquered, and since slavery had been officially outlawed in every Western Hemisphere country by 1888 (Brazil was the last one), the Indian had to be civilized and amalgamated into modern Western society and its culture. S/he had to become a useful citizen and work for the cause of the economic god of the times, capitalism. Thus the old-fashioned Indian with his/her old-fashioned civilization had to be modernized. This had been the ecomomic and social reality of the American Indian long before 1900 and the literary reality after 1900. Quite obviously, this clash of realities is in itself enough to furnish ample literary grist for the mill of a novel. At the same time, however, the newly conquered Indians were often horribly treated and quickly became the economic wage-slaves of a system whose meaning was empty for them. They were supposed to believe in the progressivist myth already discussed, or at least give their allegiance to it. Thus any lack of acceptance of the myth made whites, whose insecurity was evident, fear them and consider them treasonous. However, if they did accept the myth, then the more secure whites, counting upon their ultimate resignation and docility, could indeed make them the slaves previously described. Thus not only was there a clash of cultures, there was also the plight of the newly created economic slaves to be considered. The nineteenth-century strong Indian, whether noble or ignoble, had now become Buffon's weak and helpless figure. S/He needed to be helped, it appeared, and was "helped" through the literary and cultural efforts of of twentieth-century writers, critics, historians, and anthropologists.

This twentieth-century concern about lower-class human beings has been described in association with Clorinda Mattos de Turner's novel on Peruvian Indian life. Let us describe then the evolution of each of the four literatures' use of the Indian in the twentieth century, beginning where we left off, with Spanish-American literature. At the end of the chapter, more general observations of the most recent New World literature will be made.

Peru

After <u>Aves sin nido</u>, one of Peru's leading literary figures of the period took up the cause begun by Matto de Turner. Manuel González Prada published his <u>Indole</u> in 1891, which although an indigenist work, was more interested in the problems of corrupt priests than poor Indians.[3] Matto de Turner, herself, continued her work with other less successful volumes treating the same characters and taking place in different parts of Peru where the Indian characters were not so important. Although other writers such as José Chocano and Ventura García Calderón functioned as a type of <u>marche en arrière</u>, modern Indians, for the first time in Peruvian literature, had become worthy of interest. There was, as a result, a period of neo-Romantic writing on Indians which had to be endured until the leap forward presaged by Matto de Turner could take place. As Antonio Cornejo de Polar says in his <u>Literatura y sociedad en Peru: La novela indigenista</u>, "En términos ideológicos—no literarios—la obra de García Calderón parecería anterior a <u>Aves sin nido</u>".[4] Other Peruvian writers who wrote works in a quasi-indigenista manner were Augusto Aguirre Morales in <u>El Pueblo del Sol</u> (1927), and Abraham Valdelomar with his short stories which helped open the way, stylistically, for later indigenist writings.[5]

Some critics believe that the first real indigenist in Peru was Enrique López Albújar with his <u>Cuentos Andinos</u> (1920) and his <u>Nuevos cuentos Andinos</u> (1937). His Indians, however, are often closer to John Richardson's than to those later described by Ciro Alegría or José María Arguedas. They are violent, desperate, and often ignobly savage beings, although in terms of the majority of Latin

---

[3] Concha Melendez, <u>La novela Indianista en Hispanoamerica, 1832–1889</u>, (Madrid: Imprensa de la Libreria y Casa Editorial Hernando, 1934) 200–205.

[4] Antonio Cornejo de Polar, <u>Literatura y Sociedad en Peru: La Novela indigenista</u>, (Lima: Editora Lasontay, 1980) 92.

[5] Polar 48.

American Indian writing Albújar has pointed out a new path. Whereas Matto de Turner's Indians are seemingly hopeless passive creatures, Albújar's are ready to revolt at any time. With this work the possibility of Indian rebellion against white domination is introduced as a theme in modern Peruvian literature dealing with the Indian. However, the early key figure in the flowering of indigenism in Peru (and perhaps all of Latin America) is not Albújar but rather José María Mariátegui. His Siete ensayos de interpretación de la realidad peruana[6] are perhaps the most important single non-literary influence in twentieth-century Peruvian literature. Written in 1928 in a polemic tone and inspiring violent reactions from its readers, it still draws emotional reactions in the late twentieth century. It is basically a pro-revolutionary work which states that Indians must be brought fully into Peruvian society economically, socially, and culturally, no matter how this is done. In his discussion, Mariátegui reviews all previous Peruvian literature written about Indians and finally decides that Aves sin nido is an important but not conclusive step in the process towards the indigenist novel. At the same time he denigrates several other writers not sympathetic to reform in Peruvian society. His ultimately Marxist leanings color his cultural and literary analyses just as much as his economic and social discusssions. Nevertheless Mariátegui is important for his politicization of Peruvian literature and for giving literature treating Indians the courage to follow new paths. As a manifesto Los siete ensayos are no less important to indigenism in South America than the manifestos of surrealism were to it in France.

By the 1930's true indigenist works began appearing all over Latin America, but especially in Mexico, Ecuador, and Peru. In Mexico, after the 1917 revolution had been consolidated in the 1920's, many writers began to discuss what they saw as the evils of pre-revolutionary society with the goal of presenting the inevitability of the revolution. One work, Tierra, (1935) by Gregorio López y

---

[6] José María Mariátegui, Siete ensayos de interpretación de la realidad peruana, (Lima: Biblioteca Amauta, 1928).

Fuentes introduced the figure of the powerful and oppressive landlord who attempted to keep the Indian <u>campesinos</u> in a state of servitude. One good example of the landlord's feelings toward the people he commanded are his comments upon the death and the birth of two different Indians,

> At dawn those who have to work take their leave. The administrator an early riser, passes by. He looks in on the dead campesino:
>
> "Poor man!"
>
> That is his commentary. The father of the newborn arrives to tell him:
>
> "You have a new servant to command."
>
> "Aha."[7]

Another Mexican work of the thirties by López is <u>El Indio</u> (1935). In this work the Indians are passive although they are distrustful of the whites. At one juncture they attempt a small rebellion by refusing to furnish some white men a guide through the mountains. They relent, however, when faced with official papers served them by the whites. Later after the guide selected was crippled by the whites when he failed to tell them where a quantity of gold was hidden (in fact there was no gold), the Indians were forced to kill a white and consequently fled into the mountains. They emerged after many years, and in spite of promises of better treatment, they found nothing changed. The final passage of the novel is a colophon labeled "Distrust".

> The cripple continues hiding in his watchtower, showing distrust toward the wagon trail—which is civilization—from the rough ground. In the heights of the mountain range another awaits

---

7 John Reyna Tapia, <u>The Indian in the Spanish-American Novel</u>, (Lanham, MD: University Press of America, 1980) 92.

> the signal. Only they know, like all of their kind, that
> *people of reason* want to attack them: that in the
> mountain range and in the valley, hatreds like packs
> of hounds, show each other their teeth; and that the
> leader is enjoying his good situation.[8]

The other influential non-Peruvian indigenist novel of the thirties was Jorge Icaza's Huasipungo (1935). In this Ecuadorian work, Icaza writes another anti-clerical anti-white novel in which there are no good whites, nor a revolution to reform affairs. A poor white landowner decides to sell part of his land to a rich costeño, Mr. Chapy, who persuades him that the newly-acquired property is worthless unless there is a road built into it. To build this road hundreds of Indians are drafted and kept in a state of perpetual drunkenness to assure their compliance. The parish priest comes into the act, too, haranguing the Quechuas with stories of hellfire and eternal damnation if they do not keep on building the road. The Indians, themselves, are given no shelter to avoid the cold, wet weather of the mountains; a number of them die and many more of them become ill. Finally, after many individual stories of bravery, miscomprehension of the white world, and deaths, the road is finished. However, its purpose is now made painflully clear to the Quechua Indians. It is to be used to drive them out of their huasipungos (Quechua for houses with doors). Too late the Indians revolt and kill six whites; but their revolt is destined to failure as a whole company of the militia, using the road, arrives to put it down. The work then ends in a note of failure and deep tragic sadness, seeming to say that no real solution to the problem was possible.[9]

Ciro Alegría's La serpiente de oro (1938) and Los perros hambrientos (1939) are Peru's first entry into the arena of the true indigenist novel, presenting the Indian's plight in a dispassionate, hopeless, and even cynical light while pointing out its causes and white collusion. It shares a tendency with other Peruvian indigenist novels, appearing to be more a series of short stories bound

---

[8] Tapia 68.

[9] Tapia 71–76.

together by various diverse threads than a single story with different characters and sub-plots tied to it. In both of these works, plots similiar to those of <u>Huasipungo</u> are advanced. The Indians want to remain in the position that they hold—no matter whether it seems lowly or inconsequential to the white observer. Unfortunately their independence and their carefully-created world has to be destroyed by whites in order that they can take full advantage of the Indians, both socially and economically. In this sense the myth of the Indian world must be replaced by that of the white world.[10]

In Alegría's most famous work, <u>El mundo es ancho y ajeno</u> (1941), this conjunction of mythic and historic worlds is clearest. In the first chapters of the book, the Indian peasants try to understand the world around them much in the way they always had, via offerings, omens, and auguring. One of the most interesting plot developments in the work then resolves around the destruction of this resort to the mythic past. Concrete occurences distort the myths of the people and subtly, slowly, a white-dominated historicity replaces the mythic. With this change the Indians themselves change and begin to think of themselves in the terms of the white man. As Cornejo Polar says,

> Los comuneros que defenden Yananahui se saben integrados a un proceso histórico más ámplio, compremetido de lleno en la lucha de clases, y puede reconocer la verdadera naturaleza del conflicto que les opone al gamonel y a los grupos de poder de la sociedad nacional en su conjunto.[11]

At the end of the work Alegría expresses a political and social rationale for the actions of all of the major characters. Thus historicity and a type of marxist thought emerge dominant from the work.

---

[10] Polar 76.

[11] Polar 76–77.

In this group of committed writers we must also place the early José María Arguedas and his <u>Yawar Fiesta</u> of 1941. With this short novel or expanded short story, he resembles Alegría and Jorge Icaza to a great degree. This plot of this work tells the story of a group of Indians facing problems caused by white control over them. Here it is the collective story of one Indian village and its long struggle leading to defiance over authority. In Arguedas's description of the village he gives a detailed picture of what a small Indian town was like in the early days of the century.

> No hay calles verdaderas en ningún sítio; los comuneros han levantado sus casas, según su interés en cualquier parte; sobre la laderita, en buen sítio con su corral cuadrado o redondo, pero con sena, para conocerla bien desde los cerros. Hacia afuera una pared blanqueada, una puerta baja, una o dos ventanas, a veces un poyo pegado a la pared; por dentro un corredor de pilares bajos que se apoyan sobre bases de piedra; en un extremo del corredor una división de pared para la cocina...[12]

Such richness of detail and insistence upon the concrete renders the physical village a character in the novel. The Indians are objects associated with the village and are very infrequently discussed as individual entities. They are merely the Indians of the village and act as the village. Even at the end of the novel it is a single (and implied collective) voice which cries out against the unjust governmental "Authority".

In this novel as well as several of his others, the Quechua background of Arguedas himself is apparent. He was born in the mountains of Peru, spoke Quechua as his native tongue, and was raised in the custom of the Quechua people, although his appearance was clearly non-Indian. His white relatives had to force him to leave his Indian friends and learn the ways of the "European" Peruvian. As a result he came to know well both halves of Peru, but his childhood memories

---

[12] José María Arguedas, <u>Yawar Fiesta</u>, (Lima: Populibros Peruanas, 1958) 7.

were clearly his most positive, as he indicates in <u>Los Ríos profundos</u> which will be discussed later.[13]

Before we discuss Arguedas' later writings, other novels need to be mentioned. Even in Argentina with its earlier tradition of anti-Indian writing, an essay, "Radiografía de la pampa", strongly allied to the Andean novels of social protest, was published in 1933. A modern critic, however, shows how strongly certain attitudes continue in Argentina as she describes this essay as something which, "Aunque no puede justificar la ferocidad del índio pampero, trata de explicar su conducta, atribuyendo al blanco la perversión del indígeno."[14] This violent anti-Indian attitude shown by critic Conrado Almiñaque may help to explain the lack of Argentinian indigenist novels. If this particular pro-indigenista essay from 1933 could be described in these terms in 1981 by a respected critic, it seems that Argentina must lag behind changes in attitudes toward the Indian seen in other countries' literatures.

Yet as Braulio Muñoz points out in his <u>Sons of the Wind: The Search for Identity in Spanish American Indian Literature</u>[15], Ecuador, Peru, Bolivia, Guatemala, and Mexico were not nearly so reluctant in writing about Indian problems. Due to the numbers of Indians living in their countries, or to the quality of the writers who chose to use Indians as important characters in their novels, those countries' literatures all had important indigenist novels published during the twentieth century. Muñoz classifies indigenist novels as those tending towards a liberal or a socialist solution of the Indian problem. He adds to the list we have already presented Alcides Arguedas' <u>Raza de bronce</u> (1919), Botelho Gosávez Raúl's <u>Altiplano</u> (1945), Jorge Icaza's <u>En las calles</u> (1935) and <u>Hijos del viento</u>,

---

[13] José María Arguedas, <u>Los Ríos profundos,</u> intro., Mario Vargas Llosa, (Caracas: Biblioteca Ayacucho, 1978).

[14] Conrado Almiñaque, <u>El índio pampero en la literatura gauchesca,</u> (Miami: Ediciones universal, 1981) 53.

[15] Braulio Muñoz, <u>Sons of the Wind: The Search for Identity in Spanish American Literature,</u> (Rutgers, NJ: Rutgers University Press, 1982).

Jorge Rivadeneyra's <u>Ya está amanecido</u> (1957), Serafín Del Mot's <u>La tierra es</u> <u>hombre</u> (1943), César Falcón's <u>El pueblo sin díos</u> (1928), César Vallejo's <u>El</u> <u>Tungsteno</u> (1931), and Alfredo Yepez Miranda's <u>Los Andes Vengadores</u> (1934) among others.[16] Muñoz follows a carefully considered social scientist's route. He uses literature and literary writers to show how important movements became launched and continued in importance through their descriptions of various social realities, how these realities owed their existence to various social environmental and cultural exigencies, and how literature described these exigencies and proposed changing them. As a result Muñoz classifies Andean indigenist novels into two categories: liberal (those written before 1935) and socialist (those written after 1935). His final chapter discusses the latest trends in writing about Indians in Spanish America. This will be evaluated later.

As is clear, many writers discussing Indians had rather ambivalent feelings about the native inhabitant's future. This Muñoz ascribes to an identification with their culture, here regressivist, along with a profound modernist (even concretist) feeling that the old way of life would inexorably be eradicated. The modern positivistic world of the new Americans and Europeans could not be resisted for long. The Indians would have to give way or be annihilated. Indeed this sentiment is evident in many Spanish American indigenist novels and creates their most successful literary tensions. Although not going nearly so far as Kafka in their depersonalizing of the injustice inherent in modern civilizations, there is a sense of ultimate futility and a feeling of great loss in many of these novels. In <u>Huasipungo</u>, for example, Indians are betrayed by the landowners, the church, and the government. All of these groups combine to make the Quechuas work for their village's ultimate destruction. It is perhaps not stretching the point to call their building the road, an absurdist struggle just as in Camus' <u>Mythe de Sisyphe</u>. Unfortunately we may not imagine the Indians to be happy.

---

[16] Muñoz 73–150.

150

In José María Argueda's <u>Todas las sangres</u> (1964),[17] the last indigenist
novel written in Peru, the Indian village selects a young man of great potential to go
to Lima to learn the secrets of the whites. As he prepares to leave they admonish
him to return just as he left, with the same spirit of the village in his heart. He
returns a changed man, however, and after striving for change and reform using the
white man's language and even guerrilla warfare tactics, the young Indian succeeds
in having his people slaughtered, just like dumb animals. At the end of the book,
he himself is slaughtered, showing through his death the necessary failure of any
attempt at preserving Indian ways with white men's knowledge.

Other novels paint equally dismal pictures of the isolated failures of Indians
to preserve their way of life. One evident reason for the Indian's failure is their lack
of unity or clear-cut goals. Most of their actions are undertaken merely to preserve
the vague <u>status quo</u>. In a time in which property is an all-important concept and in
which economic well-being is an all-important collective noun, notions of soul,
spirit, and community are disregarded and unvalued. These novels, and especially
the later ones of them, do not attempt to propose solutions to the problems of the
Indians. It is true, as Muñoz says, that the novels point out the positive aspects of
Indian culture. They center on the Indian's hard-workingness, his idealism, his
intimacy with the land and nature, and his close-knit community feeling; but they
do not attempt to propose these qualities as characteristics which will "save" the
Indians. They can only serve as the beginning basis for a compromise which
might preserve the Indians as a separate cultural entity. In most later indigenist
works, the idea of ultimate reform and correction of abuses is non-existent.
Instead, the emphasis is on the failure of the present to contain both realities—white
and Indian. As Muñoz goes on to indicate, his original observations on the
literature of the Andean region of Bolivia, Ecuador, and Peru also hold true for

---

[17] José María Arguedas, <u>Todas las Sangres</u>, 2 vols. (Buenos Aires: Editora
Losada, 1970).

Guatemala and Mexico, both of which have similiar Indian populations, traditions, and problems.[18]

Nevertheless, to lose ourselves in the social-reform aspect of these novels, is just to see one part of them. Millions of people throughout the world have read and enjoyed Alegrías' El mundo es ancho y ajeno[19] and Arguedas' Los Ríos profundos without necessarily being acquainted with Peru's history or its Indians. Quite obviously, what they sensed was that the Indian's struggles in these novels against overwhelming crushing forces was in many ways similiar to their own struggles. They could identify with these characters and cared about them. The problems detailed therein became representative of the universal struggles of all modern humans in modern society. As modern humankind has become more and more alienated from the society that s/he her/himself has created, s/he looks for alternatives to the seemingly unstoppable force of civilization which has set into motion. The message of the indigenist novels is that their Indian society, although in some respects superior to modern civilization, cannot furnish an victorious, glorious, alternative to it. At best their solution is an absurdist one involving constant struggle with no possibility of victory. As a result the main Indian characters of these works become the ultimate alienated men and women of the twentieth-century modernist novels. As these works are also more nostalgic than reformist, their ultimate pessimism is quite in line with works such as Garciliano Ramos' Vidas Sêcas[20], Adonias Filhos's Memórias de Lázaro[21], Sartre's La Nausée[22], and any other novel dealing with the Verfremdung of modern

---

[18] Muñoz 200–230.

[19] Ciro Alegría, El Mundo es ancho y ajeno, (Buenos Aires: Editora Losada, 1961).

[20] Garcilano Ramos, Vidas Sêcas, (Rio de Janeiro: Olympio, 1947).

[21] Adonias Aguiar, Memórias de Lázaro, 5th ed. (Rio de Janeiro: Civilização Brasileira, 1978).

[22] Jean-Paul Sartre, La Nausée, (1938 Paris: Gallimard, 1950).

humankind, seeing what s/he thought s/he understood about reality become strange, altered, or unfamiliar to him/her.

As the Verfremdung becomes more and more marked in later novels, writers throughout the European-inspired world began to exploit their regressive mythological tendencies and to create a new combination of myth and reality. Nowhere is this trend more well-developed than in Latin America with García Marquez' Cien años de soledad, José Donoso's El obseno pájaro de la noche, Carlos Fuentes' Tierra nostra, or Peru's own Mário Vargas Llosas' La casa verde and La ciudad y los perros.[23] Muñoz, in spite of his excellent insights, refuses to acknowledge the possibility of the relevance of "magico-realism" as a solution or even a synthetic alternative to the difficulties of societies and cultures in conflict. In his insistence on the role of the negative in the creation of these novels, and his search for solutions to "problems", he fails to describe the paths that are followed by its characters. In fact, not too surprisingly, it is often the path itself which is the point of these magico-realistic works, not their moral lessons. These new authors are not trying to change and reform; they want only to see, understand, and show their conclusions in a new way—revealing a new truth. As a result these novels are not political, but rather experiential.

The Peruvian novel chosen for analysis as the first twentieth century novel is one on the border between the indigenist and the magico-realist novel. It is not purely indigenist like Yawar Fiesta which has already been discussed, nor is it totally magico-realist like El Zorro de arriba y el zorro de abajo (1969–1971)[24] to which we will return in our closing comments on the twentieth-century view of the Indian in Peruvian literature. Los Ríos profundos (1958)[25] is from the middle of

---

[23] Muñoz 225–255.

[24] For a discussion of how Arguedas' novels fit together see José Vera Morales, Die Überwindung des literarischen Indigenismo in Los Ríos profundos von José María Arguedas: Eine Untersuchung zum Beginn der Moderne in der Lateinamerikanischen Epik. (Hamburg: Deutsche Akademischen Austaschdienstes, 1974).

[25] Arguedas, Ríos.

Arguedas' career and in it he writes a largely autobiographical tale of his childhood in the mountains of Peru.

In the beginning of the book a small boy, Ernesto, is traveling with his father, a lawyer, from small town to small town in the highlands. The boy and his father, although obviously of Spanish descent and heritage, speak Quechua as well as any Indian and as a result are able to aid Indians and impoverished speakers of Spanish, something they both feel to be a worthy and important action. Yet although Indians are seen as powerless politically or economically throughout the book the power of Indian culture is a dominant theme. The music of the <u>zumballyu</u> and other instruments keep the Ernesto's spirit intact and give him a feeling of being a part of a culture, even when in difficult unfriendly situations.

The book's first description of Indians, however, is not one of the relatively free rural Indian of the <u>ayllu</u> (the communal village), but rather that of Indians functioning as the servants of Ernesto's rich uncle in Cuzco, "El Viejo". He is a powerful landowner to whom Ernesto's father had come to ask for help and advice with Ernesto's upbringing. The father had even entertained thoughts of leaving Ernesto to the care of this uncle. But after seeing the unrelenting hardness of his uncle towards other human beings, together with his hypocritical support of the church, his father realizes that Ernesto has to continue with him in his travels for a while longer. The Indians of "El Viejo" were mute during the first encounters Ernesto had with them. Although he knows that they were, at heart, like the Indians he had already encountered, they see him as belonging to the Spanish-speaking world of their master. Therefore, they hid from Ernesto. Finally his continuing to speak Quechua draws one out enough to talk with. This is his first experience with the Indian out of his element in the Spanish-speaking world.

Ernesto and his father then travel to the village of Abancay where Ernesto is to be left at the parochial school. After a tearful, yet expected parting from his father, Ernesto has to deal with Abancay and the school by himself. He quickly learns his way around the town. He finds the taverns where the best Indian music is sung or played and begins to know many of their customers. The school is another matter. Most of the students are older than he and of varying social classes.

A few of them are nearly pure Indians from higher in the mountains; and as a cultural half-breed, Ernesto finds himself drawn to them as kindred spirits. Others are from Abancay or other nearby villages. With the exception of one student, they all speak Quechua and speak it whenever they wish, although Spanish is the normal language used for instruction in the school. As the new boy, Ernest quickly finds himself on the outs with most of the other students, even though he is a natural player of the Indian musical instrument, the zumballyu.

Although the death of one of the boys is an important event, the three most crucial events of the work involve the interaction between Indian and white elements of society. The first is the revolt by the mestizo women of Abancay when they discover that the governor has been concealing precious supplies of salt. They quickly overpower all of the town's defenders and take the salt from the warehouse where it was hidden. Ernesto becomes involved in the flow of emotions that the success engenders and joins the women in a curious foray to a nearby ayllu where they give salt to their reluctant pure-blood "kinswomen". Later the rector of the school and chief priest of the town convince the Indians to give back the salt after the army invades Abencay to restore order. Ernesto is brought to the ayllu as a witness and sees the good simple Indians fall prey to the priest's casuistry.

The second incident is one involving Ernesto himself. As is inevitable in a boy's boarding school, he finds himself challenged to a fignt by another one of the boys, the fight having been set up by the school's effete false intellectual. Although Ernesto is terrified at first, at the appropriate moment he remembers Indian reactions to the name of the Quechua wargod, Wiracocha, and is inspired to take action. He quickly persuades the other boy to call off the fight and saves his anger for Lleras, the intellectual.

The last incidents directly involving Indians in Los Ríos profundos revolve around the description of the plague in Abancay. Ernesto first sees the plague in an Indian woman who dies in the school. He puts himself into danger of catching the plague by obeying the Indian funeral customs when he prepares the body so that its soul could escape. He is then quarantined and after his release he finds himself in an empty school in a town beset by panic. The school's head then tells him to go to his uncle's estate and also tells him how to reach it through mountain passes not yet guarded by the soldiers enforcing the quarantine, thus effectively breaking the law. Before Ernesto leaves, however, he heard that the Indians from the ayllus in the area had demanded a special service of healing and a mass at Abancay's main church. In spite of all that could be done to dissuade them, and in spite of troops put in their path, they manage to reach the city. From afar he hears their songs and chants and sees their candles as they arrive at the church. After the mass, their faith in God (or the Quechua Wiracocha) triumphant, they leave the village singing. In the last scene of the book, while leaving Abancay, Ernesto still hears their song reflected in the rushing of the powerful deep rivers that flow through the village, the deep rivers of the title.

In this work the dominant element is still the realistic problems of the Quechuas. Yet the magical element cannot be denied. The spirit and the presence of the Indians are important as the principal leitmotif in the work. As this is an autobiographical novel, it is noted that there are no individual important Indian characters, with the possible exception of Palacitos whose wealth puts him in different class from the Indians of the ayllu. It is more the case here that the collective group of Indians functions as a single character, much as in Yawar Fiesta. As in other indigenist novels, there is real strength assigned to Indians as a collective unit. Yet this strength is strongest in its opposition to the alienation of mestizo and white society, its basis being found in its superstition (religious faith) which is both its greatest disadvantage and advantage. It keeps the Indians subjugated politically but also unites them and frees them spiritually. One cannot say that religion is seen in only a positive or a negative light in this or other indigenist works. The answer to how religion is viewed is much more complex and tinged in grey, not black or white. This complexity also resides in the view of Indians seen as a whole in the book. Nevertheless, certain conclusions and comparisons are clear.

The Indians in Los Ríos profundos are not the colorful national symbols of the nineteenth century. They are not the last word in the perfection of civilized man, nor are they the depraved devils bent on violence and brute savagery. However,

156

there is a note of the didactic. The whites and mestizos of the novel can learn from certain positive traits of the Indians. In a limited way, the "red men" are admired and used as <u>exempla</u>. They are also pitied and abused. The main difference between these nineteenth- and twentieth-century uses of the Indian, is that in the twentieth century, the Indian has become a flesh and blood human being. He has to fit in with current white and mestizo societies, even if he cannot be thoroughly integrated into either of them. While this is a point of contact between the nineteenth century view of the Indian and <u>Los Ríos Profundo's</u> representative view of twentieth-century Spanish American Indian novels, it does not deny the possibility of points in common with eighteenth century (and older) literatures. Arguedas', Alegría's, and Icaza's Indians are all noble, hard-working, loyal, and faithful. At the same time they are ignorant, politically impotent, and gullible. In most ways they resemble both Rousseau's primitive good men and Buffon's weak men more than the nineteenth-century's composite view that was developed in the third chapter. In fact they might even be best described as being a type of intersection (I use the term from set theory) of these views since these twentieth-century Indians are similar to those described by the Jesuit priests in their simplicity and goodness as well as their susceptibility to the ravages of progress and civilization. We will return to this point in the analyses of the conclusion as well as the discussions of the other literatures of the twentieth century.

Let us return to the Peruvian literature of the nineteen seventies in order to consider briefly Arguedas' last work written about the Indian and perhaps the best magico-realist Indian novel written in Spanish America, <u>El Zorro de arriba y el zorro de abajo</u>[26]. It was never completely finished, but was interrupted by Arguedas' suicide and published posthumously with some additional notes from Arguedas' writings, just as he had requested. This is the most optimistic of any of Arguedas' novels, with the collective Indian spirit finally definitively emerging as the model for white men. As Muñoz points out, it could only have been written in

---

[26] Morales and Muñoz 247–255.

the late sixties after the military coup of 1968 had succeeded in beginning the long process of reform. However, he believes that the work's positive message is ultimately betrayed by Arguedas' suicide, an opinion which seem to have some merit.[27] In this work the spirit already noted in <u>Los Ríos profundos</u> starts to emerge triumphant and help the non-Indian population. The novel, in fact, is so surprising that Muñoz actually gives it a separate section of its own. Nevertheless and even though this might surprise Muñoz, this type of novel seems to be part of a later trend throughout twentieth-century New-World literatures to return to the literary myth of the Indian as guide. Let us save our discussion of this theme until the section on Brazilian literature whose main novel chosen for discussion outlines this tendancy admirably.

From here let us proceed to the literature which provides us with the next example, chronologically speaking, of the image of the Indian in the twentieth century. This is Québécois literature.

Quebec

Just as the numbers of Indians were a large and a troublesome economic problem in Peru, Ecuador, Bolivia, Guatemala, and Mexico, so have their numbers been treated as insignificant in French Canada until relatively recently. In Quebec itself, and indeed in all of Canada, the slow and painful process towards cultural independence was continuing. The figure of the Indian, already of minor importance in the few Quebec novels of the nineteenth century in which it appeared, disappeared totally from view for several decades only to reemerge spectacularly in Yves Thériault's novels of the 1950's and 1960's. Nevertheless there is a submerged literary continuity. Thériault's literary image of the Indians did not

---

[27] Muñoz 247.

spring full-blown without any direct links with Québécois tradition. As Jack
Warwick states in his The Long Journey

> From the coureur de bois to the voyageur and
> ultimately the lumberjack, there is a real historical
> sequence. In literature these social types inherit
> some of the characteristics which the coureurs de
> bois acquired from the happy savage [...] The result
> is that some vestiges of the happy savage survive as
> a French-Canadian literary tradition. A series of
> standard figures, displaying combinations of a list of
> standard qualities, are related to each other through
> this common origin. The figures, which sometimes
> occur in combination and are not all of the same
> literary importance, are: the persisting happy savage,
> a modified Indian, the pioneer, the bushman, the
> canoeman, the Métis, the trapper, the missionary, the
> lumberjack, the aimless wanderer, the adultress, the
> artist, and the ancestor.[28]

As he goes on to show, the happy savage, the modified Indian and the métis are of
lesser importance.

There are some novels which can help to bridge the literary gap of writing
on Indians between 1880 and 1940. One of these is G. Dugas' Un voyageur des
pays d'en haut (2nd edition, 1912). His Indians are those of the frontier. They are
men of the woods close to nature. There is a small note of modernity in that in
Dugas' other frontier novel, La première Canadienne du Nord-Ouest (1888), the
hero actually introduces his white wife to his Indian mistress, but this is the only
early change in the Quebec novel. In the 1930's the revival in interest in the literary
savage began with Alain Grandbois' Né à Québec (1933) and Léo-Paul
Desrocher's Les engagés du grand portage (1938). They returned to earlier
models, writing about the voyageurs and the great journeys of exploration with
their novels being primarily about the superior qualities of the white French

---

[28]   Jack Warwick, The Long Journey, Literary Themes of French Canada,
(Toronto: University of Toronto Press, 1968) 107.

Canadians. In an effort every bit as determined as Louis Hémon's <u>Maria Chapdelaine</u>, they attempt to restore what was seen as important Québécois virtues[29] through Indian characters. In this they were following the renewed interest in Father Gabriel Sagard's <u>Le Grand Voyage au pays des Hurons</u> (republished in 1939), which has already been discussed in the section on pre-nineteenth century literature. As Jack Warwick points out, certain characters of novels appearing in the thirties also had what were considered Indian traits, such as those of Alfred DesRochers and Claude-Henri Grignon. However, it was not until 1941 and <u>Les opiniâtres</u> by Léo-Paul DesRosiers that Indians were specifically mentioned as characters similar to what Warwick calls the "hard savage type"[30].

A few years later in 1948 Gabriel Breynat published the first volume <u>Chez les mangeurs de caribou</u> of his trilogy <u>Cinquante ans au pays des neiges</u>. An overview of Breyna's Indians presents them as characters closely allied with the Hurons of Father Sagard, in spite of individual references and stories that seem to negate such a conclusion. The first new view of Indians in Québécois literature does not appear until Aimé de Pelletier's (the pseudonym of Bertrand Vac) <u>Louise Genest</u>. Thomas Clarey, one of the central characters of the work is a <u>métis</u>. Clarey is pictured as a modified Rousseauist man of nature, born basically to do good, but with a streak of cruelty. He lives life at a richer level than other men. Arguedas' Quechuas come to mind when Pelletier can say about Clarey, "la simplicié spontanée qui était sienne ignorait les circonspections et les complications."[31] Like Argueda's Indians, Clarey is prone to omens and superstitions. It is perhaps Clarey's simplicity and spontaneity which makes his creation a new one. Older noble savages often had little common sense and sometimes appeared to have an overly fond usage of lengthy rhetorical devices. Clarey merely uses his innate common sense and rejects civilization and its society.

---

[29] Warwick 57–59.

[30] Warwick 112.

[31] Warwick 114.

He does what he wants and advises Louise to do the same thing. She tries to follow his example, but cannot, and eventually dies.

In some other works the use of Indian characters and ideas is less obvious. In Gabrielle Roy's Alexandre Chenevert (1954) the protagonist is described as dreaming of the natural bliss of the Eskimos. Here there is a mention of a Rousseauist peace that is so foreign to modern life as to make it a type of unobtainable, pleasant daydream.[32] In Gilbert Choquette's L'Intérrogation (1962) the protagonist, Charles Duhaist, is influenced by a ten-year stay he spent among the Indians in Bolivia before the work opens. After discovering that his old love has married, he suffers from unrequited love. Even the eventual and sudden death of her husband does not free her to marry Charles. Profoundly distressed, he returns to exile among the simple Indians of the uncivilized Bolivian world. Both of these works deal with fantasy Indians. They do not concern the flesh and blood Indians of twentieth-century Quebec. As such they represent a prolongation of nineteenth-century viewpoints, expressed by the work's contemporary Québécois characters. They relegate the presented images of the pure bon sauvage to the world of fantasy.

One author, Marius Barbeau and his work, Le Rêve de Kamalmouk (1948) has written an interesting work about the Indians of contemporary Quebec. This is more of an anthropological novel than anything else. In it, as in many Andean and Mexican novels, the focus is placed upon the relationships between white and Indian society.[33] As usual, the Indian society will lose out to the whites—even though the Indians are more sophisticated (in a barbaric way) with a higher culture and more complexity in their social organizations. The reason presented for the Indian's downfall is not unlike those given for the fall of Rome before the Goths. The Indians were decimated through disease, lack of confidence, and fear of the whites' power. To make matters worse, the Indians as a tribe had to fight against

---

[32] Warwick 105.

[33] Warwick 63–64.

the vague wishes of the tribes' leader, Kamalmouk, whose dream was that his people would become rugged individuals, just like the whites that he knew. Kamalmouk's misapprehension was only identified too late and although he was not ever convinced of the superiority of the old Indian ways, he began to be unsure about which path was the best way to take. Along with the other above mentioned failures of the tribe, this led to the tribe's ultimate cultural death. They were unable to act and suffered a type of collective impotence.

Barbeau's novel shares striking similarities with Arguedas' Todas las sangres and Icaza's Huasipungo. The Indians of Kamalmouk's tribe are shown as representing a society superior to the white one. The Indians described are in both cases a small isolated band of humans surrounded by a large hostile group. In Todas las sangres and Kamalmouk two young Indian leaders have learned white ways and wish to adapt their home tribe's culture to them. Where Spanish-American indigenist novels often propose white political solutions to these problems, in these novels it is the implementation of political reform—the assimilation of white progressive mythical ideas--that brings about the wrath of the whites and the ultimate destruction of the Indian villages of Kamalmouk and Todas las sangres. In the French Canadian novel it is the attempt at social reform, and the merging with white culture, which instigates the collapse of the old order without bringing about any type of superior new order. As a result, the end of the Indians' collective power is also the end of the novels, with the moral being that change or reform equals destruction. This is indexical of the conservative and regressive nostalgic trend which seems to have influenced most late twentieth-century writers on Indians.

There is only one other twentieth-century Quebec writer who uses Indians and native Americans as the main characters in his works. His works, indeed, are so powerful and influential he seems to have taken the modified anthropological novel for his own in Quebec. No other French Canadian author up to 1990 seems to have felt that he had anything new to say about the Indian after having read the works of Yves Thériault. In this sense Thériault plays a role similar to José María Arguedas in Peru or Mario Andrade in Brazil before 1970. However, the recent

reemergence of Indians as an important political issue in Quebec (and indeed in all
of Canada) makes one wonder what new works on Indians in Quebec will emerge.

Thériault has written many native-influenced works. His most famous are
Le Dompteur d'ours (1951), Agaguk (1958), Ashini (1960), and Cul de Sac
(1961).[34] His later novels show less direct Indian or native American influence,
although the major characters often share attributes with some of his earlier
non-white creations. In all of his novels there is a component describing the
problems of relationships between one individual or a between a few individuals
and a society.

Although Thériault spent a good amount of time in Ungava and had ample
opportunity to observe the people of whom he writes, many critics see his Indians
and Eskimos as metaphoric creations of modern Québécois. Thus his heros'
victories or defeats are seen as emblematic of the Québécois's own victories and
defeats. This is a possible reading of his work. Yet there is no reason to hold this
reading to be the only possible allegoric one. As has already been discussed in the
section on Spanish American literature, we could continue to a more universal level
and see these victories and failures as symptomatic of all western man's successes
and failures.

Of Thériault's four novels previously mentioned Ashini has been chosen for
analysis, being the only one of the four dealing with Indians and not Eskimos, here
the Montagnais. It is also the novel most closely resembling the other
twentieth-century novels chosen for analysis. Yet it is worth also considering
Agaguk and Cul de Sac in some detail. Both of these deal with Eskimos rather
than Indians, although the difference between the two groups from a non-native
American literary-influenced perspective is rather slight and tends to diminish
especially as these groups are used as literary characters.

Agaguk is the story of white civilization trying to infiltrate an Eskimo
village in the persons of three white representatives, Brown, the white trader, who

---

[34] Warwick 64–68, 119–124.

provided illegal whisky, McTavish, the trader, who sold legal goods but did not try to stop Brown, and Henderson the noble Mountie who tried to help the Eskimos but was totally ineffectual. Against this infiltration, the village, like Kamalmouk's tribe, was defenseless and unprepared. Agaguk, the strong and self-reliant Eskimo protagonist, took matters into his own hands and rebeled against the village elders. He demanded the freedom and independence to follow the old ways and to repulse the whisky trader. The village then cast him out.

As Thériault points out, Agaguk's story took place in the older Eskimo world before the organized white invasion, (perhaps that of the time of the famous Clarence Brown film "Nanook of the North". It showed the strongly independent nature of a people forced to live in a tight community when faced with the rigors of unrelenting nature. Agaguk was not a smiling docile creature searching constantly for blubber, but someone who tried to break free of the bonds of his culture and curiously enough succeeded. He actually freed himself and his wife although he had to pay the price that absolute freedom brought with it—absolute loneliness and insecurity. The thread of the work resolves upon his existential decision and his new life as an existential hero. The contrast between Agaguk and a work such as Camus' La peste, however, is that there is no feeling of solidarity with the village (or society as a whole) at the end of the work. Agaguk remains a loner and can never relinquish his struggle if he is to remain free of the white man's taint. An example of this type of "survival of the freeest" attitude toward life, is a list of the things that Agaguk would relish teaching his soon-to-be born child. He would say to the boy,

> Viens, viens avec moi jusqu'à ces herbes. Ici la piste du vison, regarde! Elle se confond avec celle du rat musqué. Bon, avance et regarde, là! Du sang, du poil. Un rat musqué est mort, dévoré par le vison. Pour eux aussi, l'un comme 'autre, la rançon de la survie. Pour quel vison vive, le rat musqué est sacrifié.[35]

---

[35] Warwick 122.

Agaguk later killed a bad white man so that he himself could survive—much like the muskrat that he had mentioned. In so doing he caused the downfall of his village but gained his freedom and consequently forced the village's inhabitants in the same direction. His ending is not a "living happily ever after" one. Instead, his believed that his triumph could only be assured by how he lived his whole life, including its last few free moments, just as Sartre's has his characters are judged in Huis Clos. Indeed a fuller investigation of the similarities between Thériault's heros and those of Camus and Sartre would seem to provide a fertile area for further exploration. Like them Thériault's heros' claim to triumph rests upon his understanding of death as forced upon him by the events he underwent.

In Cul de Sac and Le Dompteur d'ours Thériault uses non-Indian and non-Eskimo characters. Both protagonists are loners and are at odds with the society in which they live. One eventually leaves his society (Hermann in Le Dompteur d'ours) when he realized that his falsehoods will be discovered. Yet he has already changed and freed the village in which he was living by its belief in his lies. The other hero eventually discovers that death is the only possible way to change an urban civilized society. Nevertheless what is interesting about Thériault's heros is their consistency. Their "Indianness" or "Eskimoness" is an intregal part of the plot, along with their unease and ill-preparedness to deal with modern societies. They are rebels of one form or another and fight to change the order of their environment. Although we are interested in this "Eskimoness" or "Indianness" in these novels we also realize that the Eskimo or Indian nature given the hero is a literary device which automatically gives the twentieth-century reader a different set of values and expectations to work from. As we have argued before, one expectation in New-World literature is that Indians will be used to show the justice and compassion of a defeated society. S/He will be an alienated character who has to accept or fight the wrongs of the predominant social order. Finally, in the twentieth century, s/he will be a fatalistic poverty-stricken noble savage rather than a proud or arrogant symbol in feathers. Thériault's Ashini shows how all of these expectations can be met yet once more.

Ashini is the story of a Montagnais Indian who tries to restore the old social order of his tribe by attempting to convince his Montagnais people living on the reservation to return to their free nomadic ways. Ashini, through a series of flashbacks, remembers the glories of his youth, the strength of his tribe, and the agonies of the recent past, including the death of his children and wife. Ashini, whose name means "the rock" (perhaps a reference to Peter/Pierre of the New Testament) is alone and sees his culture's whole way of life dying without issue. He goes off in the midst of winter, hunting, trying do decide how to save his people before he himself perishes.

While in the midst of the savage wilderness, he believes that he has discovered a method. He goes to his tribe's reservation and tries to convince the Indian agent there to help restore his tribe's old hunting grounds through an agreement with the great white chief in Ottawa. He tries to explain to this white Québécois (perhaps he should be called a Canadian here!) agent, the values of his tribe which government officials normally have difficulty understanding. The young man then tries to help him but he cannot succeed in persuading the Prime Minister to come to Ungava to discuss the Indian's wishes. For the rest of the book, with the constant flashbacks alternating with the events of the present, Ashini tries three times to set up the conference. Each time the Prime Minister fails to appear. From Ashini's frame of reference, this would be a meeting of equals, of two leaders of two peoples. The failure of the white leader to appear then justifies any type of action on his part. At one point, then, Ashini appeals to his people to rise up and take back what is rightfully theirs. Their response, however, is to accuse him of being an old fool or a madman, even though his knowledge of the old ways is beyond dispute and the justice of his claims is not denied. His people are already defeated, spiritually as well as militarily. They cannot help him. As a result Ashini, in his splendid isolation, has already planned out the last act of his life. After the white chief will not show up for the third time, Ashini will sacrifice himself. He does this on the signpost shaped like a cross annnouncing the entrance to his people's reservation. In a Christ-like sacrifice offered for the remission of his people's sins, he dies. He wins a moral and a superior victory over the whites

166

with his death, and serves as a reminder to his people of their past nobility. Yet nothing changes for his people or for the whites. He is one more martyr to a cause forgotten and ignored. In this sense his existential struggle leads to an absurd death. His death appears important and inevitable in the work, especially in its symbolism, but still ultimately meaningless. As Thériault's only Indian and not Eskimo hero (although his Eskimos share many qualities of other Indians), Ashini is a classic fatalistic noble savage who fights the whole world in defense of the values he holds to be superior. He is what Professor Warwick calls an "unhappy savage", but a better term might be an alienated savage.[36] Ashini is not unhappy in all ways. He can live his old life as long as he has breath, yet he chooses to sacrifice himself for a greater goal. Just as Rendon Willka in Todas las sangres or the Indians as a group in Los Ríos profundos or Huasipungo, he forsees his tragic fate, a fate that results from his revolt against the stifling control of twentieth century white society in the New World. His people's reservation represents security and a life of ease to them, but he believes that their choice of the white man's path leads to a living death in which the Montagnais will see their true spirit and freedom depart as the decay of their bodies and soul begins. His refusal to live this way is the revolt of the righteous against corruption and decadence.

Many critics have described this as an allegory of the French Canadian's accomodations with the English Canadians believing that the Québécois have lost their true spirit by abandoning their struggle for independence in order to live a life of ease. Once again however, this allegorical reading need not stop with a purely Canadian view. This type of hopeless, yet triumphant, rebellion is common to readers in all twentieth-century literatures. What is unique to the New World, however, is the lone Indian who symbolizes it.

---

[36] Warwick 68.

English Canada

In English Canadian literature after 1880, Indians play a much more important role than they do in Québécois literature. Part of this difference is no doubt, due to the greater number of Indians still present in English Canada, especially in British Columbia, the prairie provinces, and in Western Ontario. However, as we will discover, the roles they play do not vary greatly from what we have been led to expect as a result of our analysis of twentieth-century Spanish American and French Canadian literature.

English Canadian uses of the Indian tend to resemble U.S. American more than any other New-World literature while also resembling other New World Western-Hemisphere literatures. The old antagonistic attitude towards the Indian, combined with a strong nationalistic tendency, lasts longer in English Canada than in Latin America (again with the exception of Argentina) or Quebec, although this attitude belongs more to popular culture and popular literature than it does to more serious and innovative literature. A good example of how this attitude has lasted is seen in Merrill Denison's radio plays on Pierre Radisson and the Battle of Seven Oaks (broadcast in the 1930's)[37].

This image sees its last in the novel with the end of World War II. Some works in which this Indian savage/white patriot theme was used are Egerton Ryerson Young's Stories from Indian Wigwams and Northern Campfires (1893) and Oowikapun or How the Gospel Reached the Nelson River Indians (1895) which emphasizes the hard work of the missionaries, W.D. Lighthall's The Master of Life (1908), Charles G.D. Roberts The Forge in the Forest (1896), Carroll Aiken's play The God of Gods (1919), and Bruce McKelvieıs Huldowget (1926).[38] In all of these works, Indians represent non-Christian evil forces with

---

[37] Leslie Monkman, The Image of the Indians in English Canadian Literature, (Toronto: University of Toronto Press, 1981) 11.

[38] Monkman 12–18.

whom white heroes have to struggle, whether it be on a historical or a more contemporary level. In the late thirties and forties, this image persists. Franklin McDowell's The Champlain Road (1939), E.J. Pratt's poem Brebeuf and His Brethren (1940), Alan Sullivan's Three Came to Ville Marie (1941), and finally Thomas Raddall's Roger Sudden (1944)[39] are all examples.

There are many possible explanations for the persistence of the view of the Indian as ignoble savage in English Canada until 1945. Some possible ones that might be included are: 1) the fact that Canada only really achieved their independence late in the nineteenth century and had to continue the process of national symbol-building and breast-beating much later than other Western Hemisphere countries, 2) the fact that strict Protestantism was in control in Canada until 1945, bringing with it feelings of guilt for the past treatment of the Indians and the need to justify their bad treatment by presenting a dark picture of the Indian's nature, 3) the fact that since the United States was such a strong influence to the south and had had such a strong anti-Indian vogue, it also influenced English speakers to the north, or 4) the fact that Anglo-Saxon Protestants tend to be more anti-misogynous than other peoples thus enforcing the separation of the Indians from the whites. For whatever reason, be it one or a combination of those given above, or different reasons, this image lasted longer than in any other country in the Western Hemisphere, with the exception of the United States.

Let us not believe, though, that this was the dominant myth of the Indians in English Canadian literature from 1880 until 1945. Another myth exploited in English Canadian literature, as already presented in the section on Peruvian literature, was the naturalistic decrying of the fate of the Indian and the fading of his way of life. In a sense this, as has been shown, is perhaps the most common view of the Indian in the early twentieth century. It is also, in its beginnings, very romantic in nature.

---

[39] Monkman 13–18.

Leslie Monkman, in his earlier cited book on the images of the Indian in English-Canadian literature, entitles one chapter, "The Death of the Indian".[40] Much in the same way as Yves Thériault does in Ashini, or Barbeau does in Le rêve de Kamalmouk, several twentieth-century English Canadian authors write about the Indian's fall from a culturally-integrated group into a loosely assorted grouping of ill-adapted individuals who fall prey to white domination.

Hampden Burham's The Outbreak of the Nauscopees (1902) and W.A. Fraser's The Blood Lilies (1903) stress the historical decline of the Indians in number and force with Fraser particularly emphasizing the role of alcohol. Arthur English also writes about the decline of the native in The Eastern Indians, the Beothuks in Newfoundland. Other writers have taken the story of Beothuks and used it. They include James P. Howley's The Beothuks or the Red Indians (1915) and three more recent works: Peter Such's Riverrun (1973), Paul O'Neill's Legends of a Lost Tribe (1976), and Frederick W. Rowe's The Beothuks of Newfoundland (1977).[41] The works from the 1970's, however, are rather different from those written earlier, in that they are more mythico-realistic than nostalgically romantic. As such they create new mythologies of the vanished people, and especially in Such's work, they revel in the glory of the vanishing people who make their existential defeat a moral victory. As works of later times, they share many common features with Arguedas' Los zorros de arriba, zorros de abajo.

Other works which are more "indigenist" include Hugh Garner's "One Little, Two Little, Three Little Indians," some of Al Purdy's short stories, A.M. Klein's "Indian Reservation: Caughnawaga" (1948), Herbert Evan's Mist on the River (1954), Ryga's plays Indian (1963) and the Ecstasy of Rita Joe (1967), George Alan Fry's How a People Die (1970), Wayland Dew's The Wabeno Feast

---

[40] Monkman 65–91.

[41] Monkman 74–76.

(1973), and Matt Cohen's Wooden Hunters (1975).[42] In these works from all parts of English-speaking Canada, the historical pathetic Indian emerges in force.

These are the hopeless alienated figures alredy described in Spanish American and Québécois literature. Many of the Indian protagonists of these works suffer their own death, or disease; the death of their children, imprisonment, injustice from the omnipresent and omnipotent white society, or eventual extinction as a cultural factor in North America. The stories' realistic and concrete elements link them to some of Yves Thériault's works and to all of the Spanish American indigenist novelists. These writers chronicle the hopeless plight of an individual or a small group of individuals when faced with the amorphous but ponderous shape of white society which will attempting to crush them. A few of the novels portray Indian moral strength in the face of such a foe and end with a moral yet pyrrhic victory for the Indian. In most of them, however, the end of the individual is merely a bitter and existentially absurd death in which right is overcome by an uncaring agent. In The Wabeno Feast, Wayland Drew goes one step farther.[43] His white characters, after having killed the morally superior wisdom of the Indians, destroy themselves with an ecological disaster, showing that they learned nothing from their victory over the natives.

In contrast to these extremely negative views on the power of Indian culture or the ability of white civilization to understand it and adapt it, other writers wrote about the possibility of Indian survival in a bad new world, while continuing in his romantic role as spiritual guide to the whites. In Mazo de la Roche's Possession (1923) an Indian girl marries a white farmer and teaches him the value of understanding his surroundings and other human beings. In W.O. Mitchell's The Alien (1954) and The Vanishing Point (1973), a protagonist of mixed racial heritage learns to accept himself through a mystic loss of self-awareness and

---

[42] Monkman 80–91.

[43] Monkman 91–95.

communion with all those around him.[44] The Vanishing Point is still a novel of social protest, but just as Arguedas' Los Ríos profundos is somewhat a novel of social protest while even more a celebration of Indian culture, The Vanishing Point is a voyage of self-discovery and self-acceptance as well as social protest.

Several other writers believe that through mystical or sexual love, whites can learn from Indians. These works include Martha Otenso's Wild Geese (1940), Frederick Niven's Mine Inheritance (1940), Fred Bodsworth's The Strange One (1959), Rudy Wiebe's Peace Shall Destroy Many (1962), David Williams' The Burning Wood (1975), Joanna Glass' Canadian Gothic (1977), and James Houston's Ghost Fox (1977).[45] More traditionally minded novels of social protest are Earle Birney's verse-drama The Damnation of Vancouver (1977) and James Bacque's A Man of Talent (1972), although Bacque's novel also centers around a love affair and the consequent Indian teaching the overcivilized white man what civilization in the white sense really should be.

A further development of this tradition exists in which a messianic Indian figure, instead of an Indian lover, is used as an intermediary between white and Indian worlds. Don Gutteridge's Tecumseh (1976) is a good example of this trend, as is Rudy Wiebe's The Temptations of Big Bear. Norma Sluman's Blackfoot Crossing (1959), and several poems and plays, transform old historical figures into heroes in the struggle to find a resolution between Indians and whites. One hero who has received a lot of interest is Louis Riel about whom several literary works have been written.[46]

Although the novel of social protest, as we have seen, does exist in strength in Canada, the most important English-Canadian twentieth-century Indian novels deal more with mythico-realism than with any pure form of indigenist-influenced

---

[44] Monkman 50–57.

[45] Monkman 55–64.

[46] See Monkman 120–127 for a long section about the influence of Louis Riel as a revolt leader.

172

desire for concrete social change. Let us now examine some aspects of the development of this mythico-realism in English Canada.

In the late nineteenth century many Indian "legends" and "myths" were collected and invented which served as some sort of <u>fond</u> for early twentieth century writers. In the late twentieth century, though, the works written do not deal with simply Indian characters and Indian gods but rather with the weaving of Indian myth and white reality. The Indian influence here is a positive one. In contrast to the magico-realism of Spanish America, the mythical aspects of these novels are carefully restricted in scope. The type of <u>mise en scène</u> used in these novels does not vary greatly from everyday life in the work as a whole, but only in a few critical scenes. The mythic and the real are not woven together into a beautiful and complicated pattern as is often the case in Latin America. Rather the real dominates, with the mythic serving only as a contrasting color in the Canadian design.

Several novels illustrate this tendency. <u>Tay John</u>[47] is a good example of this combination as he is half-white and half-red; half-human and half-divine. Such a combination is inherently unstable and he eventually returns to become part of the earth in a demonstration of the cyclical nature of all things. In Margaret Atwood's <u>Surfacing</u> (1970) the heroine only discovers the strength to deal with the modern world through the realization that the ancient Indian gods of the land, the water and the heavens still live in modern Canada.[48] From this cathartic understanding and the freedom it gives her to act, she finally becomes a whole person. Robert Kroetsch's trilogy based in the Western provinces uses an image of the Indian as a Hermean "trickster" who subtly and rather indirectly modifies the behavior of the white protagonists while freeing them sexually from the binding restraints of modern society. His Indians seem to advocate a particularly blatant primitive sexuality

---

[47] Howard O'Hagan, <u>Tay John</u>, (Toronto: Malcolm, Ross, McClelland and Stewart, 1974).

[48] Monkman 150–155.

which Kroetsch appears to feel is important and unfortunately lacking in modern Canada. Ultimately this sexual liberation carries over into all aspects of the protagonist's life especially in one aptly titled volume of the trilogy, <u>Jeremy Sadness has finally Gone Indian</u> (1973). Although the focus of the protagonist's escape from the bounds of modern society and his self-discovery is different from that of Margaret Atwood's, the ultimate notion that this freedom can only be found in a non-white and non-European symbol does remind us of her work.[49]

For these writers the Indian substratum still exists in mysterious and mythic ways and is bound to the land in a way that the European-based Christian culture is not. As a result it is this ancient paganism, which is sometimes consciously allied to European paganism, that holds the key for self-identification. In some ways this quest for the self is not unfamiliar to readers of nineteenth-century literature, although the struggle here is more anthropologically-oriented, more culturally-bound, and consequently more rooted in the concrete pressures of everyday life of the middle class than is the nineteenth century one. No longer is this an ill-defined struggle to understand the meaning of <u>Sehnsucht</u> or <u>saudade</u> undertaken by a member of the privileged elite. It is rather the revolt of a <u>Jedermann</u> figure against the conforming pressures of what s/he sees as a culturally-totalitarian world.

Other modern Canadian authors explore the possibilities of freedom inherent in the Indian as mythic liberator, including Susan Musgrave, Sean Virgo, Emily Carr, Florence McNeil, Tom Marshall, and Sheila Watson, but none as powerfully as Leonard Cohen in his <u>Beautiful Losers</u> (1966).[50]

This work is perhaps one of the most interesting twentieth-century Canadian novels and certainly one of the most interesting ones dealing with Indians. It chronicles the end of the narrator's life with constant flashbacks into his past, digressions into the nonsensical garbage of popular culture, while detailing his infatuation with an Iroquois saint of the seventeenth century, Catherine Tekakwitha.

---

[49] Monkman 150–165.

[50] Leonard Cohen, <u>Beautiful Losers</u>, (Toronto: McClelland and Stewart, 1966).

Catherine's story of her withdrawal from her society and her push for martyrdom becomes ever more tied into the narrator's own story as he pushes his life farther and farther away from the dictates of his society. In this quest the narrator is guided by his friend F. who tries to teach this hopelessly rational Jewish narrator the only thing that binds us to our culture is our own self-imposed limitations. The narrator's dead wife, Edith, tried to teach the same ideas, although in much subtler ways than F.

It is in Edith that we see the first inauguration of the contradiction of "beautiful losers". She is Indian from the tribe of A. which is known only for not ever having won a single battle against any opponent (perhaps something like the Algonquin tribe?). Their history is one of constant defeat and resignation—in contrast to that of the proud Iroquois. Yet Edith comes from this tribe which still exists in twentieth-century Canada. The narrator, with his obsession with the Iroquois Catherine, misunderstands the "A." Edith during her lifetime. It is his friend and mentor, F., who leads him to reassess Edith's role in the narrator's journey toward death. One particular scene that the narrator recalls is the time Edith painted herself in red greasepaint and invited him to join her in slithery sex. The narrator refuses, ashamed. Only after Edith's death and under F.'s guidance, does he begin to see that she was trying to lead him into another reality, one in which they could be other people, escaping the smallness of their basement apartment. The vision of Edith painted in red becomes one of the mainstays of his sexual fantasies. Yet Edith is still a loser. Her death is neither noble nor tragic. She is flattened beneath an elevator. A reference to the wheels of progress crushing the Indian is too obvious not to be considered. Yet as is the case with Atwood's and Kroetsch's work, the spirit and legacy of the Indian is much more important than his or her physical presence. It is not a legacy of guilt and violence but rather one of spiritual guidance. Cohen's Indians are superior moral beings, but their spirit and their mythology is all that remains of them.

The mentor in the novel, F., is not Indian. He is a blond Canadian. He absorbs other cultures, however. Through his discussions on Catherine Tekakwitha with the narrator, through his personal readings in Indian mythology, and through his own sexual coupling with Edith, F. culturally absorbs the Indian element in Canadian society. His absorption is not limited to Indians, however. He becomes involved with the problems of the new Canadian immigrants through his intellectual and sexual relationship with the narrator. He invests in the dominant North American mythology of success by acquiring a Charles Atlas body and a seat in Parliament. He and the narrator also become involved with French Canadians through their attendance at, and consequent support of, a "Québec Libre" demonstration. Nevertheless they both return again and again to Edith and Catherine and ultimately to Catherine's uncle in an attempt to understand life and death. One of the key discussions is one in which F. describes the Mohawk journey towards death, in which one of the last steps is to have the brain removed by Oscotarg, the Mohawk god of the afterlife.[51] F. understands the significance of this step as the end of rationality and beginning of suprarationality.

Through a variety of experiences he leads the narrator along the journey towards the end of rational control. His letters to the narrator finally bring the narrator to a treehouse in the Quebec forest. There F. describes his own reappraisal of Catherine's end and details how she came to her triumph over rationality through her constant mortification of the flesh. This is the path of asceticism that the narrator will have to follow in the treehouse until he can finally overcome his rationality. F. is already ahead of the narrator, having been admitted to a mental hospital. There he wrote the letters that finally explain the purpose of the path that the narrator has to follow in order to understand the spiritual teaching of Catherine.

Finally, at the end of the book, the figure in the treehouse, the narrator has his secret presence compromised by the boy with whom he had a sexual relationship and has to flee to Montreal. There he accomplishes some "miracles", including making everyone's eyes in a moviehouse flutter at the same speed, bringing them into a wholeness and unity thought to be impossible. His miracle can only last a short time, however, before rationality reemerges. But the ascetic

---

[51] Cohen 183–184.

figure then laughs and disappears in the the twinkling of an eye in a final triumph of suprarationality. Cohen does not end the book here, however. He closes it with an addendum "written" by the Jesuits, claiming once and for all the official right to the story of Catherine Tekakwitha and the miracles that she did after her death, (perhaps including the narrator's miracles). Thus, although the protagonist can succeed in his journey towards a suprarational end to his existence, the reader is left behind in a world controlled by the hyperrationality of the world of the Jesuits who accept miracles, yet have to control them and ultimately subvert them to their uses.

In summary, we can say that the English Canadian novel does reflect the trends of the other literatures. It has an indigenist phase, although not nearly as strong as in Peru. It has some anti-Indian novels, the last one appearing in 1945. Its strongest element, which has its parallel in Peru and Quebec, is the mystical and spiritual element which it ascribes to its Indian character, whether physically present or not. The main differences are that Indians are less likely to be protagonists in English Canadian novels than in Latin American novels, and Indians in Canadian novels are more important later in Canadian literature, in the 1970's, than in Peru or Quebec—perhaps due to its later development as a literature. Nevertheless, it is interesting to see how even a Protestant culture sees the Indian in a mystical manner and absorbs moral lessons from Indian mythology just as Catholic-influenced Peruvian and Quebec authors do.

Brazil

This leaves twentieth-century Brazilian literature to be discussed. It presents a curious phenomenon, a nearly total absence of the Indian as literary figure from 1930 to 1970. This is perhaps a function of its obsession with Indians during the late romantic period and the admiration in which Alencar's creations were held. Nevertheless some interesting works were written between 1880 and 1930 which deal with Indians.

The Indianist poetry of Luís Nicolau Fagundes Varella, Luis Caetano Pereira Guimarães, and Machado de Assis presents nothing new to readers of Gonçalves Días. Even the Indian verses of Olavo Bilac, the leading Brazilian Parnassian, are more or less Romantic Indianist poetry in his "Morte de Tapir". It is only a bit different from Alencar and Días in its representation of the death of the Indian chief, the last of his tribe,[52] yet we finally also do approach more recent views in this first elegiac poem dealing with Brazilian Indians. It represents the beginning of the decline in Indianism and the start of indigenism.

However, unlike in Peru or many other Spanish American countries, indigenism never became a strong movement in Brazil. One reason for this is the relative unimportance of the Indian in Brazilian economic life. The Indians, as a recognizable ethnic group, had retreated to the jungles of the Amazon. They were not constantly in the sight of the cultural elite. Another reason is more cultural. Unlike in Spanish America, the Brazilians had prided themselves on their racial mixture. They professed to be proud to be a people composed from three different races. With this as a national mythology, any attempt to single out one race as different and underprivileged, would be tantamount to national heresy. Finally, a more literary explanation would be that writers who had invested so much in a national literature based upon the Indian as noble Brazilian, were not prepared to turn around suddenly and proclaim him a wretched figure worthy of pity and paternalism. Just as Peru had almost no Indianist tradition and a very strong indigenist one, so Brazil, conversely, had a strong Indianist and a non-existent indigenist literary history.

Even in <u>O Missionário</u> (1918) by Herculano Marcos Inglez de Souza, what could be an indigenist story becomes a modern-day reinterpretation of <u>Iracema</u>. It is the story of a young priest full of romantic ideals who goes to the Amazon as a missionary and runs into some real savages who nearly succeed in putting him to

---

[52] David Miller, <u>Indians in Brazilian Literature</u>, (New York: The Hispanic Institute, 1942) 150–175.

death before he is rescued by friendly Indians. In their camp he is nursed back to health by a beautiful Indian girl but decides to respect his vows and returns to the coast and urban life. Although it is set in the present day and deals with "psychological" dilemmas, it could be pure Indianist romance in terms of its plot.[53]

Among other writers who discussed the Indians in early twentieth-century Brazilian literature, one of the most famous is Euclides da Cunha who with his <u>Os Sertões</u> is perhaps the greatest non-fiction writer of twentieth century Brazil. Da Cunha succeeded in capturing a regional and disappearing world. As a result of his importance as a popular writer, the fact that he did once write about Peruvian Indians in his vast corpus of writing is interesting. In contrast he does not treat Brazilian Indians as a separate entity, although his "backwoods" characters certainly have some Indian blood.[54]

Alberto Rangel, a friend of Cunha, has Indian characters in his work who are different from those of Alencar. They symbolize the present-day degraded state of the Amazonian Indians. His collection of short stories about the Amazon <u>Inferno Verde</u> (1907) includes a story in which the Indian maiden ends up sacrificed to a white rubber entrepreneur, bound to a rubber tree and having her "sap" bled much in the same way a rubber tree would. In another short story, the last remnant of a once powerful Amazonian tribe speaks with a white traveler in her village. This last Indian is no romantic maiden who will throw herself off a cliff into the setting sun above a waterfall. Rather it is an old, ugly, and embittered woman who seeks to make the white man understand that he is responsible for her fate. In its pessimistic realism and its refusal to uphold the mythology of the Indianists, this selection is probably the first real indigenist collection of short stories in Brazilian literary history.[55]

---

[53] Miller 158–160.

[54] Miller 161–162.

[55] Miller 162–164.

Salvador Mendonça's poem <u>João Caboclo</u> (1910) continues in this strain. It is the story of a backwoodsman (undoubtedly with Indian blood) who is charged with the task of clearing a forest which has been sacred to his family in order that a white man may farm it. In spite of his attempts at refusal, João must burn it down. Finally he manages to set the fire, and in a fit of hallucinogenic guilt sacrifices his dogs to the fire and finally himself. The reference to the death of the land's beauty and the subsequent death of its keepers is obvious. Alexander José de Melho Morães also wrote literature on the Indians, his of a historical nature. However, his work reflects his seventeenth century sources more than any modern notions about them and thus can remain unanalyzed.

One last early Brazilian writer who wrote some poetry with Indian characters is Humberto de Campos. His poems are earlier than even Rangel's short stories and are much less interesting in terms of the use they make of Indians. He writes about the last days of various Indians and Indian tribes, but he writes of soft misty endings and lacks even Rangel's attempts at a blunter presentation of the Indian's defeats.[56]

By the time of Rangel and de Campos, Brazil's Indianist past had been superseded. Due to the factors mentioned above, indigenism did not take hold in Brazil in the first two decades of the twentieth century. Then in the 1920's two events occurred which drove Indians out of their formerly privileged position until 1970. The first was the growth of regionalism that gave realist modern writers a new focus. They could write about poor whites or persons of mixed heritage without having to write specifically about Indians. By giving names and not ethnic or racial identities to their characters, the regionalists could proclaim themselves more universal even while using a concrete setting for their works, reflecting some of the attitudes of other Western-Hemisphere writers. Secondly, most of the regionalists were from the Northeast coastal areas. In these areas, the first areas heavily settled by whites, the Indians as a separate culture had been eradicated a

---

[56] Miller 165–171.

very long time ago and subsequently replaced by blacks. The blacks, with their own culture of candomblé and their African heritage, served the role of ethnic interest and added regional realism to the works of these writers. As a result, Indians, as Indians, could have no role to play here.

The second major literary development of the early twentieth century was the introduction of modernism in 1922 with the "Semana da Arte Moderna" led by Mário and Oswald de Andrade, featuring modernist musicians and artists as well as writers and thinkers. From out of this group of exciting cultural revolutionaries, came many of Brazi's best twentieth century writers. The followers of modernism, as it was instigated by this group, numbered most of the rest (the non-regionalist) of Brazil's great writers up to 1960. Indeed very few good Brazilian writers of the first six decades of the twentieth century were not either regionalist or modernist. Regionalist disinterest in the Indian was matched, for the most part, by modernist disinterest. Most modernist works were set in the new urban centers of São Paulo or Rio de Janeiro. The novels were progressively- or socially-oriented if there was any political discussion in them.

However the most important factor in the later modernist lack of interest in the Indian was the early modernist use Oswald and Mário made of him. Oswald used Indians in only a mocking sense. He ridiculed their early literary use with his ironic espousal of "antropofagía", a clear reference to Montaigne's "Des cannibales", and he made fun of the Indianists with his essay entitled "Tupi or not Tupi", refering to the debate over whether to adopt Tupi as the national language. [57] Thus Oswald took the Indianist glamor away from the natives. Mário Andrade then wrote what might be called the "definitive" modernist Indian novel. This ensured that only with the decline of modernism would the Indian again interest Brazilian novelists in an important manner.

As David Haberly has written, Macunaíma by Mario Andrade, may be the best Brazilian novel of the twentieth century. It is certainly one of the most

---

[57] Oswald de Andrade, Obras completas, 2 vols. (Rio de Janeiro: Civilização Brasileira, 1970).

complex and controversial ones.[58] It is the story of Macunaíma, a divine Indian and his adventures in the interior of the country and in São Paulo. Haberly argues that the book reflects Mário's own ethnic diversity—that it is a harlequinesque binding of three opposing colors and races, white, black, and red, just as Mário was himself. Be that as it may, it is the Indian or native American element, as represented by Macunaíma, that dominates the work and ultimately provides the tragic end. Macunaíma is more than Indian to Andrade. He is a divine figure representing old Brazil struggling against the new immigrants and their greed. He eventually must lose and fall before the great new god who will take over from him. The first sign of his decline is his inability to control the affairs of São Paulo or its people. He becomes physically weaker and weaker as he also eventually becomes sexually impotent. This is a great contrast to his beginnings in the jungle as the extremely ribald trickster and powerful god. He is born a black-skinned Indian, but later becomes blond, white, and blue-eyed after bathing in water that filled a footprint left by St. Thomas. Jiguê, another god-figure bathes second and becomes Indian, and Maanapé bathes last and stays black. Interestingly enough, perhaps showing the effect of Indianism even in 1927, Maanapé loses himself in São Paulo and eventually fades away, but Jiguê acquires sexually potency and attractiveness in direct relationship to how Macunaíma loses them. Macunaíma obtains his ultimate revenge, however, by infecting Jiguê with leprosy. This effectively rids him of the Indian. Macunaíma, himself, will later depart the world, too, to become head of the Big Dipper after piranhas eat his body when he dives in a river seeking an elusive water spirit. Thus Macunaíma destroys himself and symbolically destroys the Indian race and old Brazil when he leaves the earth. Haberly believes that

> the book is not only an etiological myth of national
> creation, but an explanation of the annihilation of the

---

[58] David Haberly, <u>Three Sad Races: Racial Identity and National Consciousness in Brazilian Literature</u>, (New York: Cambridge University Press, 1983) 146.

future, a myth of national destruction. Macunaíma is the Brazil that might have been: the creative balanced coexistence of the three races within a culture rooted in the traditions of the past conscious of the potential of its multiplicity, and destined to flourish as a great tropical civilization. When the mutilated and impotent hero departs for the heavens, still clutching his chickens, his watch and his revolver, he leaves no descendents; his tribe and Brazil's future vanishes. All that remains is the world of ants and machines and disease, the city of stone and its petrous inhabitants.[59]

As so many critics have stated, this was the last gasp of the Indian as hero for many years. David Miller in his work on Indians in Brazilian literature even went so far as to say that Indians would never again play a major role in Brazilian literature.[60] Yet he has been proven wrong with the Indian staging a comeback after 1970. We might wonder why this is. But as we saw, it seems more logical to wonder why it took Brazilian writers so long to come back to the Indian when writers in many other major New World countries had already discovered the potential of the Indian as both myth-maker and myth-breaker. All of the above, however, does not mean to suggest that Indians did not appear in Brazilian works written between 1930 and 1960. It is clear that they did. Yet most of the Indians are extraneous to the heart of these works. They merely add a touch of the exotic. Mixed-breed characters such as Jorge Amado's Gabriela take the place of pure Indians such as Iracema. Pure Indians or culturally-pure Indians function simply as local color—not as a major part of a work.

This all changes finally in the 1960's. One of the main agents of change is Antônio Callado's Quarup which in its hundreds of pages describes the adventures of white heros in the Amazon region.[61] There is finally some some important

---

[59] Haberly 159.

[60] Miller 172.

[61] Antônio Callado, Quarup, (1972 Rio de Janeiro: Pluarte, 1984).

description of Indians in this work even if they often still function merely as elements leading to a successful <u>mise en scène</u>. Here many different elements of Brazilian society—and especially the plantation culture—are discussed in a long work with many plots and sub-plots. Yet on the whole, this novel is not primarily about Indians or Indian life.

This focus contrasts with Callado's recent novel <u>A expedição Montaigne</u> (1982) and Darcy Ribeiro's <u>Maíra</u> (1972).[62] Ribeiro, a sociologist, has undertaken to write a novel about the way a small Amazonian tribe influences the white world around it. A young man, who should be the future chief of the Mairun tribe, is taken away and eventually ends up in Rome where he studies to take holy orders. A young woman from Rio de Janeiro named Alma distraught at the death of her saintly father, blames her sinful behavior for his agonizing final few days. She then decides that she needs to redeem herself by helping to establish a proposed mission of French nuns in the Indian territory. In the Mairun community itself, the old chief dies and his spirit joins the legion of other Mairuns who watch over the village. His successor will be the young priest apparent, Isaías or Avá. At this same time, a group of young men becomes the predominant group in the villages. Led by Jaguar, they coalesce around him and became more and more powerful. These events, however, are not presented in a normal chronological order. Rather the story begins with the death of a young white woman during the birth of stillborn twins along the Mairun's river. Only later do we learn that the woman was Alma ("soul" in Portuguese), the woman from Rio, and that an investigation has been undertaken to explore the death of a beautiful young white woman in Indian territory. The author weaves all of these diverse elements together into a story in which the cohesiveness of the Indians and their tenacity to their ways, in spite of their declining numbers, changes their destiny and that of the non-Indian characters in the book. As the author states himself,

---

[62] Antônio Callado, <u>A Expedição Montaigne</u>. (Rio de Janeiro: Nova Fronteira, 1982), and Darcy Ribeiro, <u>Maíra</u>, 5th ed. (Rio de Janeiro: Editora Civilização Brasileira, 1983).

> Rola a roda que rola e torna a roder. Tudo rola ao redor do umbigo do mundo: esse pátio mairúm com o tuxauá Anacã plantado no meio. Só ele e fixo no mundo que roda a girar. Gira a luz na cova do ceu azul da amplidão. Nas alturas Maíra [the sun] e Micura [the moon] bebem cauím, giram e dançam, caem de bêbadas, cantam e rolar de rir. Roda tudo e rolam despencando do fundo do céu, as estrelas tombando de bêbadas, girando sem eixo, na pele azulona do jaguarouí de Deus Pai. Lá-embaixo, rodam que rolam no espaço ambir os mortos-manon bebendo cauím e esperando Anacã. Até os mamães dos oxins esvoaçam e grasnam chumbados.[63]

Throughout the work these highly descriptive passages detailing the life and customs of the Mairuns predominate. As in this passage, the intimate relationship of the tribe with the sun god, the powerful snake spirits and the spirits of the jaguars of the forest serve to bring out the primitive, yet spiritually wealthy fabric of their lives. Every member of the tribe holds an honored spot in the cosmos and knows, that as Mairun, s/he has a destiny to uphold. It is this strength and assurance that pulls Isaías back to the Amazon region. It is the same power that pulls Alma to the village—the center of the universe as it describes itself. It is that same self-confidence that makes Juca (an expelled member of the tribe) anxious to destroy the society from which he has been outcast. It is that same power that keeps the Brazilian government from interfering in the internal affairs of the tribe. Yet this is a poetically-based integrative unity of the individuals with the whole (tribe) and with the universe. The very primitive ancientness of the power of the unity is what makes it so appealing.

Callado's latest work, and the one chosen for primary analysis is his A Expedição Montaigne. In this work, unlike in Quarup his protagonist is an Indian, Ipavu, although his white character, Vincentino Beirão, is also an important figure. Ipavu is from a small tribe in the interior of Amazonas. He develops tuberculosis, and his consequent ill-health attracts the attention of a do-gooder missionary who

---

[63] Ribeiro 96.

has him placed in a hospital. There Ipavu does not recover but does not deteriorate physically either. His mental state alters, however, as he misses his beloved companion, his turkey vulture, who had become his alter-ego. Finally, he winds up in a small mental hospital where he watches an unchanging pocket watch and coughs for hours on end. The warden of the mental hospital took a liking to him as well as the other two inmates, and treats them as family—the only family the white keeper had—although they were Indians. Suddenly the cozy little world is disturbed by the entrance of Beirão, a famous journalist who had campaigned for years for the re-indianization of Brazil. Taking to the extreme the doctrines of Alencar's supporters and ignoring the humor inherent in Oswald de Andrade's Antropofagía and his "Tupi or not Tupi", he decides that the terminally-ill Ipavu will be his country's savior from the problems outlined in Mário Andrade's Macunaíma. Beirão and Ipavu make a long pilgrimmage together upriver, searching for Ipavu's village which will serve as the locus for the revolt and home base. During the journey the roles of the two principal figures became reversed. The patron Beirão who paid for the beer and the alcohol and led the way up the river becomes impoverished through his spendthrift ways and Ipavu has to resort to begging and portraying himself as the last of his tribe to feed the pair.

While they are inching their way up the river, Callado in parallel chapters begins to present the current happenings in Ipavu's home village. He tells the story of Ieropê, the medicine man and chief of the village who denied penicillin to many of his tribe during a ravaging epidemic, keeping it for himself, thus splitting the tribe and fomenting a serious division in the village. During the course of the work, Ieropê falls more and more into self-doubting, seeing the remnants of his faction leave him for the other group of the tribe.

At the same time in the alternate chapters relating Ipavu's story, Ipavu becomes more and more confident, although losing what physical force remains to him. Beirão collapses as Ipavu grows and begins to mirror Ieropê, falling more and more into a state of helpless passivity and eventually becoming physically ill as well. In one of the key scenes of the work, as the pilgrimmage is at its lowest point, Beirão finally shares his last secret with Ipavu. He reveals a small plaster bust of Montaigne which he had been carrying with him as a personal icon of their spiritual journey. This pitiful attempt to recapture the spirit of Montaigne, using Montaigne's own writing on the Indians (see chapter one), strikes Ipavu as particularly child-like. This incident is more than a vignette showing the development of the work's characters. As is indicated by the title, it symbolizes the absurd nature of the quest for what cannot be had.

It should not surprise anyone who has read the earlier chapters of this work to discover that this novel relates a quest attempting to find a part of the New World that never existed, in fact this is a quest for an eden created in Europe by writers who never traveled to the new found lands. Yet even a quest as absurd as this speaks to a deeply-felt need of Europeans and European descendents both in Europe and in the Western Hemisphere.

The duo finally reach the village, with Ipavu at the edge of death. Then the ultimate irony occurs. Beirão is roasted at the stake and eaten by Ieropê and the remnants of the tribe. Just as Montaigne indicated in "Des Cannibales" they sought to acquire his strength and force through his flesh. Then in a sudden shift in the last scene of the book, the dead Ipavu is seen floating down the river in a canoe past the rival faction's village, with a black turkey vulture seemingly piloting the boat. The rival faction seeks for a few minutes to corral the craft, but quickly desists when the vulture prepares to attack them. Their medicine man then bids them observe the bird and man carefully. They see that Ipavu's face is possessed with a divine joy and they realize the near supernatural loyalty of the bird must not be interfered with. Thus they see the final perfection and realization of what had become Ipavu's pilgrimmage as much as Beirão's. They could not disturb

> o vau de passagem entre um mundo e outro,
> o vão dos encontros, onde o homen tem seu juízo e a
> alma tem seu corpo, mesmo porque, como qualquer
> um pode ver, a canoa estava indo direita, feito quem
> marcou hora, pro Morena, pro moitará dos ríos e das
> almas.[...] a qual canoa, em miniatura, numa rosca

> distante do Tuatuarí já pareça uma escura serpente
> com topete de garça.[64]

In this mystical ending, the Indian, at one with the cosmos and the gods of nature, emerges heroically. Ipavu made the journey towards his death and salvation—the only real salvation open to him. Callado thus has used several Indian literary myths, drawing his work from its indigenist opening to its magico-realist ending while using some Indianist coloring to achieve his purpose.

The mystical elements in the work are extremely strong and help place it in the larger tradition of Western Hemisphere writing on the Indians. Throughout the Western Hemisphere, as we have seen, just as the positivistic-scientific and technical culture's progressive mythology seems to be dominating the future of western man, so do writers retreat into the regressive mythology of the superior, primitive, and mystical Indians. The world of magico-realism, with its ancestry of absurdist existentialism faced with the concrete and asphalt of modern life, leaps to embrace the incongruities of this life, while both retreating and advancing into a mystical suprarationality with the Indians as guide.

In Los Ríos profundos, written before Arguedas' adoption of magico-realism, the Indians' legacy of strength, perserverance, overwhelming emotion, love of their surrounding environment, and moral superiority emerges through their music and poetry and can be called forth magically through the sound of the zumballyu or the inherent poeticity of the people. These Indians' primitive faith rejects modern western man's cynical Weltmüdigkeit and his amorality as having departed from the true nature of the New World and its age-old ways.

In Ashini the hero's superhuman power to withstand the rigors of his environment, his powerful and intuitive comprehension of his tribe's past and place in the cosmos, makes his self-crucifixion a powerful note of protest to the European-influenced western man. He seeks, through his self-sacrifice, to provide an example of what has been lost and has to be regained. His mystical

---

[64] Callado 128–129.

188

understanding of nature and his complete integration with it is killed. Yet the open ending of the work and the evident Christ imitation of Ashini's death are enough to allow one to believe that his death is not for nought. One can even entertain the hope that he will rise again through the writing of his life, a life that will serve as an inspiration to the cynical, uncaring western men of the novel.

In Beautiful Losers the clearest example is given of the hopelessness and depravity of modern urban man's existence. Yet western man is not without a nineteenth-century type of longing for a better way, for a meaningfulness that is lacking in his life, or even for some magic in his life. He has no relationship with the outer world and therefore creates restricted inner worlds which gradually shrink until the western man begins to choke himself with his own mental creations. The narrator embraces Catherine Tekakwitha as an example of higher humankind, just as Ernesto views the Indians as culturally and morally superior in Los Ríos profundos. The narrator uses the tradition of Catherine's life to admit himself to a reality higher than the one in which he lives. As he admits to F. "I didn't want to work to change myself. I wanted miracles."[65] Catherine Tekakwitha's miracles are the miracles he finally adopts. Yet only F. with his sublime presence as illuminator and guide, can lead the narrator down the path to his ultimate salvation. Only he can force the narrator to abandon the world of pop radio and elevators to purge ascetically his soul just as Catherine purged hers. Both of them finally produce miracles at the end of their lives. The life to come, however, requires their consequent figurative self-immolation. Much more powerful and more attractive is the way to salvation followed by the Mohawks and Catherine's uncle. Yet unless one is enough *of* the world to *be* the world and able to dance between the crashing boulders and the river described in the Mohawk story of the death journey, s/he must purge her/himself. Catherine's uncle and F. do not have to do this. They glory in the gifts of the primitive world, including its sexual gifts, and attempt to aid others with their suprarationality. But although Catherine's uncle finally fails, F. and Catherine, herself, do succeed with the narrator. He finally does become a god.

[65] Monkman 158.

In <u>A Expedição Montaigne</u> and in <u>Maíra</u> this suprarationality of the Indians also emerges triumphant. In <u>Maíra</u> the mystical power of the Mairuns converts the reader into longing to participate in their totally self-assured and confident world—even as it declines. Although certain critics suggest that this world is a metaphor for the need for Brazil to stand strong against the rest of the world, it seems to be more a call for Brazilian and other western humankind to return to the simultaneous inner direction and outward comprehension of the mystically-superior Indian. In <u>A Expedição Montaigne</u> the moral lesson is that white men, seeking to grasp an idealized past associated with the Indians, should be aware of what is Indian and what is not. The true Indian heritage is still powerful and admirable but it is probable that few white men and even few Indians can understand it or benefit from it.

This striving of European-influenced western man to understand the conquered traditions and their legacy, the desire of western man to adopt and adapt the perceived mystical suprarationality of the Indian is a constant in these four twentieth-century works and in most of the twentieth-century works here surveyed. Just as the nineteenth-century literary myth that emerged dominant was that of the white or European-influenced man seeking to define his superiority through descent from the Indian or struggle against him, so the dominant myth of the last half of the twentieth century is that of the mystical suprarational Indian guiding the western man, seeking to help him fight the inhumanity and absurdity of modern existence. Let us now challenge these assumptions and summary notions about the image of the Indian in both of these centuries by analyzing these eight works on a more elemental level—that of the individual passage.

SEMIOTIC ANALYSIS AND FINAL CONCLUSIONS
ABOUT THE MYTHS AND IMAGES OF INDIANS
IN THE FOUR LITERATURES

After having examined the development of the way that the American Indian is viewed in New World literature, and specifically, how s/he is viewed in eight novels, let us review the images of the Indian taken from the eight novels of chapters three and four with different critical eyeglasses in order to test the preliminary conclusions that were made in these chapters. Then we may proceed to our final conclusions.

Until this point in this work the images of the Indian have been treated in a standard critic-centered fashion. We have discussed the images of the Indian used in nineteenth- and twentieth-century literature with special emphasis given to eight novels. Having done this, it is now possible to take the eight novels and use a different type of literary analysis in order to derive conclusions from them to add to the views of the more traditional critical method already used. With an eye to a new type of literary analysis that will be particularly appropriate to our main problem of Indian myths and images, let us consider, extremely briefly, the different types of literary analysis currently practiced.

Traditional critics who take their training from forebears ranging from Aristotle to St. Beuve analyze a passage or a work by reading it several times, drawing on their experiences, their readings of other similar works, and their knowledge of the author's life to describe the author's intentions in the work under consideration as a means of explaining the plot and philosophy of the particular work. They write in clear language trying to show how their traditionally semantic and/or biographical approach is the soundest for understanding the work in question. Other, less-traditional, critics do not use this way of analyzing a text. Some instead use linguistically-based analyses, based upon the work of Saussure, Greimas, Jakobson, and Kristeva or other linguists, grammatical semiologists, and/or "structuralists". That is to say, they study the grammatical, syntactical, and semantic structure of the work, looking for specific and unique combinations of subjects, verbs, and adjectives; unique being defined by the critics' acquaintance with similar semantically-and/or chronologically-defined literature. An individual critic may choose to perform such an analysis while ignoring larger elements of the text, such as plot or characterization as well as any historical or authorial intention. Complicated diagrams of the linguistic relationships can be studied to look for patterns. Another level of reading is often then accomplished by adding the word-patterns to the level of plot structure creating significant smaller and larger meaning-units from either a diachronic or a synchronic perspective. Other groups of critics make what we can call a more "semiotic" or "sign-based" reading (especially as influenced by the work of Charles S. Peirce and Umberto Eco). The meaning-units of a text become signs pointing to components of the linguistic level—the meaning-unit level of the other levels—or to "higher" levels such as that of semantics. The meaning-units in the linguistic structure are considered to convey meaning or significance in a semiotic manner, but once the semiotic communication is established, a significance in the reader's mind is created which is related to the basal object itself through the interpretants that the object automatically generates. What semioticians often mean by the semantic level of reading then is the relationship between groups of "simpler" signs. Obviously this series of "complex" signs does not exist independently of other levels of reading and it is not a "higher" level of reading except in that it cannot exist without the level of "simpler signs".

Once the informed semiotic reader or critic has established some type of semantic understanding (and my previous discussion only hints at the complexity that a thorough theoretical consideration would include), s/he must then place his/her understanding in some type of historic context, that is to say to realize the interpretants represented by this context. This does not necessarily mean that s/he

193

has to spend hours studying the life of an author and discovering whether the author prefered crumpets or scones with his or her tea. It does mean that the critic has to be aware of certain social or cultural notions held by the author or his/her public. Whether s/he chooses to treat this notion in a particular specific analysis is, analysis-dependant. Some types of analyses will not need this context to be explored. Others will. However it is important for differences between an author's and a critic's cultural and social milieu to be noted by the critic, especially when looking at semantic questions. It is certain modern critics' (both "structural" and "new" critics, for example) greatest innovation and worst drawback that they do not treat the historical aspects of their texts more. Some of them cannot conceive of hermeneutic differences between their own critical perspective and that of others. This type of egocentric privileging of their own perspective should be obvious—yet in the worst readings from this group (especially noteworthy are the social scientists among them) they seem to believe that their own currently held psychological, cultural and social attitudes are extremely similar to those held by writers of the past—no matter what the writer's individual circumstances may have been. In the best readings provided by this group, on the contrary, these critics put their greatest emphasis on the linguistic or semiotic levels of their reading and include historic contextualizations as they are relevant to the analysis at hand. What they attempt to do is to bring new insights into a well-known passage or work in which certain important features have been ignored. Then by using these insights they can reformulate their ideas concerning older conclusions written about the text discussed.

During our own discussion of the development of the non-Indian's view of the Indian, we have been careful not to ignore the historical circumstances of the Indian and those who described him or her. Since the question of what types of generally-describable literary myths were used by nineteenth- and twentieth-century writers in New-World literature has not been addressed before this present work, it was felt that a more "traditional" manner of criticism had to be used to give the background for further commentaries. This is the reason for the type of presentation used in the first, third, and fourth chapters. Both the specific historical events and the <u>Zeitgeist</u> of all of the important writers had to be chronicled. In the later chapters, comparative readings were emphasized in order to discuss works of the nineteenth and twentieth centuries.

The second chapter is an interruption of this flow. Yet the second chapter summarizes pre-Romantic feelings about the Indians, showing how these feelings relate to one of the most important watersheds in European intellectual history, the Enlightenment, and how the Indian becomes the central focus in a mythology whose immediacy is no less great in the late twentieth century. Therefore it provided a framework upon which to place the changes and adaptations modern writers made in the mythology. Finally, the type of textual analysis and vocabulary used in the last two chapters was presented to refine our vision of these changes as introduced in key texts of the last two centuries. However almost all of the analysis of novels beyond the eight specific novels discussed in the last two chapters not only is "traditional criticism" but also relies to at least some extent upon other scholars' interpretations as to how each work is significant in the role it played during the development of the mythology of the Indian. Here, in the conclusion, it is appropriate to reexamine some of these other critical interpretations as well as the ones we have made ourselves earlier.

To go back to the original point of this concluding chapter, that is to address each passage or work cited in a new and perhaps more useful way, we have to begin by looking at different ways of comparing works and passages such as the importance of "intertextuality" in comparing texts.

The notion of intertextuality, that is generally speaking some texts influence others, has been discussed imprecisely. Let us now refine certain ideas about it. Enough historically-based criticism has been done to know that certain authors, or a critical elite, actually read certain works which influenced them—whether the works were by a Montaigne, Marmontel, Cooper, or a Matto Turner. Some critics who deal with this type of analysis would then make the broad and general assertation that "x was influenced by y in his writing on z". The field of comparative literature was created from such statements with the added note that y's work did not have to be written in the same language or in the same country as x's. Thus the field of comparing/comparative literature(s) was first strengthened by using certain semantic understandings as a basis for comparison and only later by forcing all of the texts to be considered through specific methodological analyses. As a result social and cultural differences between works, authors, literatures, and critics have been largely not well discussed by these critics, as if these differences would negate discovered similarities. It is my point that the social and cultural differences do exist and must be considered as I have done in this work. Yet it is also my point and the point of most comparative literature scholars that the writers of various literatures often tend to search for truths beyond cultural and social boundaries. Very different works from very different authors and literatures can be compared in spite of obvious contextual differences when they are attempting to accomplish similar goals.

After putting aside the question of what type of intertextuality is really at work in these Indian novels (whether it be the traditional "x" influenced "y" type of intertextuality or the the Kristeva <u>Zeitgeist</u> type of intertextuality), the question remains, however, as to how an "objective", effective, and thorough comparison can be made between works from different times and different languages even if some type of similar goal is hypothesized? The answer to this is multi-fold.

A more traditional critic's answer is to create narrow taxonymies which strait-jacket each work dealing with the subject into the frameworks these critics have created. There are two major problems with this approach. One is that the critic usually creates the categories only after having read all of the works. Thus s/he anticipates these categories and tailors them to fit what s/he already knows. A category may either be so specific that it does not serve a general range of works, or so general that works which should be kept separate are placed together.

The second major problem is that this approach requires the critic to make assumptions about the overall use of the subject. S/He must interpret the text in such a skilled manner that s/he takes her or his own intentions, the author's intentions, and all of the probable complexity of the work into account. Coming up with any general impression of a work that would permit *a single person* to categorize it completely, thoroughly, and "objectively" becomes an attempt fraught with difficulties.

Perhaps the most important problem with a traditional nineteenth-century approach is its assumed "objectivity". Most late twentieth-century critics, having been through the rigors of multiculturalism, look at the term "objective" with a jaundiced eye. These critics now know that it is impossible and even undesirable to avoid the subjectivity of critical evaluations and impressions because this is the very heart of literary analysis. As Umberto Eco and many others have indicated, the fact that some works require skilled critical analysis and that said analyses will often not resemble each other explains why some works are still read centuries after their first appearance. Their very complex semantic and semiotic configurations lead us to call such examples "rich works of art". Nevertheless, if we concentrate on *a single* semantic aspect of these works we reduce the confusion and complexity inherent in analyzing them by a large factor.

In this study of images and myths of Indians we can hope to establish a less difficult basis for comparison by dealing with the presentation of the Indian through *the* most complete description of the major Indian characters. This could be a single paragraph, connected paragraphs, or short passages taken from a well-defined portion of the text under consideration. To test the accuracy of the choice of this particular passage, several passages from a long text could be compared to see how the chosen passage varied from an impression created by the combined passages. Then the chosen passage, or series of sentences which create a passage, could be discarded or kept depending upon its variation from the collective norm. Such a passage, *if* carefully selected, can then summarize in a not too reductive fashion the work's viewpoint on its Indian characters—the focus of our study—while at the same time presenting a text small enough for intensive study and analysis.

A major problem with using a single passage to portray a complex image is that of representing chronological changes in the image. What if the most important Indian character actually changes during the course of the work studied? The only answer is, if the changes are exceedingly great, then two passages must serve as _exempla_ of a single character. We shall find however that this problem, perhaps surprisingly, appears to be rather uncommon, a fact which by itself is very interesting and sheds additional light on the rationale behind the creation and use of Indian images. A final problem is that of two, similarly-important, images of the Indian occuring whose attributes vary greatly, for example where an author presents "good" and "bad" Indians in conflict in a particular work. Quite obviously, then, if neither image dominates the work, both images must be used.

Before going on to discuss how the images can be compared in a systematic manner, it is necessary to refine the focus of analysis. In considering these Indian images we are not always discussing what some critics would call the primary characters of these novels. If the Indian is not a protagonist and serves only as a foil to the white man, then our creation of the composite Indian image will not attempt to illuminate the work as a complete entity. Indeed our current study of Indian images alone will certainly ignore certain important aspects of the novels.

It is possible that negative criticism can be directed at this, perhaps, overly sociological use of literature. However, an analysis of images and character-attributes need not be used only for sociological purposes. Here they are used in an attempt to see how an author's notions or ideas are expressed through his or her use of literature and how s/he makes an intentionally or unintentionally cultural statement about the way Indians are used in the creation of a Pan-American literary myth. Extrapolating the results of a literary study to make more general statements of a purely sociological or cultural nature is, of course, possible and perhaps even inevitable. Such a use is what makes the sociology of literature an interesting field. My own goal is not to argue for a specific type of sociological theory based upon the findings that will be presented; rather, it is to present my findings as objectively as is possible in a subjective area. Then sociological philosophers can use my results to further their own studies.

To begin our new type of literary analysis, let us decide where to start by imagining different ways of analyzing passages after selecting those which best describe the most important Indian characters. We could first simply discuss each passage's descriptive adjectives, adverbs, or verbs and isolate from the other words in the passages in order to make a simple listing[1]. Viewing such a list, however, will automatically induce the reader to make several conclusions of a higher level, based upon the knowledge that s/he brings with him or her. A second method could involve be a listing of meaning-units. These may be individual words or combinations which express a complex idea. Some of these combinations might then be discussed in more detail. Finally, a summary of meaning-units could be presented to show how this passage relates to the higher levels of the text and ultimately the myth and the mythologies discussed earlier.

Yet, although perhaps valuable and certainly interesting, this type of analysis is not sufficient to discuss the degree of adherence to a particular image of the Indian. We can say either yes, the passages conform to a certain view, or no, they do not. We cannot say how well or to what extent the different images reflect similar images or myths.

Let us go back to the level of words and meaning-units. To be able to compare individual passages from one work with each other and/or with similar extracts taken from other works, it is necessary to use a different, more quantitative type of analysis. Let us consider a comparison on the level of words. An obvious first level would be a type of concordance which would list the words and number of times they are used in a certain textual segment with French, Spanish, or Portuguese (or any other language's) words being translated into their closest English equivalent. As a result all of the passages could then be compared on the level of the individual word with the frequency of each noted to make the most basic types of conclusions.

From a quantitative standpoint, comparing the numbers of identical words as taken from different texts allows an interesting and fairly objective analysis and is a defensible activity in itself much like the types of analyses considered earlier. I feel a need to go beyond this level however, using a comparison of degree of

---

[1] This is not done here, due to the limitations of space that a one volume book imposes; however, this particular type of study could be done in a different format.

similarity and difference. It is possible to do this through the creation of "semantic tables" which can be compared with the help of several different statistical methods, although I will only use the simplest of methods in this work[2].

To set up a semantic table we must first treat each individual passage as our primary unit of analysis. We will consider the semiotic import of all of the words and/or "simple meaning-units" in the passage as a series of "simple signs". Then we will group our "simple signs" together to create a "complex sign" or "complex meaning-unit" which reflects the Indian character's image contained in the whole passage. Having gone this far, then in connection with the works as a whole, we will be able to group these passages together and rank them in terms of discrete categories. The discrete categories created will be semantic descriptive-listings. I propose to name one category "bravery", one "strength", and one "maliciousness", for example (see a complete listing of categories in tables one and two and note six of this chapter). I will use many different semiotically-charged categories in order to lower personal bias by using a variety of words, which although they may have similar "meanings", may be interpreted differently in different places on the semantic table since they will be chosen from suggestions by a group of people from different backgrounds.[3] Once these categories have been created, I will then consider each passage from a text as a single entry. This passage or microtext will then receive a numerical ranking in each of the

---

[2] Certain program packages such as "SAS" and "SPSS" could be used for the determination of specific statistical items, such as standard deviation and correlation coefficients. For an example of how these could be implemented, see my unpublished master's thesis "Ethnic Groups on the Frontier in Rowan County, North Carolina, 1753–1778", Vanderbilt University, Nashville, TN, 1977. (It is also available from the North Carolina Collection at the University of North Carolina's Davis Library in Chapel Hill, NC.)

[3] I asked a variety of people what words they would use to describe Indians. These acquaintances included a number of graduate students from a variety of disciplines and secretaries in the Romance Languages department at UNC Chapel Hill and Chapel Hill office workers. See also note 6 in this chapter for a discussion of how the advantages of these categories outweigh obvious problems.

categories[4]. After the rankings are finished (three separate rankings have been done over a period of six months), then the categories will be analyzed for similarity of intent.

It is necessary to stop here and explain that I am using numerical rankings to reveal my prejudices as an individual critic. Giving a microtext a numerical value in many different summary categories is a method that is easily followed by others wishing to examine my critical judgment and possible prejudices. If, for example, the use of Ponteach in the description given of him by John Richardson in Wacousta is given a "five" in "maliciousness" (out of ten, zero being not malicious, ten being extremely malicious), this ranking is clear enough so another critic can easily discuss it. By this ranking of "five" on a ten-point scale I hope it is clear that I am saying that after a careful consideration of all of my knowledge of this microtext and the other relevant microtexts possible in the novel Wacousta, I believe that Ponteach is neither an overly malicious and wicked character, nor is he an innocent or naive creature of the forest. If a particular reader would wish to dispute my judgment s/he could pointing to other passages in the novel. Yet my answer would be that although Ponteach could be malicious, perhaps, he does not necessarily show this trait in this microtext and that "maliciousness" is not a word that I feel has a strong association with Ponteach, either positively or negatively in these texts. Therefore on a scale of one to ten he would be given a middle ranking of five.

The great problem with using numerical rankings is now obvious. The last paragraph gives a much more detailed explanation of my view on the extent of Ponteach's maliciousness than the simple number five can. Yet at the same time, with this sample explanation in mind, the sum total of my reading can be represented by the number and this number can be more easily and quickly

---

[4] A discussion of numerical categories will be given later in the chapter, as well as the categories selected. For the importance of careful selection of character-attributes see my article "Character-Function in Romanian Ballads" Romance Notes (Fall 1983) 36–42. See also note 6 in this chapter.

compared to other conclusions about the applicability of the word "maliciousness" to other characters and other texts, such as a "zero" for a sample text from Iracema or a "ten" for the description of the character, Wacousta, himself. When comparing five, ten, twenty, or even one hundred microtexts composed of a similar number of characters, the advantages of numerical comparisons are even more salient.

In addition to simple one-to-one comparisons, numerical rankings are essential for higher-level statistical comparisons. Determining the means and medians for each category can give an idea of how homogenous an author's views are on certain character-facets. A high mean or a low mean is of obvious interest. Secondly, a high standard deviation from the mean would show that certain entries or microtexts are not actually closely associated with the mean. Rank-order analysis could find which microtexts are then out of line with the mean. Then these isolated microtexts can be grouped together and viewed to see why they were similar. Aiding in this quest would be the use of statistical correlations of the different semantic categories for each variable to see which categories should be grouped together and could be repeated by using other category-groupings. If so, larger generalizations about groupings could then be made as well as informed discussions of what types of groupings are both statistically- and semantically-important. Yet this particular example is but a single example of the types of analyses that can created by using statistics on large amounts of data leading to interesting conclusions. With this method, which obviously requires numerical ranking, old relationships between texts and microtexts, between different texts, or different microtexts, can be thoroughly examined and tested, and new and perhaps surprising relationships can be discovered[5].

One must not, however, be blind to the ultimately subjective nature of these statistics, both in terms of the origins of the numbers, and in terms of the types of

---

[5] Many different texts can thus be used. These might then be such diverse microtexts as the first Norse view of the Indian cited in the first chapter, Montaigne's "Des cannibales", or a modern magazine account.

analysis which are chosen—a most subjective undertaking itself, as statisticians are aware. It is recognized that numbers are not an ultimate answer which can eliminate other types of analysis and explanations. If this were so then the first four chapters of this work and the subsequent analysis of the statistical findings would be superfluous. Nevertheless, numbers are indispensable in comparing large amounts of information in a comprehensible manner. Therefore, I believe that a subjective reading, after highlighting as much of its knowable subjectivity as possible, can be converted into a numerical form and then reconverted into "alpha notation" (words) without losing its informational content and, of course, its continued subjectivity. Finally, I feel there is little risk of a high level of "entropy" or "noise" interfering with this communication of information, as the encoder and decoder are the same person. As a result the traduttore may only become a tradittore to him or herself.

In this particular study, I chose many different semantic meaning-units for analysis with twenty-six categories that I decided were positive and twenty-five that I labeled as negative[6]. I took a total of thirty passages from the eight novels for

---

[6] The positive categories are: "good poverty", "honorable", "powerful", "fierce", "generous", "strict moral code", "stoic", "primitive/powerful", "brave", "natural man", "merciful", "silent", "environmentalist", "in total cosmic communion", "proud", "intelligent", "self-reliant", "honest", "thrifty", "peaceful", "prudent", "straight-forward", "open", "friendly", "superior", and "American". The negative categories are: "indigent", "dishonorable", "physically weak", "cowardly", "malicious", "merciless", "no moral sense", "barbaric", "wild/pagan", "unhuman", "inhumane", "earthy", "cruel", "pitiable", "suffering", "stupid", "lying", "cheating", "stealing", "alcoholic", "crafty", "warlike", "superstitious", "treacherous", and "wretched". It has been noted by some scholars with whom I have discussed the idea of "semantic tables" that all linguistic signs are fundamentally ambiguous as well as arbitrary, meaning that any word can create different signs in their interpreters' minds. (I thank Charles Pearson, Umberto Eco, Kathy Harring and others for their help in these discussions.) I accept the truth of this statement. However I reply to this assertion by noting Charles Peirce's own creation of the "community of scholars" who would agree upon the possibility of "final interpretants"; i.e., some type of disagreement upon the "meaning" of these terms is quite possible; however, agreement will always be stronger than disagreement in any educated speaker of a language. To deny this is to deny *any* possibility of communication between individuals and to deny even the possibility of any type of communication between human beings.

analysis, using these semantic categories. Some works have only two passages chosen for analysis, while others have as many as five passages. I was careful to take passages from several different places in the "macrotexts" (the novels), which gave as many different views of the Indians as possible. These different views will be noted in the data tables. Before finishing the analysis, I had an outside person (a natural scientist) give her own categoric reading of two different English passages, one from nineteenth- and one from twentieth-century English Canadian literature, in order to check the relevance of the concept, the categories, the rating system, and finally my subjective evaluation. Although she did have some valuable suggestions to make[7], she agreed that this type of rating did have relevance and could by done by someone not involved in the original literary studies.

When the data-collecting was finished I averaged the three (or four) readings to generate a summary number[8]. Once these numbers were collected I made two tables (Tables One and Two) in which only very high numbers (eight to ten) and very low numbers (zero to two) were given, making the assumption that only very high correlations, whether positive or negative, are truly significant in this particular context. In addition I developed a primitive version of a standard deviation quotient. I added up the total variation from the highest to the lowest figure given in the three readings and found that the maximum figure possible would be ten (with at least one reading of a passage giving a number of zero and another one giving a figure of ten). If the total variation was five or higher, the

---

[7] One of her suggestions (Fayanne E. Thorngate's) was that I should be careful about confusing which variables are not applicable at all (a "five") and which variables really do indicate a strong negative correlation (a "zero"). Another suggestion was that I should have a variable labeled "ignorant" instead of "stupid". Both suggestions have been incorporated in the body of this work.

[8] The most important factor was the time element for the completion of this work. It is important for other scholars to have this work on Indians now when Columbus and Indian films have renewed interest in the subject. It is also important for scholars after the recent publication of Eco's work on interpretation. If I have to occasion to do more study in this area I will certainly refine some of my statistical assumptions and methods.

TABLE ONE:
POSITIVE TRAITS

	#	OBSERVATION	GOOD POVERTY	HONORABLE	POWERFUL	FIERCE	GENEROUS	STRICT MORAL CODE	STOIC	PRIMITIVE/POSITIVE	BRAVE	NATURAL MAN	MERCIFUL	SILENT	ENVIRONMENTALIST	TOTAL COSMIC COMMUNION	PROUD	INTELLIGENT	SELF-RELIANT	HONEST	THRIFTY	PEACEFUL	PRUDENT	STRAIGHT-FORWARD	OPEN	SUPERIOR	FRIENDLY	AMERICAN
WACOUSTA	1	0	0	10	10	0	0	0	1	10	9	0	0					1	2	0	0					0	0	0
	2			10	10	0	9	9	9	2	9	8	0					9	8	0					0	0	0	0
	3			10	1	9	10	9	10	9	9	9						8	8	8	10	10				9	9	
ANCIENS CANADIENS	1	10				9	10	10	10	9	10		8				10		8	10				9	8	9	9	10
	2		9	9	10			9	9			9	9					9	8	8								
IRACEMA	1									10		10				10	10	8	8							8	9	10
	2				9	9	8	10	9	10	9							9	8	9			1			8	9	9
	3								8	10	9								9							8	8	
	4		8						8	10	9							8	8	9		1						
AVES SIN NIDO	1		8	0	0	1	8				8								9		9			9	9	9		
	2		8	0	0		8												9		8				8	9		
	3	1	8	0	0														8					8	9	8		
	4			0	0																					8	8	
	5	0	8	0		1			8		8				8				8							9	8	
LOS RÍOS PROFUNDOS	1				0						9																	
	2		8	1	0		8												8							8	8	9
	3			0	0		8																	8	8			
	4					8	9	8											8					8	9			
	5			9	9				9	9						10	9	9						9		9	8	9
ASHINI	1	10	10				9	10	10	10	10			10	10	10	10	10	10	8						10	9	9
	2		10	2	2		9	10	10	10	10		9	8	10	10			9							10	10	
BEAUTIFUL LOSERS	1	0			0	0	2		0	1	0					1	0	0		10					8	0	10	0
	2		9	9			8	9	9	9	10	9	9		8	10	8		8			8				10	8	
	3		8						10	10	8	8	10			10	8								10	8	8	
	4	8							8	10					8													0
	5	8		8					9	8	8					10			8			8				10		
EXPEDIÇÃO MONTAIGNE	1	0	2	0	0				0	0	0	1	1	2	1	1	0											0
	2			1	1					8	8															10		
	3			0	0		0	1																				
	4								8	8	10	8	10	8	8	10											9	

TABLE TWO:
NEGATIVE TRAITS

	OBSERVATION	INDIGENT	DISHONORABLE	PHYSICALLY WEAK	COWARDLY	MALICIOUS	MERCILESS	NO MORAL SENSE	BARBARIC	WILD/PAGAN	UNHUMAN	INHUMANE	EARTHY	CRUEL	PITIABLE	SUFFERING	STUPID	LYING	CHEATING	STEALING	ALCOHOLIC	CRAFTY	WARLIKE	SUPERSTITIOUS	TREACHEROUS	WRETCHED
WACOUSTA	1	10	0		9	10	10	10	10	10	10	9	10									9		9	9	10
	2		0	0	8	9		10	10	10				10	0	0	0	9			2	2	8	9	9	10
	3		0	0	0	0	0	0	0		0	0	1	0	8	8	0	0	0	0	0	0	0		1	
ANCIENS CANADIENS	1	0	0	0	0	0	0		8	0	0			0			0	0	0	0		0			0	0
	2	0	0	0	1				8	1				0	0	0	0	0	0	0				8		0
IRACEMA	1			0	0				8	0	1			0	0	0	0	0	0	0	0				1	0
	2	1	0	0	0					0	0			0			0	1	1	0	0				0	1
	3	0	1	0	0	0	0	0		0	0						0	0	0	0	0					
	4	0	0	0	0	0				0	0		1	0	1			0	0	0	0				0	0
AVES SIN NIDO	1	10	0		0	0	0	0	0	1	0	0	2	0	10	10	1	0	0	0	0	0	0		0	10
	2	10	0	8	0	0	0	0	0	0	1	0	0	0	10	10	0	0	0	0	0	0	0		0	10
	3	10	0		1	0	0	0	0	1	0	0	2	0	10	10	0	0	0	0	0	1	0		0	10
	4	0	0	0	0	0	0	0	0	0	0	0	0	0			0	0	0	0	0	0	0	1	0	2
	5	10	0	8	0	0	0	0	0	0	0	0	0	0	10	10	0	0	0	0	0	0	0	0	0	10
LOS RÍOS PROFUNDOS	1	2	0	0	0	0	0	0	0	0	0	0	0	0	8	8	1	0	0	0	0	0	0		0	
	2	8	0	0	0	0	0	0	0	0	1	0	0	0			2	0	0	0	8	0	0	0	0	0
	3	9	0	1	0	0	0	0	0	0	0	0	0	0	8	8	1	0	0	0	0	1	0		0	
	4	0		0	0	0	0	0	0	0	0	0	0	0	8	8	0	0	0	0	0	0	0	0	9	0
	5	0	1	0	0	0	0	0	0	0	0	2	0	0	8	2	0	0	0	0	0	0	0	0	0	0
ASHINI	1	0	0	0	0	0	0	0	0	0	0			0	9	9	0	0	0	0	0	0	0	0	0	0
	2	0	1	0	0	0	0	0	0	0	0			0	9	10	0	0	0	0	0	0		0		0
BEAUTIFUL LOSERS	1	10	0	10	8	0	0	0	0	0	0			0	10	9	0	0	0	0		0	0	0	0	10
	2	0	0	0	0	0	0	0	0	0	0	0	1	1		1	0	0	0	0	0	0	0	8	0	
	3	0	0	0	0	0	0	0	0	0	0			0	0	0	0	0	0	0	2	0		8	0	
	4	0	0	0	0	0	0	0		0	0			0	1	9	0	0	0	0				0		
	5		0	0	0	0	0			0	0			0	9	0	0	0	0	0	0	0		0		
EXPEDIÇÃO MONTAIGNE	1		8		0	0			0	0				1			1	0	0	1	0			0	0	
	2			0	0			0			0	0	2	0			0	0	0	0	1	0	0	0	0	
	3			0	0			0	0	0	0		0	8	8	0	1			9		2				
	4	0	0	0	0	0	0	0	10		0			0			0	0	0	0	0	0	0	0	0	

result would not be used, even if the summary number expressed a high positive or negative correlation.

After looking at Tables One and Two, certain conclusions are obvious. Starting with the negative table, which is a bit easier to read, it is evident that the vast majority of the negative categories—especially the violent and actively negative ones—are only given highly positive correlations in the first two passages taken from Wacousta. These Indians are clearly "malicious", "merciless", "barbaric", "wild" or "pagan", "unhuman", "inhumane", "cruel", "warlike" and "treacherous". The last passage, which describes the noble Indian, Oucanacousta, has a high rating only in the categories of "pitiable" and "suffering". This shows the bi-valent view Richardson had of the native New World inhabitants. In Les anciens Canadiens the only high negative categories are those of "wild/pagan" and "warlike", groupings which could be thought of as positive in some senses. There is only one high negative number in Iracema out of a possible one hundred. This shows, rather dramatically, the idyllic picture painted of the Indian in this work. In contrast, demonstrating its revolutionary nature, Aves sin nidos' Indians are "indigent", "pitiable", "suffering", "wretched", and occasionally "physically weak".

In the twentieth century Los Ríos profundos' and Ashini's Indians have consistently high ratings only in the areas of "pitiable" and "suffering". Beautiful Losers' Indians also have high summary numbers in some areas, but with its several different uses of the native New-World inhabitants; it does not have as much consistency as some of the other novels. Finally, A Expedição Montaigne has almost no high negative correlations.

Thus on the negative side, with the exception of the first two passages taken from Wacousta, most of the negative categories do not apply to these passages in both centuries except in a very strong negative manner. Most of the traits that we tend to associate with Indians in much of popular U.S. American literature and art are not reflected in these works. In the two works from the middle of the century, and the only true romantic works, there are no really negative characteristics ascribed to their Indians. Aves sin nido clearly reflects its naturalistic nature and not its romantic style with its rating in these categories, showing more similarity to Los Ríos profundos than to Iracema (and, incidentally, justifying the place most critics give it in Latin American literature as representing a break from what went before in terms of writing on Indians). What is perhaps most remarkable here in the negative table is the near unanimity in viewing Indians as "pitiable" and "suffering" from 1880 until the present, despite the many other differences between the images from different parts of this period.

In the positive table, reading the results is much more complicated. However the grouping of positive readings dovetails with the descriptions already given in the negative table analysis while giving us additional details. In Wacousta Richardson's Indians are always viewed as "powerful" and "brave" "natural men". However, the passage describing the meeting between Ponteach and Haldimar also has many characteristics in common with the last passage describing Oucanousta. His "bad" Indians also have a "strict moral code", are "stoic", "proud", and "intelligent". A comparison between the last two passages of Wacousta and all of the passages of Les anciens Canadiens would show a great deal of similarity. Together with Iracema all of these works attribute the characteristics of "primitive/positive", "brave", "natural man", "proud", "intelligent", "self-reliant", "open", and "superior" to Indians.

As we have already posited in our discussion on the negative tables, Aves sin nido represents a change in the view of the Indian. There is some continuation in the high ratings given to the characteristics of open and honorable, but it gives precedence to "honest", "straight-forward", and "friendly" for the first time. We see support for the theory that has been put forward that this work seeks to combine some of Rousseau's and Buffon's qualities in order to create a wonderful pitiable creature worthy of altruistic white help. Los Ríos profundos continues the trend established by Aves sin nido. It has several high ratings in the same categories. Ashini, however, is in some ways a throwback to Les anciens Canadiens with the categories of "strict moral code", "honest", "stoic", "brave", and "natural man" being important. However, it breaks new ground in the areas of "environmentalist" and "in total cosmic communion". It also has a high negative correlation in the area of "powerful" and "fierce". This, together with high ratings in the areas of "pitiable" and "fierce" shows that Ashini is not exactly like the Indians of <u>Les anciens Canadiens</u>. In <u>Beautiful Losers</u> and <u>A Expedição Montaigne</u> the positive ratings reflect those of <u>Ashini</u> with the differences being that <u>Beautiful Losers</u> gives more weight to "good poverty" and "peaceful" and that <u>A Expedição Montaigne</u> has few high positive ratings at all, except for the last selection detailing Ipavu's funeral cortege.

Thus certain new similarities and differences have been isolated through the use of these semantic tables. It is now easier to detail the development of the nineteenth and twentieth centuries' use of Indian myths and complex images. Certain shadings and surprising comparisons can also now be isolated. Finally, and perhaps most importantly in terms of future use of these semantically-derived tables, not only can these results be easily discussed (and perhaps disagreed with) by other readers, both critically and non-critically trained, but these same readers can now add *their own* readings of the passages chosen and include these readings in the table. Since the tables are numerically-based, it is now possible for "macro-reader reception" or group reader analysis as opposed to individual reader analysis to be carried out in an effective manner.

This method has proved to be a valuable one in providing a new perspective on important critical areas and in allowing the creation of a new and different type of viewpoint in these areas. Such a method is especially important in a field as charged with emotion and pre-conceived notions as the sociology of literature. If a whole group of readers can now interpret texts in such a way that their group analysis can be studied and compared, then groups from different cultures, classes, and eventually different historical contexts can be compared. I do not believe I can underestimate the benefit possible to theorists of interpretation with this method.[9]

---

[9] I, myself, have done some other work in this area, mostly in the form of oral communications I had Charles Pearson, in the same form. I may be contacted personally for copies of some of these papers. Some of Charles Pearson's work, especially his discussions of how Peircean semiotics deal with the problem of stereotype interpretation can be found in <u>Semiotics</u>, the refereed publication of selected proceedings from the meetings of the Semiotics Society of America.

Let us return to the focus of our work, the Indian images, now and using all of the material discussed in all of our chapters proceed to our final conclusions about this work.

As in any work of such wide scope and such limited length, this study suffers from some large lacunae. Although this work provides a thorough consideration of eight novels and some details of almost all major works that deal with Indians as characters in these four New-World literatures, it does not address some other important questions such as the relationship of the more "popular" image of the Indian to the more "intellectual" one. Neither does it differentiate between the image and myth of Indian women as opposed to Indian men. A full-length study of the role of Indian women, as opposed to Indian men, cries out to be done. Other areas for further study include more complete consideration of the summary uses of the Indian by the various white literatures as well as a further investigation of the use of underlying European mythologies in dealing with subordinate peoples. In addition the roles of Indians and blacks could be compared in terms of New-World literature along with the role of half-breeds in certain literatures, such as the voyageurs and the métis of Canada, the mestizos of Peru,and the gauchos of the southern part of South America. Expanding now beyond the limits of the current work other literatures of the New World, especially U.S. American and Mexican, could be analyzed in more detail in order to ensure a fair consideration of the summary picture this particular study has produced. Finally, it would be fascinating to take the literature of the Native Americans, themselves, into account and compare it with the white-authored works on Indians in terms of the images and myths that each produces.

Even with all of the above taken into account, this study has produced some important analyses and conclusions. First of all it sheds important light on the images and myths of Indians in four representative New World literatures. We have discovered that beginning with the Greco-Roman Christian civilization of renaissance Europe Europeans automatically treated unknown human beings as others, as infidels, as aliens—in the strongest sense of the word. We have seen how the eighteenth-century French summarized all opinions on Indians, both favorable and unfavorable, through the argument between Rousseau and Buffon and then saw how these two author's composite images became literary myths which through their strength, clarity, and cohesion defined the stage that later writing on Indians took, whether the works could be called noble or ignoble savage works.

We saw in the nineteenth century that the new New-World literatures took earlier European ideas about Indians and tweaked them slightly for their own new purposes. When each country of the New World became independent, Indians became a idealized symbol of non-European excellence. Tied in with Romanticism, Indians were removed from the present time and became strong, historicized characters. With the exception of a few prominent English-language examples in the early twentieth century, the ignoble savage had disappeared from the greater part of these four literatures' novels by 1880 (1820 in Latin America), never to return. The resultant composite early and mid-nineteenth century Indian character was indeed a noble savage, an edenic Adam or Eve living in a world of chivalresque romance who had little or no contact with white Europeans or their descendants. Only in the last part of the nineteenth and in the early twentieth century do these bucolic idylls become supplanted and do "real" Indians return to these literatures.

Starting with <u>Aves sin nido</u> at the turn of the century, "real" Indians become characters in works advocating social and economic reform. Indians are seen as Buffonian poor, pitiable creatures whose ignorance and naïvete puts them into thrall to non-Indians. The most extreme examples of this image are found in Latin American literature yet the other literatures discussed in this study all have some examples of the Indian described as a "red" Uncle Tom-like "good nigger". Still, the importance and prevalence of this composite image of "The Poor, Suffering, Child-like Native" is not nearly as great as that of the "New American Noble Savage" before it or the image to follow—even if it helps create the latter.

The next and so-far final Indian image of the twentieth century is a final tweaking and combination of Rousseau and Buffon. Whereas the early part of the century was most interested in socio-economic reformist critiques, later writers are much more involved in spiritual and psychological reform. While Indians might still be poor and economically powerless they now have ascribed to them strengths worthy of emulation in the areas of emotional and spiritual power—especially in the area of spiritual oneness with the natural world surrounding them. They do become guides to the alienated European-descended whites who have suppressed them and their summary title can be therefore "The Spiritual, Ecological, Indian Guide".

Our understanding of this series of Indian-inspired composite images, myths, and their relationship to the Western world's mythological understanding of non-Western peoples is not the only important conclusion we can make, however, nor is our fascination with the possibility of semantic tables. What we have learned as well is that not only is the area of comparative New World literature a possibility but that it is extremely valuable to the continuing development of greater literary understanding. No longer can comparative literature be limited to its old area of Europe or its new area of Asia. The Americas are just as important as any other literary region and perhaps most important of all to those of us who live within their boundaries.

Therefore this work has demonstrated that New-World or Inter-American Comparative Literature is a viable, important field of study that needs to be developed much farther. It has also shown through its conclusions future paths of analysis in the area of Indian images as well as providing new ideas on methodological research in the area of image analysis and interpretation theory. As such this study represents the important first step in a variety of areas. It is now hoped that other scholars will take it and expand it yet farther into all of the areas to which its conclusions shed light.

BIBLIOGRAPHY

A. The eight novels:

Alencar, José de. <u>Iracema, Lenda de Ceará</u>. Rio de Janeiro: Edições de Ouro,

Arguedas, José María. <u>Los Ríos profundos</u>. intro. Mário Vargas Llosa. Caracas: Biblioteca Ayacucho, 1978.

Callado, Antônio. <u>A expedição Montaigne</u>. Rio de Janeiro: Nova Fronteira, 1982.

Cohen, Leonard. <u>Beautiful Losers</u>. Toronto: McClelland and Stewart, 1966.

Gaspé, Aubert de. <u>Les anciens Canadiens</u>. Montréal: Fides, 1967.

Thériault, Yves. <u>Ashini</u>. Montréal: Fides, 1961.

Turner, Clorinda Matto de. <u>Aves sin nido</u>. Cuzco: Universidad Nacional del Cuzco, 1949.

Richardson, John. <u>Wacousta; or the Prophecy, a Tale of the Canadas</u>. Philadelphia: Key and Biddle, 1833.

B. Journals and reviews:

<u>Journal of Canadian Literature</u>. 1 1956.

Ledgerwood, Mikle D. "Character-Function in Romanian Ballads" <u>Romance Notes</u> 1982, pp. 52–57.

Segal, D.M. "Problems in the Semiotic Study of Mythology" in <u>Soviet Semiotics</u> D. Lucid gen. ed. Baltimore: Johns Hopkins University Press, 1982.

214

C. Unpublished works:

Hrushovski, Benjamin. "Integrational Semantics."

Ledgerwood, Mikle D. "Ethnic Groups on the Frontier in Rowan County, NC 1753–1778". Master's thesis, Vanderbilt University, Nashville TN, 1977.

Ransdell, Charles. "Peirce: The Conception of a Sign."

Romer, James. "Rabelais and the Voyages to the new World." Unpublished dissertation, University of North Carolina, Chapel Hill, NC, 1977.

D. Other works:

Aguiar, Adonias. Memorias de Lázaro. 5th ed. Rio de Janeiro: Civilização Brasileira, 1978.

Alegría, Ciro. El mundo es ancho y ajeno. Buenos Aires: Editora Losada, 1961.

Almiñaque, Conrado. El indio pampero en la literatura gauchesca. Miami: Ediciones universal, 1981.

Amadís de Gaula, Edwin B. Place, ed. Madrid: Consejo Superior de Investigaciones Científicas, Instituto Miguel de Cervantes, 1971.

Andrade, Oswald de. Obras completas. 2 vols. Rio de Janeiro: Civilização Brasileira, 1970.

Arguedas, José María. Todas las sangres. 2 vols. Buenos Aires: Editora Losada, 1970.

Arguedas, José María. Yawar Fiesta. Lima: Populibros peruanas, 1958.

Atwood, Margaret. Survival: Thematic Guide to Canadian Literature. Toronto: Anasi, 1972.

Barnett, Louise K. The Ignoble Savage: American Literary Racism 1790–1890. Westport, CT: Greenwood Press, 1975.

Barthes, Roland. Le Degré zéro de l'écriture suivie de: Eléments de sémiologie. Paris: Gontier, 1965.

Baudet, Henri. Paradise on Earth: Some Thoughts on European Images of Non-European Man. Elizabeth Wentholt, trans. New Haven: Yale University Press, 1964.

Beltrão, Luis. O Indio, um mito brasileiro. Petroposis: Vozes, 1977.

Bergerac, Cyrano de. Voyage dans la lune. Maurice Lauguna, ed. Paris: Garnier-Flammarion, 1970.

Boscán, Guillermo Yepes. La novela indianista en Venezuela. Zulia, Venezuela: Editorial Universitaria de la Universidad del Zulia, 1967.

Buffon, Georges Louis LeClerc. A Natural History, General and Particular, Translated by William Smellie, a New Edition Corrected and Edited to which is aded a History of Birds, Fishes, Reptiles, and Insects. London: Henry Augustus Chambers for R. Evans, 1817.

Caillet-Bois, Julio. Análisis de la Araucana. Buenos Aires: Centro Editor de America Latina, 1967.

Callado, Antonio. Quarup. Rio de Janeiro: Pluarte, 1972 rpt. 1984.

Cazeneuve, Jean. Les mythologies à travers le monde. Paris: Hachette, 1966.

Cervantes, Miguel de. Don Quijote de la Mancha. Juan Bautista Avalle-Arce ed. Madrid: Editorial Alhambra, 1976.

Chiapelli, Fredi, gen. ed. First Images of America, The Impact of the new World on the Old. 2 vols. Berkeley: University of California Press, 1976.

Chinard, Gilbert. L'Amérique et le rêve éxotique dans la littérature française au XVIIème at au XVIIIème siècle. Paris: E. Droz, 1934.

.....L'éxotisme américain dans la littérature française au XVIe siècle d'après Rabelais, Montaigne, etc. Paris: Hachette et Cie., 1911.

.....L'éxotisme américain dans l'oeuvre de Chateaubriand. Paris: Hachette et Cie., 1910.

Cortázar, Augusto Raúl. Indios y gauchos en la literatura argentina. Buenos Aires: Instituto Amigos del Libro Argentino, 1952.

Cortés, Hernán. Cartas de relación de la conquista de México. 5th ed. Madrid: Espasa-Calpa, 1970.

Courtes, Joseph. Lévi-Strauss et les contraintes de la pensée mythique: Une lecture sémiotique des "Mythologiques". Tours: Mame, 1973.

Defoe, Daniel. The Life and Adventures of Robinson Crusoe. London: Oxford University Press, 1910.

Diderot, Denis de. Oeuvres philosophiques. Paul Vernière, ed. Paris: Garnier frères, 1964.

Driver, David. The Indian in Brazilian Literature. New York: The Hispanic Institute, 1942.

Dudley, Edward and Novak Maxmillian E., eds. The Wild Man Within: An Image in Western Thought from the Renaissance to Romanticism. Pittsburgh: University of Pittsburgh Press, 1972.

Eco, Umberto. The Limits of Interpretation. Bloomington: Indiana University Press, 1991.

Eggleston, Wilfrid. The Frontier and Canadian Letters. Toronto: Ryerson Press, 1957.

Ercilla y Zuñiga, Alfonso de. La Araucana. Santiago de Chile: Escritores coloniales de Chile, Editorial universitaria, 1969.

France, Marie de. Les lais. Jean Rychner, ed. Paris: Librairie Honoré Champion, 1977.

Franco, Alfonso Arinos de Melo. O Indio brasileiro e a revolução francesa. Rio de Janeiro: Libraria Jose Olympio Editora, rpt. 1976.

Frye, Northrup. The Bush Garden: Essays on the Canadian Imagination. Toronto: Anasi, 1971.

Gerbi, Antonello. The Dispute of the New World: The History of a Polemic, 1750–1900. Pittsburgh: University of Pittsburgh Press, 1955, rpt. 1973.

Haberly, David. Three Sad Races: Racial Identity and National Consciousness in Brazilian Literature. New York: Cambridge University Press, 1983.

Harrington, K. P., ed. Medieaval Latin. Chicago: University of Chicago Press, 1962.

Hillman, James. The Dream and the Underworld. New York: Harper and Row, 1979.

....."Further Notes on Images," Spring: An Annual of Archetypal Psychology and Jungian Thought 1978.

..... "An Inquiry into Image," Spring: An Annual of Archetypal Psychology and Jungian Thought 1977.

Hodgins, Jack., ed. The Frontier Experience. Toronto: Macmillan of Canada, 1975.

Horowitz, Louise K. Honore d'Urfé. Boston: Twayne Publishers, 1984.

Jung, C.G. and Kerenyi, C. Essays on a Science of Mythology. trans. R. F. C. Hull. New York: Harper Torch Books, 1949.

Keiser, Albert. The Indian in American Literature. New York: Oxford University, 1933.

LaFrance, Jeanne. Les personnages dans le roman Canadien-français. Sherbrooke: Editions Naaman, 1977.

Laing, R. D. The Facts of Life. New York: Ballantine Books, 1972.

Leach, D. Edmund. Claude Lévi-Strauss. New York: Viking Press, 1974.

Lemire, Maurice. Les grands thèmes nationalistes du roman historique canadien-français. Quebec: Les presses de l'Université de Laval, 1970.

Léry, Jean de. Indiens de la Renaissance. Anne-Marie Cheuser, ed. Paris: Episa éditeurs, 1972.

Lévi-Strauss, Claude. Fonction symbolique: Essais d'anthropologie. compilateurs, P. Smith et M. Izard. Paris: Gallimard, 1979.

Lévi-Strauss, Claude. L'Homme nu. Paris: Plon, 1971.

.....Myth and Meaning. New York: Schocken Books, 1979.

.....Tristes tropiques. Paris: Union générale d'éditions, 1955, rpt. 1965.

Lewis, Clive Staples. The Discarded Image, an Introduction to Medieval and Renaissance Literature. Cambridge: Cambridge University Press, 1964.

Lorand de Olazagasti, Adelaida. El indio en la narrativa gualtemalteca. Barcelona: Manuel Pareja por la Editorial Universitaria de la Universidad de Puerto Rico, 1968.

Manzoni, Cometta Aida. El indio en la novela de America. Buenos Aires: Editorial futuro, 1960.

......El indio en la poesía de América Española. Buenos Aires: J. Torres, 1939.

Mariátegui, José Carlos. Siete ensayos de interpretación de la realidad peruana. Lima: Biblioteca Amauta, 1928 rpt. 1975.

Melatti, Julio Cezar. Indios do Brasil. Brasilia: Coordenada Editora de Brasilia Limitada, 1972.

Melendez, Concha. La novela indianista en Hispanoamérica, 1832–1889. Madrid: Imprensa de la Libreria y Casa Editorial Hernando, 1934.

Miller, David. Indians in Brazilian Literature. Nee York: The Hispanic Institute, 1942.

Miller, Perry. The New England Mind: The Seventeenth Century. Cambridge, MA: Harvard University Press, 1954.

Monkman, Leslie. A Native Heritage: Images of the Indian in English-Canadian Literature. Toronto: University of Toronto Press, 1981.

Montaigne, Michel de. Les essais. Maurice Rat, ed. 2 vols. Paris: Editions Garnier Frères, 1962.

Montemayor, Jorge de. Los siete libros de la Diana. Enrique Moreno Baéz, ed. Madrid: Editora nacional, 1976.

Montesquieu, Charles Secondat Baron de. Lettres persanes. Paris: Garnier, 1975.

Morales, José Vera. Die Überwindung des literarischen Indigenismo in Los Ríos Profundos von José María Arguedas: Eine Üntersuchung zum Beginn der Moderne in der Lateinamerikanischen Epik. Hamburg: Deutsche Akademischen Austaschdienst, 1974.

Muñoz, Braulio. Sons of the Wind. Rutjers, NJ: Rutgers University Press, 1982.

Nash, Gary B. Red, White, and Black: The Peoples of Early America. 2nd ed. Englewood Cliffs, NJ: Prentice Hall, 1982.

Northey, Margot. The Haunted Wilderness: The Gothic and Grotesque in Canadian Fiction. Toronto: University of Toronto Press, 1976.

Nuñez de Pineda, Francisco. Feliz cautiverio en Chile. Madrid: Colecciones Austral, 1965.

O'Hagan, Howard. Tay John. Toronto: Malcolm, Ross, McClelland and Stewart, 1974.

Pandolfo, Maria do Carmo Peixoto. Mito e literatura. Rio de Janeiro: Pluarte, 1981.

Pascal, Manuel Corrales. Jorge Icaza: Frontera del relato indigenista. Quito: Centro de Publicaciones de la Pontifícia Universidad Catolica del Ecuador, 1974.

Pearce, Roy H. The Savages of America: A Study of the Indian and the Idea of Civilization. Baltimore: Johns Hopkins Press, 1965.

Plato. The Dialogues of Plato. B. Jewett, trans. New York: Scribner, Armstrong and Co., 1873.

Polar, Antonio Conejo de. Literatura y sociedad en Peru: La novela indigenista. Lima: Editora Lasontay, 1980.

Ramos, Garcilano. Vidas Sêcas. Rio de Janeiro: Olympio, 1947.

Ribeiro, Darcy. Maíra. 5th ed. Rio de Janeiro: Editora Civilização Brasileira, 1983.

Riffaterre, Michael. Semiotics of Poetry. Bloomington, IN: Indiana University Press, 1980.

Rodriguez-Luís, Júlio. Hermeneútica y praxis del indigenismo: la novela indigenista, de Clorinda Matto de Turner a José María Arguedas. Mexico City: Fondación de la Cultura Economica, 1980.

Rousseau, Jean-Jacques. Oeuvres complètes. Paris: Garnier frères, 1965.

Saint Brendan, The Anglo-Norman Voyage of St. Brendan by Benedeit, A Poem of the Early Twelfth Century. ed. Edwin George Ross Walters. Geneva: Slatkine Reprints, 1974.

Sartre, Jean-Paul. La Nausée. Paris: Gallimard, 1938, rpt. 1950.

Scroggins, Daniel C. A Concordance of José Hernandez' Martín Fierro. Columbia, MO: University of Missouri Press, 1971.

Steblin-Kamenskij, M. I. Myths.

Stevenson, Lionel. Appraisals of Canadian Literature. Toronto: MacMillan Co. of Canada Ltd., 1926.

Sutherland, Ronald. Second Image, Comparative Studies in Quebec/Canadian Literature. Toronto: New Press, 1971.

.....The New Hero, Essays in Comparative Quebec/Canadian Literature. Toronto: McMillan of Canada, 1977.

Swift, Jonathan. Travels into Several Remote Nations of the World by Lemuel Gulliver, First a Surgeon and then a Captain of Several Ships. New York: The MacMillan Company, 1922.

Tacitus. The Histories. W. Hamilton Fyfe, trans. 2 vols. Oxford: The Clarendon Press, 1912.

Tapia, John Reyna. The Indian in the Spanish-American Novel. Lanham, MD: University Press of America, 1980.

Urrello, Antonio. José María Arguedas, el nuevo rostro del indio: Una estructura mítico-poetica. Lima: Libreria-Editorial Juan Mejia Baca, 1975.

Warwick, Jack. The Long Journey, Literary Themes of French Canada. Toronto: University of Toronto Press, 1968.

Zolla, Elemire. The Writer and the Shaman: A Morphology of The American Indian. New York: Harcourt, Brace, and Jovanovich, 1973.

INDEX

222

NATIVE AMERICAN STUDIES